The Horse in the Furrow

by the same author

★

ACKY

ASK THE FELLOWS WHO CUT THE HAY

THE PATTERN UNDER THE PLOUGH:
ASPECTS OF THE FOLK LIFE OF EAST ANGLIA

WHERE BEARDS WAG ALL:
THE RELEVANCE OF THE ORAL TRADITION

THE FARM AND THE VILLAGE

THE DAYS THAT WE HAVE SEEN

★

Edited by George Ewart Evans:
WELSH SHORT STORIES

The Horse in the Furrow

by

GEORGE EWART EVANS

Illustrated by
C. F. TUNNICLIFFE

FABER AND FABER
3 Queen Square
London

First published in 1960
by Faber and Faber Limited
3 *Queen Square London W.C.*1
First published in this edition 1967
Reprinted 1971 *and* 1975
Printed in Great Britain by
Whitstable Litho Ltd., Whitstable, Kent
All rights reserved

ISBN 0 571 08164 9

© 1960 by George Ewart Evans

Acknowledgments

The author thanks all those who have so generously helped by giving much of the information contained in this book. In addition to those mentioned in the text he is grateful to Messrs H. H. Dawson and C. W. H. Cullingford of Ransome, Sims and Jefferies: F. E. Thirtle of James Smyth Ltd of Peasenhall; Philip J. Butler, E. Duncan Lofts, W. H. Thurlow and James Wilson.

He makes grateful acknowledgment to the Ipswich Borough Libraries (Reference Section) and Ipswich Borough Record Office for the facilities given him for research; and he wishes to thank the staff, especially Miss M. Maynard and Mr J. M. Collinson, for their help. He is also grateful to the Suffolk Agricultural Association for allowing him to consult their records. He owes a great debt to the Suffolk Horse Society and its Secretary, Mr Raymond Keer. Mr Keer gave a great deal of his time to the author's questions and kindly read that section of the manuscript dealing with the Suffolk horse. Whatever inaccuracies now remain in this section are the author's sole responsibility.

The author thanks all those who kindly lent photographs, and he makes grateful acknowledgement to Mrs. Barbara Woodhouse, Mr D. C. Horton and Mr Thomas Davidson for permission to quote from their works. He also thanks Mr Morley Kennerley for his real encouragement at all stages in the preparation of the manuscript, and Mr G. E. Fussell who read the proofs. Finally, he thanks his wife for being an occasional listener to his ruminations while he was gathering material for the book.

Y mae, fodd bynnag, reswm arall dros ymdrin yn fanwl a'r creaduriaid amyneddgar y bu'r ddynoliaeth mor ddyledus iddynt, sef y sicrwydd y derfydd am anifeiliaid gwedd cyn bo hir iawn. Trist gan wladwr sylweddoli hyn.

There is, however, another reason for a detailed study of these patient creatures in whose debt we all remain: the certainty that the plough teams will come to an end in the very near future—a sobering thought for the countryman.

Ffransis Payne,
Yr Aradr Gymreig
(The Welsh Plough)
1954.

Contents

CONTENTS

IV. FOLKLORE CONNECTED WITH THE HORSE

Abbreviations
used for those sources most frequently cited

G.V.A.C.S.: A General View of the Agriculture of the County of Suffolk: Arthur Young: London, Third Edition, 1804.

E.V.C.: The English Village Community: Frederic Seebohm: Longmans, Green, 1884.

E.F.P.P.: English Farming Past and Present: Lord Ernle: Longmans, 1922.

B.O.H.: The Book of the Horse: edited by Brian Vesey-Fitzgerald: Nicholson and Watson, 1946.

S.H.S.B.: The Suffolk Horse Stud Book: Volume One: by Herman Biddell: Cupiss, Diss, 1880.

Y.A.G.: *Yr Aradr Gymreig* (The Welsh Plough): Ffransis Payne: University of Wales Press, 1954.

A.O.S.: The Agriculture of Suffolk: Wm & Hugh Raynbird: 1849.

A.F.C.H.: Ask the Fellows who Cut the Hay: George Ewart Evans: Faber and Faber, 1956.

Introduction

The purpose of this book is to record the history of the farming associated with the horse in a part of East Anglia. Although he has by no means ceased to be used on the farms of Suffolk, the era when the horse was the pivot of the corn-husbandry of this area has come to an end; and the generation of horsemen or ploughmen who best remember the full 'horse-regime' has gone from the land. Many of the farmers who were brought up on, and practised, the old system of farming for the greater part of their lives have also retired or are near retiring age. The book has been attempted at this particular time —so near to the passing of the horse as the main power on the farm —chiefly in order to take down first-hand information from the men who knew the old regime in its most complete form, before the changes of the last fifty years had begun to revolutionise agriculture. The farm, especially in Suffolk, revolved round the horse; and the care and attention which the old type of farmer and his men bestowed on his horses and on their breeding was a recognition of their import-ance. *Good horses: good farm*, was more than a saying: it pointed to the mainspring of a system of husbandry—the *four-course*—that had its home in the Eastern Counties.

Much of the material set down here has been collected from farmers and farm-workers whose evidence has been checked and cor-related with documents and records of Suffolk farming methods during the past two hundred years. I had no hesitation in seeking agricultural history from the working farmer in Suffolk. As Sir Frank Stenton,[1] the authority on the mediaeval manor, has confessed: a farmer of the old school is able to give immeasurable help to the student who is attempting to interpret some of the problems of

[1] Address at the inaugural conference of *The British Agricultural History Society*, 13th April, 1953.

manorial farming. When the period studied is nearer the present day, the farmer is naturally able to give much greater assistance still.

During the preparation and writing of this book I found the Suffolk farmer an invaluable help, both in supplementing and expounding the written sources. For the farmer in this county is usually in the direct line of a very long tradition: not only has farming been the whole of *his* life but it has been the life of his family for the past two hundred years. Often when studying records of the late eighteenth and early nineteenth centuries I came up against little problems that could not be solved by reference to any known book or document: I sought the help of the older generation of farmer and in nearly every instance I got what I was looking for. I discovered that not only did their farming knowledge extend over the period covered by their own working life, but often embraced the experiences of their fathers and grandfathers, reaching back into the first half of the nineteenth century.

Similarly, I did not hesitate to go for help and enlightenment to the old hands who had spent most of their life with the horses on the farm. It would be accurate to say of these horsemen, during the period before the First World War, that horses and farming were the whole of their lives: they had a seven-day-a-week job; they talked, lived, and almost dreamed horses; and when they did 'go abroad' it was either to an agricultural show or to an event that was connected either directly or indirectly with their work. I found the old horseman —wherever I met him in the county—helpful, highly intelligent within the field of his own experience, and accurate to a degree that many people would find it difficult to credit. But when one reflects that farming was his sole interest, from the time he started as a boy of about twelve years of age—perhaps sixty years before—and that he had trained his mind to hold all the data he needed in his job, without the aid of books, or at the most with only the barest of written memoranda, it is not surprising that he was able to recount in accurate detail something he was interested in and had perhaps not seen for thirty or forty years—an early corn-drill, for example; which checked against an old catalogue showed that not one essential fact had escaped his memory.

It seems that in this respect the old countryman has been much neglected. Indeed, he has been more patronised than respected as someone who can make a real contribution to the history of the most profound changes that have ever occurred in agriculture. The old countryman is worth getting to know for his own sake: he is worth regarding against his natural background—the pre-tractor farming and the community which it nourished. So viewed he will appear as a living social document, and his true worth and dignity will emerge. And as for being a simple country swain, as many people seem to look upon him (the *yokel* of the country week-enders) the saying, *If you want to find a fool in the country you'll have to bring him with you*, is a good deal nearer the mark. Admittedly some of his talk is strange; but it should be remembered that it is so from long use and preference, and not from cussedness; and if he speaks a language nearer that of the First Elizabeth rather than that of the Second, it should be a matter of wonder and of interest. The old countryman has largely stood out against the town system of education[1] that was imposed on the countryside by the 1870 Act and he might lack the graces of what passes for a typical twentieth century product. Yet were some of his limitations in this respect to be brought to his notice, he could ask with point: 'Who is the truly educated man: the one who can grow onions or the man who can only spell 'em? '

The reader will notice that 'They don't do it like they used to', or 'Times are not what they were' is the undersong of much of the information given by many of the people I have talked to in preparing this book. But times were never what they were: men have never worked as hard, been as strong and as noble and as thick in the thews as they were a generation or two in the past. Distance in time is a powerful enchanter of the eye. Yet in these later days the older men have a greater sanction for repeating the old theme than perhaps ever before. For in their life-time they have seen, not merely the passing of a few generations, but the passing of an era. They are praisers of past time because less than any men before do they understand the age they have survived into. How can they, when so few of their

[1] cf. *Rural England: Sir H. Rider Haggard*, Longmans 1902 pp. 542-3.

superior and educated contemporaries have an inkling where the present age is tending and what it is all about?

A word should be said about the use of the dialect in this book. I have not attempted to translate the information the old horsemen gave me into precise English: to do this would have deprived it of a good deal of its colour and would have given an altogether false impression. Moreover, there was another additional reason for keeping at least some of the dialect: this was to emphasise what has been written above, and to underline the rather obvious but apparently neglected truth that information should be judged not so much by its provenance as by its usefulness and ultimately by its accuracy. On the other hand, neither have I attempted to transcribe phonetically the true Suffolk dialect: had I done this I might possibly have won the approval of a few purists, yet at the same time added immeasurably to the general reader's difficulties. My aim has been to give what I hope is an authentic flavour of the dialect. Wherever there was a dialect word of interest—interest in itself or in the object or process it described—it has been scrupulously kept and usually commented upon.

One final point: the reader should not expect this book to be solely about the farm-horse in Suffolk. Even if I had the technical equipment to write what would necessarily be an exhaustive study, it is doubtful whether it would be desirable to focus it completely on the horse himself. More I think has been gained by placing the farm-horse in the social and economic setting that called him forth and made him such a use and an ornament to East Anglian farming during the last couple of centuries.

Part One

THE HORSEMAN

I

The Horseman's Day

The term *horseman* as used in Suffolk meant a farm-worker who possessed two distinct skills: one in the care and management of horses, the other in field work—the ploughing, drilling, cultivating and so on, of arable land using a team of horses that varied in number according to the nature of the task and the nature of the land under cultivation. In this second skill the horseman in other parts of the country was referred to as a ploughman; but in Suffolk this term was very rarely heard.

The horseman was the earliest riser on the farm. He got up at 4.00 a.m.; took a bite of bread and cheese and hurried to the stables to feed the horses. For between the time when the horses had their first *bait* (or meal) and their *turning out* to plough at 6.30 a.m. two hours must elapse. This was an unalterable rule in Suffolk; and to give the Suffolk breed of horse a shorter time than this for his morning bait, was to treat him less than well, since he had no nosebag to feed from in the field; and he had nothing more to eat until he returned to the stable at 2.30 in the afternoon. It was essential, therefore, that the horse should have a good morning meal and plenty of time in which to digest it. The horseman kept the above hours throughout the spring and summer months: during the other half of the year (October to April) he turned out to plough half an hour later—7 a.m. instead of 6.30.

William Cobbold (born 1883), who was for twenty years bailiff of a 570 acre estate at Battisford in Suffolk, has said: 'The horseman was always regular to the minute. You could set your watch by him. He thought a lot of his horses and took a pride in looking after them. You'd rarely have to speak to a horseman for being late.' From the

time he arrived at the stables until about 5.30 the horseman was busy
baiting and cleaning down the horses. This early morning activity
is tightly woven into the memories of those people who were brought
up on the farms before the coming of the tractor: one of them has
described it thus: 'I was born on a Suffolk farm; and when I was a
boy I used to lie in bed in the early morning and listen to the quiet
champing of the horses, the clink of their shoes on the cobbles of the
stable, and the horsemen whistling or hissing through their teeth
to soothe the horses as they brushed and curry-combed them before
turning out.'

On the Battisford estate there were twenty-four horses—eight
plough-teams—with two horsemen and two *mates* or under-horsemen
to look after them. The order of precedence of the horsemen on
Suffolk farms was fixed with almost military precision; and at no
time was this precedence more jealously guarded than when the
teams turned out in the morning and returned to the stable after
work in the afternoon. The horsemen and their mates went first in
proper order with their teams of horses; and if there were more
teams needed on a particular morning the remaining ones were in
the charge of *day-men*, ordinary farm-workers, who followed on
behind. The distinction between day-men and horsemen was an
important one; for it meant that prior to the fixing of a minimum
wage[1] for farm-workers the day-men were liable to be *stood-off* on
wet days or when the land could not be worked. The farmer sent
them home, and they received no pay for the days they lost. But the
horsemen were paid a fixed weekly wage, and also had certain
perquisites which put them higher in the farm organisation, on the
same level as the stockman or the shepherd.

The actual feeding of the horses was important, chiefly for two
reasons: the need to keep them in perfect working condition; and, in
the interest of farm economy, to bait them as regularly and effectively
as possible without any of the corn going to waste. How important it
was may be gathered from the following: in the Battisford estate, as
in many other districts of Suffolk, the head horseman was known as

[1] Fixed under the *Corn Production Act*, 1917. The figure was 25s. 0d.
per week.

the *first baiter*, and the second in command as the *second baiter*. Arthur Chaplin (born 1885), a contemporary of William Cobbold, was for many years baiter at a similar estate àt Stowupland. He has described how he managed the feeding of his horses. The first baiter was in complete charge. He was responsible to the farmer for the condition of the working horses and for a proper method in feeding them.

In the stable was a *corn-hutch* or bin and the baiter filled it twice a week—Mondays and Thursdays—as it was not big enough to take a full week's ration. He drew the corn from the granary where he measured out the quantities scrupulously: he became so expert in gauging the right amount that he could apportion the ration without actually weighing it. He allowed each horse a stone of corn (oats and beans mixed) for a working day—six stones a week. Therefore, a little of each day's ration had to be kept back to make up the Sunday feed when the horses were resting: they were allowed unlimited amounts of chaff or *stover*. The utensil used for actually placing the food in the manger was a *baiting-sieve*. This was a round sieve with a fine cane bottom, something like one type of brewing-sieve. When it was full of chaff the baiter shook it gently to ensure that all the dust fell out; for if this was inhaled by the horse it caused him discomfort and, consequently, uneasy feeding.

At Battisford the corn consisted of beans and maize, *ground up rough*; and it was mixed with wheat chaff that came off the threshing *drum*. As it came out of the drum or threshing machine the farmer had it bagged and stored near the stable, over or alongside it, in a room or loft called the *chaffin'*. At this particular farm the baiters damped the chaff with water before giving it to the horses. But the methods of feeding and the kind of fodder differed considerably within the county. In the light land district—the *sandlings* or coastal area of East Suffolk—feeding beans to horses was a practice that was seldom held in high regard. In 1797 Arthur Young noted:[1] 'The quantity of beans given to horses is not very considerable, and the consumption for hogs or fattening cattle is still less'; and Newton Pratt, a Trimley farmer whose family has been connected with the

[1] *G.V.A.C.S.*, p. 80.

Suffolk horse ever since the time Young referred to, has stated: 'This is not bean country. Our horses were fed on oats, chaff, ground up roots and stover.' In this, the light-land farmers of Suffolk appear to agree with many of the Scottish farmers who have come into Suffolk during the last hundred or so years: the Scots considered beans were 'too hot for horses'.

James (Benhall) Wilding (born 1886) worked for the Pratt family for over half a century and was head horseman for the greater part of the time. He stated that beans caused a lot of feet-fever, especially in horses being prepared for shows, and he never used them for that reason. 'We used a lot of carrots—the red kind. Carrots kept the horses in good condition. We reckoned they were good for the water.' To bear out this use of carrots the Pratt stables have, as well as the usual chaff-house, a *root-house* alongside the stalls: here the roots—carrots and cattle-beet or mangel-wurzels—were stored before being ground up and fed to the horses.

Arthur Young has a note on the growing of carrots in this area:[1] 'The culture of carrots in the *Sandlings* (of Suffolk) . . . is one of the most interesting objects to be met with in the agriculture of Britain. It appears from Norden's *Surveyors Dialogue* that carrots were commonly cultivated in this district two hundred years ago, which is a remarkable fact, and shews how extremely local such practices long remain, and what ages are necessary to spread them. For many years (generally till about six or seven past) the principal object in the cultivation, was sending carrots to the London market by sea; but other parts of the kingdom having rivalled them in this supply they have of late years been cultivated for feeding horses; and thus they now ascertain, by the common husbandry of a large district, that it will answer well to raise carrots for the mere object of the teams. . . . In feeding they give about eighty bushels a week to six horses with plenty of chaff, but no corn, and thus fed, they eat little hay. Some farmers, as the carrots are not so good to Christmas as in the spring, give forty bushels and four of oats, a week, in the fore-part of the winter, but in the spring eighty bushels and no corn.'

[1] *G.V.A.C.S.*, p. 125.

Carrots are still grown by farmers as a field-crop in this area but chiefly now with the purpose of selling them to the town markets—especially Covent Garden. And Arthur Young's note emphasizes the persistent quality of traditional farming practices, founded no

doubt as much on the inherited skill and knowledge of the best way to treat the crop as on the suitability of the soil for growing it. It is noteworthy also that down the years some of the best Suffolk horses have come from this area which is indeed the cradle of the Suffolk as we know him today.

The baiters took immense pains in grooming their horses, out of pride in the beasts in their care, also out of a spirit of rivalry. One baiter did not care to fall behind another in the amount of *shine* or *bloom* that was on his horses' coats; and it was one of the first baiter's duties to see that the farm's horses turned out to the plough looking at least as well as the horses belonging to the neighbouring farms.

To make the coat shine each horseman had his own, usually secret, recipe. One used tansy leaves: 'You dried them and then rubbed them atween your hands. You kept this powder in a little linen bag and you sprinkled a bit now and then in their bait.' Another used sweet saffron leaves, baked to dry and fed in the same way: 'Only you had to be some careful not to give the horse too much of the powder or else the sweat would bring it out and you could smell the herb on his coat.' Another horseman used bryony root—a fairly common remedy in Suffolk: 'Bryony is a big root like a passnip. You cut it up; let it dry, and feed it with the chaff.' One horseman knew bryony as *big-root*: 'We used to come across it while we were ditching. I used to borrow my wife's nutmeg grater and then I'd grate up some of the root and feed it to 'em with the chaff.' One horseman asserted that the best device to make the coat shine was to wet the chaff occasionally with a little urine.

A chemist remembered that some old horsemen put their faith in black antimony for getting *bloom*; while a farmer stated that a device to bring up quickly the shine on a horse's coat was to rub him down lightly with a rag that had been dipped in paraffin: this also had the advantage of keeping the flies off and thus helping him to stand his steadiest in the show-ring. One horseman recalled that a few leaves taken from a box hedge and dried and fed in a powder in the chaff helped to keep down excessive sweat which tended to spoil the look of a horse; and this same horseman prescribed gentian or felwort for inducing a horse that had lost his appetite to use the rack and the manger once more.

Nicholas Culpeper confirms the property of this herb. He says: 'The power of the dry roots (of gentian) help (*sic*) the biting of mad dogs and venomous beasts, opens obstructions of the liver, and restoreth an appetite of their meat to such as have lost it.' He also commends bryony: 'The root cleaneth the skin wonderfully'—presumably in men and in animals. But yet another horseman, while commending the old simples and remedies, stated baldly: 'If you grow your corn and stover, you won't want vet nor medicines for your horses'.

William Cobbold has mentioned that: 'Some of the old horsemen liked to *nick* a few mangels from the bullocks' barn. (This was in the 'bean country') They ground up the mangels and mixed it with the stover. They reckoned the mangels toned the horses up. They acted as a medicine, especially when they were ripe, just after coming out of the clamp about April time. We also used to feed mangels to sheep at this time, but we had to be careful to rub off the young shoots or else they would cause the lambs to *scour*.'

At many farms there was, for keeping up an unlimited supply of chaff, a horse-powered chaff-cutter or *Old Roundabout*, as it was known in this district. One such machine was made by Ransome, Sims and Jefferies, the Ipswich firm, and was catalogued in 1860 as 'A New and Improved Horse Gear with Intermediate Motion for Driving a Small Chaff Engine'. The machine itself was housed in the barn or a specially built shed; and was geared to a capstan-like arrangement in the yard outside. To the single lever or shaft of this *capstan* a horse was fixed, by traces, and by a thin, quarter-inch steel rod—from the inside end of the shaft to the bridle—'to stop it from going off'. The horse walked in a circle pulling the lever and working the machine. Behind the horse walked a man or a boy to keep him pulling steadily.

Two men inside the barn were occupied with feeding the machine. One man picked up the hay or straw and placed it at the end of the feed-box; the other pushed it gently forward to engage it with the knives of the cutter. The man who picked up the hay arranged it in *yelms*—that is, disposed it in more or less regular bundles or *shuffs* ready for feeding into the cutter. A man, who had walked behind the horse when he was a boy, recalled: 'It wasn't hard work; but it was tedious work both for the boy and the horse. You had to keep the horse going steady. If you didn't watch out, he'd gradually slow down—he'd get bored with his job; but as soon as you urged him he'd go forward with a start like a thunder-bolt and the old machine started to revolve like fury. Then there was some swearing. A head poked out of the barn window and there was a shout: 'Keep thet hoss steady, can't you?' You see, as the cogs quickened up, the machine took the yelms too quickly: the feeder couldn't keep pace and there was a danger of him getting his fingers in the knives. If the old horse started a-loitering, on the other hand, the yelms didn't travel fast enough and the chaff-cutting wouldn't go forrard.'

As soon as he had completed the baiting the horseman slipped home for a *snap* and he returned to the stable about 6 o'clock. If he lived some distance away from the farm it was necessary for him to bring sufficient *bait* to last him the whole of the working day. If he lived near he returned from breakfast with a packet of bread and cheese his wife had prepared for his mid-morning break. As soon as he was back he began to harness the horses for the day's work: *a-collaring up* it was known as in this district. Then at 6.30 he turned out. The farmer was usually in the yard about that time to allot the jobs to each team; and if he had any doubts about a particular horseman's grooming of his charges he had only to take out a white handkerchief, and surreptitiously hold it against the flank of one of the horses as they passed, either to justify his doubts or to dispel them.

As already stated there was a quasi-ritual atmosphere about *turning out*. The head horseman or first baiter went first; then came the first baiter's mate; then the second baiter who was followed by his mate. If a horseman, either through perversity or absent-mindedness, took his team out of the stable before his turn in the ordered procession, there was a true disturbance. A head horseman has been known to throw a brush at a man rash enough to lead his horses out of the stable before his proper turn. Another method of arresting the undisciplined was to rattle a stick suddenly against the side of the stall, thus temporarily frightening the two horses, and causing them to throw back their heads. As soon as he had got them under control again the erring groom was rated with a peremptory: 'Don't you know where your place is?'

The same precedence was carefully observed at the end of the day when the teams had completed their work in the field. If a second horseman, for instance, happened to finish ploughing somewhere near the gate, it would not do for him to proceed out. He had to 'hold to one side', draw his horses away from the gate until the first horseman and his mate had passed through. Only then could he move his team into the procession that both horses and men had looked forward to, at least during the latter hours of their long task in the field. The horses walked in pairs, as they had ploughed, on the right-hand side of the road; and if a horseman rode, he sat sideways on the *land* horse, the horse on the outside, nearer to the oncoming traffic.

2

In the Field

In many ways the part of a horseman's job calling for most of his skill was that concerned with working the land, and using a standard of craftsmanship set immeasurably high both by the tradition of his craft and by the immediate needs of cultivation; and a horseman served a long and disciplined apprenticeship before he could attain to the standard demanded. Briefly, this meant the ability to 'take his work and leave it': to start and finish the ploughing; that is, to open and shut up a furrow and leave every *stetch*, or parcel of furrows, straight and level and without a wrinkle to mar the whole length of it.

In Suffolk it was customary until recent years to plough a field in stetches or lands of varying widths. Each stetch was limited on its two sides by *water-cuts* or deep furrows that made easy the escape of surface water from the soil; and in fact the main purpose of ploughing in stetches was—and still is, where stetches continue to be used—to ensure effective draining of the land. The lighter the soil the fewer water-furrows were needed and, therefore, the wider were the stetches. In the *strong-loam* belt of Suffolk—the heavy-land districts —however, very narrow stetches of two yards and upwards were necessary effectively to take off the surface water. As the ploughshare most commonly used in this county was one that turned a nine-inch furrow, the two-yard stetches were characterised as *eight-furrow work*; the two-and-a-half yard stetches as *ten-furrow work*; and the three-yard as *twelve-furrow*. But the narrow stetches were used only where the heaviness of the land made them inescapably necessary; for their disadvantages were many. First of all, the more water-furrows in a field the more land is wasted; secondly a field that is ploughed in narrow stetches that are ridged up slightly to assist the drainage is not the best seed-bed for a crop of corn, as the ridges are bound, to some degree, to cause an unequal ripening of the seed. Again, as it was impossible for wheeled implements to cross the frequent deep water-cuts of a field ploughed in this way, all cultivation had to be done along the stetch itself; and this meant that implements—drills, hoes, harrows, etc.—had to be adapted to fit the width of stetch used.

But the introduction of the reaping machine, the self-binder and latterly the combine-harvester made the use of narrow stetches impossible, as the continual jolting over the deep furrows soon put the most robust machine out of action. Under the surface draining or *thorough water-draining* of the land had to be undertaken on a more planned and workmanlike scale than had been done formerly; for now the below-surface drains had to take off *most* of the water and conduct it to the ditches, and had not merely to assist the wasteful system of frequent water-furrows on the surface, as the old bush-drains had done when they were almost the sole method of under-draining. Therefore the narrow stetches gradually went out of use as more machinery was introduced, and they were replaced by *flat-work*—wide stetches with water-furrows at as great an interval as was compatible with efficient overall draining.

But when the first baiter led his teams on to an unploughed field he did not have to trouble his head about the width of the stetches: that had been fixed by long usage and probably appeared to him then as unalterable an aspect of the landscape as the roads and the hedges. His first job was to start his teams to plough: he had already been on the field the day before to mark out the stetches. He had laid out their width, at each end of the field, with the help of a *stetch-pole*, a pole equal in length to the width of the stetch they were working—a nine-foot one in twelve-furrow work. This use of a pole to measure arable land is very ancient. Old Welsh laws, quoted by Seebohm,[1] specify how the strips of plough-land were to be measured—in some provinces—with a rod equal in 'length to the *long-yoke* used in ploughing with four oxen abreast'.

[1] *E.V.C.*, pp. 119, 120.

At each end of the centre or *top* of the stetch he placed a hazel-stick, taken from the hedge and peeled so that the white pith acted as a *sight* for drawing his first furrow. He, or the second horseman, did this for the whole of the field until it was marked out in equally spaced stetches. He then drew the first furrow of the stetch himself. If the first furrow was straight, example and actual guidance helped to persuade the ploughman who followed after him to draw the other furrows in the stetch in like manner: if the first furrow was *bent*

nothing could prevent the others from being less than perfect also. The responsibility for drawing the first furrow on a narrow stetch was one the head horseman could not afford to delegate, unless it was to a man equally skilled as himself; for a stetch that did not come out, at every point, exactly to the inch would render ineffective the use of implements that had been designed specially for it; again, a botched stetch was visible to all—to the casual passer-by and to the practised eye of his neighbour; and the 'loss of face' a head horseman suffered through allowing the standard of his own work to be below that of the next farm's was enough to make him ensure that every field was laid out and ploughed with as much care as patience and long-practised skill made possible. But another important reason for the head horseman's care was that he was directly responsible to the farmer for the way the field was cultivated; and if the farmer brought forward a complaint, the head man had to bear the full burden of it.

After he had drawn the first furrow in the stetch he returned alongside, ploughing a second furrow against the first, thus completing the *laying of the top* or centre-furrows—in shape, exactly like the ridge of a roof. He then left the first stetch and did the same with the next. Robert Youngman (born 1889) a retired horseman of Stratford St Andrew, has described how he started work at Marlesford Hall. His account illustrates how jealously the standard of workmanship was kept up, even when coaching a beginner in his first bout of ploughing was involved: 'I started on the farm when I was thirteen, but I was eighteen before they let me plough. The first time I put my hand on a plough-handle they placed me between the first horseman and the second. It was ten-furrow work at that time. The head horseman laid the top, and then I gathered a *round* (two furrows around the *top*) then the second horseman followed after me; and someone else followed after him and so on till the *moul' furrow* (the mould furrow was the last in the stetch) had been ploughed.' In other words, the beginner was made to plough directly after the head man, who gave him guidance and a high standard, and any mistakes he made were covered up by those coming after him. Consequently when they had finished the stetch, it would not, even at its worst, fall much below the usual standard, as the beginner's errors were corrected or at least made less obtrusive by the skill of the older men coming after him.

Perhaps the deep concern of the horsemen to keep their high standard of work even in the ordinary day-to-day ploughing can best be understood when we look at it against the background of a practice that was once common in many parts of Suffolk. On Sunday mornings during the time of the spring and autumn ploughing, the horsemen often strolled around the parish to view one another's work, estimating its quality with the eye for detail of an exacting *sticker*[1] at a furrow-drawing match. And if a man had a *bent* furrow or a *hog's trough* (a hollow between two furrow slices) in his work, the mistake would soon be recorded in every farm and public house in the parish.

Arthur Chaplin has given an account of the responsibility of the first baiter in the field: 'Supposing he had to plough a field of thirteen acres and he had eight plough-teams working. His first job was to calculate when they should finish, how long they should take to plough the whole field, each man ploughing at the rate of three quarters of an acre in one day. Next he had to calculate how many *rounds* each man had to plough. Then he had to remember that even after the rounds had been allocated and the stetches accounted for, he still had to include the acre or so of *headland*, the land on the outside of the field where the ploughs turned, which had to be ploughed the last of all.' The procedure followed at Stowupland with the twelve-furrow work was similar to that already described for the ten-furrow: the head horseman, or first baiter, laid the top and the other horsemen followed him, each ploughing a round at least on a stetch.

'If there were only six stetches in the field and eight ploughs working, the first baiter then put the second baiter and another to open up the furrows and lay the tops, so all the ploughs were employed. If there were six ploughs on the field and six stetches then it worked out easily: each man did one round (two furrows) on every stetch, making up the twelve furrows—or, to be more exact, eleven furrows and the *brew* or *moul' furrow*. The *brew* was very important as it completed or *shut up* the work. We called ploughing the last furrow in a stetch *taking up the brew*. In twelve-furrow work, or any narrow-stetch work for that matter, it was important that all the brews lay in one direction. If they didn't, the width of the stetches wouldn't be exact; and the drill and so on wouldn't fit the stetch; there was a waste of land or a waste of seed-corn. And if that happened you might as well hide your head in the hedge.

'The first baiter had a responsible job when he had a field full of ploughs to look after. He was a kind of foreman; and he had con-

---

[1] A judge: he uses upright sticks to estimate the straightness of the furrow.

tinually to be looking at his watch and calculating whether they were forrard enough. And as they came towards the end of the day he had to do some quick thinking to find out whether he'd have to keep the men working right up to the last minute in order to get the stint, of three-quarter of an acre's ploughing for each man, finished.

'After they gave up twelve-furrow work—when the machines came in—they went in for *flat-work*, wide stetches, even on the heaviest land, of anything up to eighteen yards. Then each man ploughed his own stetch after the first baiter had laid the top. That system was better in a way. It kept you on your toes. As soon as you had a break in your ploughing you'd walk along the *headlings* to have a look at your neighbour's work, to see where he had gone wrong, or if his ploughing was better than yours. It wouldn't do just to have straight furrows: a good ploughman also had to have a good *top* to the stetch—the furrows lying all flat and even. If there was a bit of *low* in the land, he had to let his plough bite in a little deeper at this spot to bring his furrows up level. You had to have level furrows as the drill coulters[1] had to enter the land at equal depth everywhere. Some say: 'Oh, don't worry about that! The harrows will level it off when they go over it.' But the harrows would never level off. You can pick out a furrow after the harrow has gone over it. If a first baiter knew his job, as soon as a man had ploughed a stetch he'd drop his stick across the furrows. If the stick didn't lie flat, but went all *tittymatawta* (like a seesaw), he then wanted to know the reason for it. It was *work* in the days I'm telling you about. Now, if you see a ploughed field today, it looks exactly as if a lot of pigs have been a-hoggin' and a-rootin' on it up.'

A *level top*, apart from its looking well, was emphasised for a good economic reason: if the ploughland was level, the drill coulters would bite in at an uniform depth, and sow the seed in the same way; the ears of corn would then mature at approximately the same time and all the seeds of corn would be approximately the same size. This was a big point in a barley-grower's favour when he took some of his corn to show to a maltster. For one of the first things the maltster

---

[1] The metal 'spouts' down which the seed from the drill runs into the soil; often called *counters* in the dialect.

looked for was just this: uniformity of seed in the samples that the farmer showed to him.

But there is a long tradition of skilful ploughing in this county. Arthur Young wrote of it:[1] 'The ploughmen are remarkable for straight furrows; and also for drawing them by the eye to any object, usually a stick whitened by peeling, either for water cuts or for new laying out broad ridges, called here *stitches*; and a favourite amusement is ploughing such furrows as candidates for a hat, a pair of breeches given by ale-house keepers or subscribed amongst themselves as a prize for the straightest furrow. The skill of many of them in this work is remarkable'.

Furrow-drawing and ploughing matches with horses remained popular until recent years, and even now have not gone out altogether. William Cobbold tells how the ploughmen at Battisford often had a small sweepstake amongst themselves during the day's work in the field—an ounce of tobacco for the best furrow or the best laid stetch. Or sometimes one horseman said to another while they were ploughing: 'See you across the field for a pint o' beer'. If this challenge to plough the straighter furrow was accepted the head horseman was called in to judge the winner.

The efficient horseman was a highly valued member of the old pre-machine, rural community; and his skill at the plough earned for him a notable place in the regard of his fellows. William Cobbold recalls one of them in this district: 'Frank Botwright was my first horseman at Hill Farm. He was a very quiet horseman but a real good 'un. You could hear some horsemen three or four fields away; but you wouldn't hear Frank even if you were in the next. He was ploughing the headlands of a field just by the farm one day and I had to go over to see him about something. Do you know, his two horses went right round the headlands without him touching the *cords* (reins)'.

Other ploughmen have been known to set the plough in the furrow, start the horses off and then release the plough handles, walking a few yards away from the plough till it neared the headland when they took hold of the plough again to turn it. One of the men who did this

[1] *G.V.A.C.S.*, p. 46.

confessed: 'It was a bit of a trick. Of course you had to have two good horses. But the real knack was in setting the two wheels of the plough—the land and the furrow wheel. Even so, you couldn't go very far away from the plough; because if the coulter or the share struck a flint and started to dance, you had to be at hand quick to put it right.'

The more formal ploughing—and furrow-drawing matches have been described elsewhere,[1] but Arthur Chaplin has recalled his father at one of these in a story that is worth quoting: 'My father tied with another man at an Old Newton furrow-drawing match: both had a quarter-inch *deviation*—it must have been about sixty years ago. Now he had one peculiarity when he was a-ploughin': he had to have his pipe going before he could start. So this particular day at Old Newton, just before he started, he stopped to do the usual: get a good light on his owd pipe. One of the stewards saw him a-doin' this and he say:

' "Hurry up there! We're waiting for you to start. You can't smoke and draw a furrow at the same time."

' "Dew you be quiet. I know what I'm a-dewin' on."

So he lit up his owd bit of clay pipe, put his hands to the plough and went after his horses. When he had drawn a furrow that everybody could see was one of the best—even before the *stickers* put the sticks on it—they say:

' "See! It's child's play for him. He smokes at it as if he's just a-diggin' in his own garden!"

They didn't know that he couldn't have drawn a proper furrow let alone a real good 'un if he hadn't got his owd pipe a-drawin' in his mouth! It just shows you: what you're used to, you must do—even if it's in a competition.'

James Edward Ransome, writing in 1865,[2] summarised the regard in which good ploughing was held: 'I have done my best to explain the construction and mode of using the most useful and most general of all agricultural implements (the plough), and when we consider that good ploughing lies at the root of good farming and that good

[1] *A.F.C.H.*, p. 126.
[2] *Ploughs and Ploughing*, Thomas Constable, Edinburgh (pamphlet).

farming produces food for the world, we shall see that it is worthy of our attentive study. Nor ought the ploughman himself to be despised. He has not often had the advantages of education which make the scholar, but he has had an implement to study and work to perform which requires years of patient daily toil to master and become proficient at. I have found many a warm and honest heart beneath the rough hand of the ploughman. Nor has his work been despised by those in higher stations'.

At eleven o'clock the teams stopped working. The horseman threw a couple of sacks over the backs of his horses and sat under the hedge to eat his *elevenses*. The break lasted twenty minutes; but it was not a complete break for the horseman for he was still in charge of the horses; and as they were not feeding they sometimes got restless, especially in the summer time when the flies worried them and sometimes caused a horse to get his foot over a trace. Even when he was resting the horseman had to be on the alert for incidents like this to see that nothing untoward happened to his team. After the break he resumed work and continued until 2.30 in the afternoon when it was the end of the day as far as the horses were concerned.

But why this peculiar organisation of the horseman's day which to a large extent cut across the hours of the other workers on the farm? The answer appears to be that such was the traditional day for the ploughman from time immemorial when his team was made up solely of oxen. Mediaeval records show that the oxen ploughed only in the morning and returned to their stalls shortly after mid-day. The old Welsh laws, dating from the middle of the tenth century, make it clear that the oxen were not to be used in the afternoon; and as Seebohm[1] points out a *cyvar* (or co-ploughing, where different people contributed different members of the ox-team and the plough itself) ended at noon. Ffransis Payne,[2] in a very valuable book that deals, in its early chapters, with the history of the plough in Britain, quotes three Welsh poets of the fifteenth and sixteenth centuries to show that the ox-team ploughed only until noon and spent the rest of the day in feeding and in resting.

But, someone will say, what has Wales to do with England, and

[1] *E.V.C.*, p. 124.   [2] *Y.A.G.*, p. 171.

especially with Suffolk from which it is so far removed? Frederic Seebohm,[1] has stated why the Welsh evidence is so relevant:

'In these (Welsh) laws is much trustworthy evidence from which might be drawn a very graphic picture of the social and economic condition of the unconquered Welsh people, at a time parallel to the centuries of Saxon rule in England. And amongst other things fortunately there is an almost perfect picture of the method of ploughing. Nor is it too much to say that in this picture we have a key which completely fits the lock, and explains the riddle of the English open field system.

'For the ancient Welsh laws describe a simple form of the open field system at an earlier stage than that in which we have yet seen it—at a time, in fact, when it was a living system at work, and everything about it had a present and obvious meaning, and its details were consistent and intelligible'.

But why start early and finish in the middle of the day? Ffransis Payne suggests that ploughing was particularly burdensome to the oxen during the heat of the day, and that by finishing at noon they would escape the greater part of it. But an important reason for the long, unbroken stretch of work in the field was undoubtedly the amount of time and trouble that was necessary to yoke and unyoke a team of eight, or even four, oxen. A break during the middle of the day and a return to the stables—apart from the question of distance from the field where the work was being done—would have meant unyoking and yoking up a second time for another stint in the afternoon; and this would have lengthened the day without appreciably lengthening the working time. Therefore it was natural that the ploughing should be done in one extended visit to the field: it was convenient that this should fall in the forepart of the day while the afternoon was spent, by the oxen in resting, and by their driver and ploughman in feeding them and seeing to their wants.

That the traditional shape of the old horseman's day was a continuation of the much older discipline submitted to by the ox-driver and the ploughman is borne out by some of the terms that still survive in Suffolk. One old horseman put forward his opinion that the reason

[1] *E.V.C.*, p. 118.

for the teams' long stretch of work in the early part of the day was, in fact, to save *taking off* (the harness etc.) in the middle of the day; and—what is more interesting—he referred to the day's visit to the field as a *journey*. Seebohm has pointed out[1] how ancient this term is when it is connected with ploughing; for in mediaeval times the acre or strip, which was the average day's ploughing for an ox-team, was sometimes called a *jurnalis* (or *diurnalis*) in monks' Latin and *journel* in French—that is, the amount of ploughing that could be done in one day.

George Izzard, a Kentish man who is in charge of the large farm of H.M. Prison Commissioners at Hollesley Bay, in Suffolk, also revealed the antiquity of the practice when he recently referred to it as *one yoke*. He has a large stable of Suffolk horses which he still uses for ploughing: he said, however: 'We don't have the old system of *one yoke* now: the horses now return to the stable at mid-day, and go back into the field for another stretch of ploughing in the afternoon.' This procedure has also been adopted by most Suffolk farmers who still work horses: the old, traditional one *journey*, or one *yoke* fell out of use just before or during the last war. Though there are farms in the county where it was retained up to nine or ten years ago—or even later; and it is likely that in other parts of the country the old system is still kept, at least in vestigial form.

It appears that in some parts of Essex the organisation of the ploughing bore even greater resemblance to the old mediaeval system. Charles Bugg (born 1883) a Barking (Suffolk) farmer, re-called: 'The horseman didn't plough in Essex. They went on different there—at least in parts of Essex. There was a baiter who did nothing but feed the horses; and when they were ploughing two men went with every plough-team—the ploughman and the driver. The ploughman had nothing to do with the horses.'

This is exactly how the mediaeval team was organised: the plough-man at the handles, the team of oxen—yoked in pairs or four abreast —and the driver who walked alongside with his goad. This is clearly shown in an illustration in the Luttrell Psalter. It is also worth noting that in the Welsh organisation, referred to in the old laws already

[1] *E.V.C.*, p. 124 and 382: see also *A.O.S.*, p. 295.

mentioned, the counterpart of the driver was termed *y geilwad* or the *caller*. He walked *backwards* in front of the oxen singing to them as they worked. Songs were specially composed to suit the rhythm of the oxen's work; and some of these songs were still used for their ancient purpose in the county of Glamorgan until the latter half of the nineteenth century.

If the day's ploughing was originally conditioned, as seems likely, by the length of time it was possible to keep a team of oxen working in the field without taking from them more of their strength than they could recoup during a night's rest, it follows that the amount of ploughing done—or at least aimed at—during a day was fairly constant. This amount was, in fact, the acre. The Roman acre (about two thirds of an English acre) was the amount of land that could be ploughed by a single yoke of oxen in a day; and the Latin word for an acre, *iugerum*, is almost identical with that for a yoke—*iugum*: an additional argument in favour of this theory of the acre's origin. Seebohm also mentions that the extent of a *cyvar*,[1] or co-aration in the early Welsh laws, was an *erw* or acre; and he quotes the name for a similar strip in the German open field: this was *morgen*—a clearer indication still that the day's ploughing ended at noon.

As already mentioned three-quarters of an acre was the usual ploughing task for a day in the heavy-land districts of Suffolk; but in the light-land districts an acre a day was the rule. It was so at Morston Hall, an 800 acre farm near Trimley: Newton Pratt and his present head horseman, Jack Lancaster, used six or seven plough-teams of two horses, drawing single-furrow ploughs, and two teams of three horses, harnessed abreast, for the double-furrow ploughs. Incidentally, at this light-land farm, the men who worked the double-furrow ploughs earned a shilling a week extra to compensate them for having to work the extra horse. If at first sight it appears that an acre is not much land for a man and a team of horses to plough in a day, one fact may help to correct the view-point: if they were turning a nine-inch furrow—mostly commonly used in this county—the horses and the ploughman would have walked eleven miles by the

---

[1] *E.V.C.*, pp. 382–3 He also quotes Varro: *iugum—quod juncti boves uno die exarare possint.*

time they had completed their stint; and walking, both for the horse-man and his charges, was by no means the most arduous part of the business.

But ploughing was of necessity not continuous throughout the time they were in the field. The horses had a 'breather' every hour or so; and during that time the men were able to walk along the headland to have a chat and inspect one another's work, or to observe the trivial but absorbing happenings of the countryside—the movement of the birds and small animals about the field. One interesting fact may be mentioned before leaving this: Charles Bugg has related how nervous plough-horses became, when they heard the baying of the hounds in a hunt. The horses frequently became distressed even before the horsemen could hear the hounds; and it was difficult then to work them. The old farmer knew of a ploughman who worked a horse that was particularly affected by the sounds—or the scent—of a hunt. To soothe him the ploughman used to take off his coat, spread it on the ground and get the horse to lie on it until the hunt had gone out of the immediate neighbourhood. Confirmation of this comes from Essex[1] where an old horseman was able—much to the amazement of his fellows—to divine from the behaviour of one of his horses that the hounds were meeting in the neighbourhood on a particular morning.

As soon as the teams had returned to the stable and had been uncollared, the baiters gave the horses a handful or two of stover as a prelude to their main meal of the day; and then they went home to have their own dinner. They returned at 3.30 and for the rest of the afternoon until they finished at 5.30 they were busy baiting the horses and taking off the mud and dust of the day. Arthur Young has given an account of what happened to the horses; and although he was writing at the end of the eighteenth century the account des-cribes accurately the practice that was generally retained in Suffolk until nine or ten years ago and which is still followed on the few farms where horses are worked in any number:[2]

'In the east district, in winter, horses are never permitted to remain in the stable at night; but about eight o'clock are turned out into a

[1] *The Times*, 1st March, 1958.   [2] *G.V.A.C.S.*, p. 219.

yard, well littered with straw, and plenty of good sweet oat or barley straw to eat but never clover or hay. By this treatment, a horse is never swelled in his legs, or seldom has any ailment about him. Horses in this county are as good as any in England and are kept in fine condition. A horse turned out every night will hold his work several years longer than one confined in a stable.'

The recent practice did, however, differ in one particular from the above: the baiters' mates, who were not normally allowed to feed the horses, were expected in addition to cleaning out this yard, to *rack the horses up* for the night—that is, to fill their racks with fodder. And they usually filled the racks with stover.

A yard such as Arthur Young described is to be seen in its classical form at Morston Hall, Trimley. With the stables and the stalls and the sheds around it, it covers three-quarters of an acre; and the whole is as compact and square as a Roman fort. On one side are the long stables, without stall divisions, with the root-house at one end, the chaff-house in the middle with the corn-bin not very far away from the chaff; and, at the other end, the groom's room where the head horseman sat up at night whenever a mare was expected to foal. On the adjoining side, on the left of the yard, is the open shed, complete with stover-racks, where at night the horses could shelter and take their bait. On the other two sides of the square are the boxes, or separate stalls for horses. At the time of writing this huge agricultural fort held one horse, though at one time it held a hundred—thirty or forty working horses, and the rest a breeding stud of Suffolks.

Mrs Leslie More (born 1884), of the family of Newson Garrett of Aldeburgh and Richard Garrett a well-known breeder of Suffolks, gave a glimpse of the way the horses were stabled before they were turned out into the yard in the evening:

'On many farms the Suffolks were all crammed into a long barn and head-roped to a rail running its length. No stall divisions. When staying, years ago, with my mother at Thorpe, I saw the Punches crowding into their barn, on a farm near Friston. "Is that safe?" I asked. "Won't they get snagged up and do each other harm?" The farmer laughed: "*They?* Not likely. They fare to be all one family and each knows his place." '

Yet another quotation[1] serves to pick out and sum up the salient points in a horseman's day. Although, like the Arthur Young account just quoted, it refers to a period about 150 years ago, it is in its essentials a true description of a horseman's life right up to the First World War—a time that brought in so many changes in the organisation of the farm and the rural village community:

'When I became a horseman, a day's work was to be out with the horses from breakfast to nearly three o'clock. In summer this was, except for busy times such as haysel, very easy work; and I had simply, when I returned, to give the horses a bait of corn and chaff, rub them down and then turn them out to grass. But in winter it was different. The horses' coats were thicker, and they perspired heavily at their work, so to thoroughly groom them took a long time. Besides, as they had worked on heavy land a considerable quantity of soil adhered to their legs and bodies, all of which I had to remove. . . . In winter they were turned out, after I had my supper, into a straw-yard, which had an open shed. The rule was "early to bed and early to rise" so that as soon as we had done with the horses we were off to bed. When hoeing wheat the men worked from six to six, and a day's work on haysel depended on the weather. Men living in the house (as this man was) were not expected to leave the premises without the master's permission; and in winter there was not much opportunity to do so even if desired.

'Before coming to the farm I had considerable practice with the plough; but I could not, as it was called "take my work and leave it", and it was a long time before I could draw a furrow so as to satisfy the farmer's critical eye.'

A family memory, dating back to the end of last century, gives a final view of the horseman's job. George Garrard (born 1891) farmed, until a few years ago, at Gislingham; and it is from north Suffolk that this story comes: 'My father went to work on the farm as a boy of eleven. Later, when he started ploughing he had to go into the fields before it was light, so he'd have to scheme round in the dark to

[1] *The Autobiography of a Farm Labourer with Recollections of Incidents etc in Suffolk* (1816–1876), The Suffolk Mercury, 1894.

find the *whipple-trees*.[1] He became a head horseman on that farm; and on Saturday night the farmer used to give him a gold sovereign and tell him:

' "Pay owd Sam out o' thet."

That were ten shillings and sixpence for the head horseman and nine-and-six for the second.'

[1] Or *swingle-trees*; a whipple-tree is a wooden cross-bar (pivoted at the middle) to which the traces of the horse are fastened. The whipple-trees were fixed to a pommel-tree, a similar but longer cross-bar, which in turn was fixed to the plough.

3

The Horseman's Year

In order to show how essential was the horse at almost every step
in the progress of the farming year, it would be profitable at this
stage to list the various tasks that lay before the horseman in fixed
order—as far as weather and circumstance permitted—as soon as
that year began. The account is based mainly on Arthur Chaplin's
relating of the sequence at Stowupland Hall: each farm had its own
variations but the main framework of events was, from their nature,
the same in all essentials.

Once the harvest was in the stack-yard, there was the seed-clover
to cut, make and cart. Then the farmer set the men and horses to the
spreading of muck on to the stubble. The details of this process will
be recorded in a later chapter; but one can state at this point that
muck-spreading was no casual, haphazard work but as carefully
calculated and managed as the sowing of the corn. When they had
finished muck-spreading at least two jobs were waiting—the pulling
and topping of cattle-beet, and the winter ploughing. The beet was
usually ready about the last week of October or the first week in
November; therefore, if the previous job had finished early, the teams
started on the long job of winter-ploughing before the men tackled
the root-crop.

Winter tares were then sown for use in the spring—mainly as food
for the horses; and the sowing of winter beans came next—a task that
was usually completed by a fortnight after Michaelmas—the 29th
of September. 'But you had to start early if you were a-ploughing the
beans in, as that was a very slow job.' When the beans had been
sown they began drilling the winter-wheat. Two, three or even four
horses were used for this job, according to the size of the drill and

46

the nature of the land. On the very heavy land where they used a full stetch drill (a nine-foot one for twelve-furrow work, for instance), they harnessed four horses to the drill—two walking *at length* in each furrow.

After the wheat-drilling the mangels or cattle-beet were ready for carting off and clamping. As soon as this job was over the horsemen returned to the winter-ploughing; for all the ploughing had to be finished, and the ploughs *set-up*—taken off the fields and stored away in barn or shed—before Christmas. It was bad husbandry if the

ploughing was not done by this time; and the horsemen went to great lengths to avoid the reproach of 'being behind'. Harry Groom (born 1894) a Needham Market horseman, recalled: 'If you were behind with pulling your turnips or mangels, and it were getting near Christmas, you used to plough right up to 'em—as soon as they'd pulled a row of roots we came along with the plough; so when the last row was off, the field was almost ploughed.'

After Christmas, when bad weather was usual, the horses had a rest; and the horsemen kept themselves busy with fencing and various jobs about the farm—cleaning out stack-yards and repairing implements and gear. At this time, too, there was an occasional day of threshing. 'The seed-barley was thrashed and stored as a regular procedure; and sometimes, when the farmer was short of money, he'd have one of his stacks of corn thrashed. But, of course, he didn't put it just like that: 'We're getting short of chaff for the horses," he say, "we'll have to have the engine". A rare bit o' chaff that was, and it used to make us men smile.'

If the weather in February was at all good they drilled the spring beans and the peas; and the spring tares or vetches were sown for use when the autumn crop had been eaten. They drilled the oats and the barley as soon as the weather allowed—in March during most years. Then they made the ridges or *baulks* ready for the mangels, and sowed the seed straight afterwards. (The preparation of the ground and the traditional culture of cattle-beet in Suffolk deserves detailed recording and will be treated in a later chapter on old methods of cultivation.) After the cattle-beet or mangels had been sown the winter-wheat and the beans were ready for harrowing and rolling. Mention of this prompted the horseman to a piece of farming lore:

'We used to be told: "Never harrow wheat or beans in an east wind". As you know the harrow scratches out the weeds and snatches blades off the young wheat and makes it branch out and shoot better. But the young corn won't do this if it's perished at the same time by an east wind: a cold wind wounds the wheat when it's bruised by the harrow, and it's bound to take harm. If a man were in charge of an *off-hand* place, and the farmer say to him: "Harrow the wheat or the beans tomorrow", he'd have enough sense, if an east wind sprung up during the night, not to go on with the harrowing but to do some other job instead. But they don't pay any attention to that sort of thing today. I saw a man harrowing wheat in a perishin' east wind—only recently; and it made me say to myself: Where are the old methods? It's all rush today. You hear a young chap say in the pub: "I done thirty acres today". But it ain't messed over, let alone done. You take the rolling, for instance. Two mile an hour is fast enough for a roll or a harrow. With a roll, the slower the better. If you roll fast, the clods are not broken up, they're just pressed in further. Speed is everything; just jump on the tractor and way across the field as if it's a dirt-track. You see it when a farmer takes over a new farm: he goes and plants straight-way, right out of the book. But if

48

one of the old farmers took a new farm, and you walked round the land with him and asked him: "What are you going to plant here and here and here?" he'd look at you some queer; because he wouldn't plant nothing much at first. He'd wait a bit and see what the land was like: he'd *prove* the land first. A good practical man would hold on for a few weeks, and get the feel of the land under his feet. He'd walk on it and feel it through his boots and see if it was in good heart, before he planted anything: he'd sow only when he knew what the land was fit for. But the new farmers they go in and plant slap out of the book. It's a good job some these book-farmers weren't a-farming fifty years ago: most of 'em would have starved themselves to *dead*.'

This is a familiar plaint: experienced age bewailing the unorthodoxy and over-confidence of the new. But the plaint is worth a hearing at the present time, if only because farming in this county—in common with many other areas in the country—is fast becoming purely extractive. It would be a gross misrepresentation to say that under the old system of farming, that has just been displaced, the farmer was not much bothered by the need to make a profit. He was, certainly. A nineteenth century farmer's accounts given later, show that he was actively concerned, not only in getting a living for himself and his family, but in making his farming pay. But at the same time the farmer of the old school balanced this motive with a real regard for the land he was farming. The whole temper of the age, nourished by the Norfolk four-course orthodoxy, was such that one of the most sacred articles in the farmer's creed was: The land's potential must be preserved; and it was one of farming's unwritten laws that no man should mulct posterity by degenerating into *a landskimmer*—a term of abuse that was as bitter to the ears of a farmer of the old school as the accusation of being a common criminal.

Today the prevailing climate is different: the old symbiotic relation with the land has been broken. 'It's all money; get what you can; that's the story today,' is the despairing admission of an old farmer, despairing because it goes right against his real instinct. *Words, words, words*, someone will say. *Just tell me what is the old farmer's real instinct*. Briefly, it is this: a traditional knowledge, not acquired from books, direct instruction or even the conscious taking of thought; it is a knowledge that is instinct in the community in which he lives; and it tells him that a rural society's first concern has always been and can only be *continuity*; and if the over-riding need to make money threatens to imperil that continuity, he is uneasy. And the economist's or the historian's assurance that the money-motive in rural production is historically recent and must needs, in the nature of things, soon be modified or even superseded, is not likely to encourage him, when he sees the land around him, at this moment, being treated not as a partner but as an adversary that must be exploited right up to a point just this side of immediate retribution. Moreover, this instinct tells him that the real tragedy of purely extractive farming is that its evil effects are insidious and cumulative, and that when they make themselves known it is already too late to apply a remedy.

The next job after harrowing the wheat and beans was to harrow and roll the clover-leys in order to break down the stubble that would be standing. 'Earlier in the year you *spreed* (spread) all the mole-hills with a spade. If you left the mole-hills untouched until the harrowing and rolling you'd be doing harm, because the harrow would just skim them off and then you'd have a pancake of pressed mud, caked hard—and no grass could get through that easily. We did the meadows with an old bush-harrow, and it was sight to see the wheat or the meadow just after it had been harrowed—especially when the sun was on it. If there was a tree in the middle of the pasture I was harrowing I did my best to keep the harrow *square*; to go right round the tree and carry on the other side in exactly the same line. So if somebody were to look at the field as they were passing, they'd think and wonder, because it would look as though the harrow had gone plumb through the tree without stopping.'

The next jobs were hoeing the wheat and the beans and *chopping-out* cattle-beet. The beet-seed was sown in rows and the young plants were chopped out with a hoe, leaving isolated bunches of plants every eighteen inches—in fact a little less, for when the beet-plants were *singled* out by hand they had then to be eighteen inches apart, no more no less.'Women and children did the singling. They got on their knees and picked out the plants with their fingers, leaving them in *oneses*. They got 1s. 6d., and for chopping-out we got 3s. 6d., an acre.'

Next came *ploughing 'tween beet*. They took the breast off the plough and used the share only, ploughing three times up and down between the rows or *baulks*, going up one furrow and down the next, to kill the weeds. The first week in June saw the cutting of the clover, its making and carting. This was the stover that formed a large part of the horses' fodder. Then they cut the hay; made it and carted it. Once the haysel was over there was a respite until the harvest. This is the period of the agricultural shows, the real holiday-time in the farming year. But on the farm the job was to clean out all the stock-yards and to cart the manure to make *muck-hales* or *hills* in the fields whose turn is was to be dressed. The hills were left on, or near, the field so that as soon as the corn was off the stubble, later in the autumn, the muck could be spread and the winter-ploughing go forward without delay.

Finally came the harvest, the climax of the farming year and the busiest time for both men and horses. Then they cut and carted the corn, and afterwards had their brief rest and *frolic* before the in-exorable farming round began once more.

4

Some of the Ploughs

Closely linked with the old horseman in Suffolk is the firm of Ransome, Sims and Jefferies of Ipswich. This firm has made most of the horse-ploughs used in this county during the last 150 years; and their researches here have had a great influence on plough-design and plough-making all over the world. Robert Ransome, the founder of the firm, was born at Wells, Norfolk in 1753, the son of a Quaker schoolmaster. With the help of the Gurney's, the Quaker bankers, he started a foundry business in Norwich; but a few years later, in 1789, he removed his foundry to Ipswich.

At Norwich Robert Ransome had been experimenting with the making of cast-iron plough-shares: he continued his experiments at the Old Foundry, Ipswich. But he failed to discover a process of manufacture that would correct the one big disadvantage connected with their use: the constant re-sharpening the cast-iron plough-share required to keep it fit for ploughing. Wrought-iron shares, although more laboriously and hence expensively made, were therefore still preferred. Then in 1803, by one of those lucky accidents that have had such a great effect on the course of agriculture, as they have on that of science, he discovered how to manufacture a cast-iron plough-share that would remain sharp in use and be at least as effective as a wrought-iron share but much more economical to produce. George A. Biddell (born 1824), grandson of Robert Ransome and a member of a Suffolk farming family, described[1] how his grandfather made the discovery:

'Some little time after he started here (in Ipswich) an accident

[1] *Reminiscences of George A. Biddell* (Ransome; Sims and Jefferies: MS. in Archives).

occurred through the bursting of a Furnace, which gave way and all the molten metal ran out and some of it ran on to some iron plates and cooled rapidly—of course much more quickly than that which ran on to the sandy ground of the foundry. When the metal had cooled down it was broken up and he observed that wherever it had run on to the iron plates it had changed its character; and the surface which had come immediately into contact with the iron

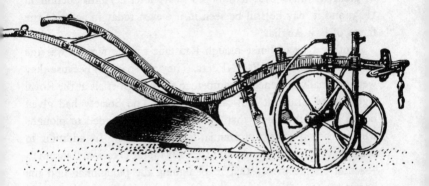

plates was "chilled" and very hard and white in texture for quite a good way into the metal.

'Mr Robert Ransome was a man of great observation and, in fact, was a natural engineer; and the idea struck him that the chilled metal possessed just the qualities for a good plough-share because the lower side being hard and the upper side soft, the friction of the upper soil would form a good cutting edge. Up to that time this class of Shares was always made in wrot. iron. This, in the year 1803, is believed to be the first application of chilling for any purpose.'

Later in the century George Biddell himself gained some fame for applying the same principle to the case-hardening of rails used on railway crossings.

After the invention of the chilled plough-share the firm became widely known as specialists in the making of agricultural implements; and at the first Royal Show at Oxford in 1839 they won the Royal Agricultural Society's gold medal for their display of implements and machinery. They exhibited altogether six tons of goods—quite an amount for those days; for the material had to be carried on its hundred miles' journey by teams of horses and wagons.

One of the landmarks in the history of plough-making was Ransome's manufacture of their famous Y.L. plough with iron beam and handles. The design of this plough arose out of the complaint of one of their customers: no customer ever complained to better purpose, for the Y.L. plough was still being manufactured and sold in great numbers over a hundred years after its introduction in 1843; and it may be still be seen in use even today in some of the farms of East Anglia.

Another type of horse-plough Ransome's made famous was the Newcastle series—RNE, RNF, etc. They are so called because they were originally designed to compete in the plough-trials at the Royal Agricultural Show at Newcastle in 1864. The Society had given notice before the Show that 'prizes would be awarded to ploughs which reached a certain standard of excellence'. In addition to designing a series of new ploughs specially for the occasion, Ransome's —acting on the theory that in ploughing the ploughman and the horses are at least as important as the plough itself—sought around for a skilled ploughman to join up with their selected team of Suffolk horses. In 1863 James Edward Ransome, another grandson of the founder, discovered James Barker, an Essex man who had a great local reputation as a ploughman. Ransome engaged him not only for the Newcastle trials but afterwards to attend plough-trials wherever they were held up and down the country.

About this time the firm was beginning a new policy: in previous years, during the railway boom, they had been so engaged in manufacturing railway material that the agricultural side of the business had been to a certain extent neglected. The appointment of the professional ploughman was the beginning of a new trend; for James Barker soon justified his engagement. The firm won five prizes at the Newcastle Show, and during the same year, fifteen out of twenty all-England prizes, all with the newly designed ploughs and the new ploughman. In 1865 they carried off twenty-one. For many years after this Barker was acknowledged as the champion ploughman of England; and he continued competing until 1879. During this period he won £2000 in prizes. After this date Ransome's gave up the idea of competing, and Barker concentrated on coaching local men. His visits to ploughing matches in Suffolk became a great attraction. It was said at the time that 'the farmers and labourers regarded with almost as much interest his grand team of Suffolk horses from the stables at Ipswich as his own matchless ploughing.'

The firm ceased to make horse-ploughs in 1948; and a few years later they gave up their stables. Although they did not compete in ploughing-matches after Barker's time, they always kept a team of Suffolk horses and an expert ploughman to try out experimental designs of new ploughs and to demonstrate the merits of designs that had already been approved.

The head horseman of the Ransome's stable kept a diary, and here is one of the entries from recent years:

'7th November, 1934; Punch, when ploughing on 5.11.34 developed a slight lameness in the right foot. The following morning (6.11) I had the vet. down to the Works to see him. The farrier removed the shoe and found that the hoof had been pricked near the frog. This he cut open, cleaned and ordered bran poultices to be put on.

The vet. has seen him this morning and reports that the lameness is much better. (Signed) S. Hazell.'

By 1950 the Ransome's stable of Suffolk horses had dwindled to a pair—the last in a long line. The last entry in the diary records what happened to them:

'March 21st, 1950; Punch and Rex
These two horses were sold to Mr. M. I. Wood, Pearls Farm, Helmingham. (Signed) W. F. Garnham.'

It would be instructive to trace the steps by which the tractor has displaced the horse-plough in Suffolk. To do this fully over a fairly wide area is beyond the scope of the present work; but one or two related facts may be mentioned. James Edward Ransome introduced one of the first motor tractors in England in the year 1903; and during the following year the firm staged a demonstration of the petrol motor-tractor together with the first tractor plough on Rushmere Heath, near Ipswich. This demonstration was for the benefit of a certain Prince Schoenburg-Hartenstein. There does not seem to have been much use of the tractor plough in Suffolk before the 1914–18 war; but this period established the worth of the internal combustion engine beyond doubt; and the development of the tractor and the spread of tractor-ploughing quickened up enormously immediately after the war ended. In 1919 Ransome's introduced the self-lift tractor-plough at the Tractor Trials held at South Carlton Lincolnshire; and in the early 'twenties the tractor found its way on to the Suffolk farms in increasing numbers.

William Cobbold of Battisford—then bailiff at Hitcham—first used a tractor in 1919: 'It was a Sanderson, made at Bedford; and I used to work it with my thirteen-year old son.' George Garrard who had a *six-horse farm* at Gislingham bought his first tractor in 1927: 'I had an Emerson-Brantigan, a big owd thing that drew a three-furrow plough. There were only about half a dozen of them in the county.' When he bought the tractor he sold two of his horses, working his land with four horses and the tractor. Later, he bought another tractor—a Standard Fordson, and sold another two horses. He kept two tractors and two horses right up to the 1939–45 war when, to a certain extent, the farm-horse came into his own again. This is what happened on George Garrard's farm: 'During the war one of my tractors broke down and it was difficult to get spare parts. So I say: "I got two tractors and one is no good, so I'm going to get some good horses". I went to a sale and saw some Suffolks a-going at 150 guineas apiece. I saw an owd bor there and he say: "Don't have 'em". So I went hoom and on the way I met a man I knew. I told him about the horses and he say: "If you want a pair of good horses and don't mind a-going back with me a little way, I can show you where you'll find a couple o' good uns." He took me to a place where there were two Suffolks—one forty-five guineas and one forty-two—a gelding and a mare. They say the mare was two year old and had now been at work a-carting beet. I say: "I want something that can work," so I bought the mare. I took her hoom and soon found she was a right good worker. But one day one of the men say to me, he say: "Thet mare is in foal". "No!" I say. But he were

56

right. I kept her in the yard and on light work; and one morning I went into the yard; and there was a beautiful little foal. The man I bought her from wanted to buy the mare and foal back for a hundred guineas; but I wouldn't part with them. And a little later I bought another colt to run in with mine. For a long time I worked the horses along with the tractors: I used the horses for ploughing the headlands after the tractors had ploughed the stetches; and for *finishing-up*, as we called it. We used to plough the last two furrows in the stetch with the horses so that the tractor-wheel wouldn't go on land that already been ploughed. In the heavy owd land where I was, the tractor wheels can very easy form a *hard pan*—a hard layer of mud that you wouldn't be able to break up till the following winter. I sold the colts; and then I sold the two horses in 1953— they went to the knackers. They brought in sixty guineas each, much more than I paid for 'em.'

As this account indicates the tractor gained ground very quickly after the last war; and during the early 'fifties the tractor-plough ousted the horse-plough from most of the farms in Suffolk.

5

Outside Jobs

In addition to his work about the farm the horseman, not infrequently, went with a wagon and a team of horses on an 'outside job'. He acted, in fact, as a carrier or a wagoner. One horseman remembers taking pigs twelve miles' distance into Ipswich; also loads of wool after a sheep-shearing. He drove three horses in his wagon—two shaft-horses and a trace-horse; and he got half-a-crown *outside allowance* for the day. But he had to stable his horses out of this. Stabling meant just putting up the horses, as he took fodder with him in the wagon. The price was fourpence for each horse. Therefore, he had one-and-sixpence—at the most—left for his own meals; and considering that on occasions such as this he got up much earlier than usual and did not return until well after his normal finishing-time, he needed the money for sustenance and compensation for the extra hours he worked. 'You didn't have many spare pence then. If, when you were in the town, you treated yourself to a hair-cut, you'd probably have to go without your usual pint.'

One of the inns at Ipswich used by the wagoners was The Rose and Crown. Each wagoner unharnessed his horses and placed them in the stable until they were needed: if the stables were full he threw a few sacks over the horses' backs and tethered them, leaving them with a nosebag each to feed from. At this particular inn, the wagoners living north of Ipswich sometimes arranged a little sweepstake amongst themselves for the return journey. They clubbed together and collected half-a-crown—as a prize for the first team to get to the Barham Sorrel Horse, an inn about five miles' distance along the Norwich road. Arthur Chaplin has described some of his carting jobs from Stowupland Hall: 'We used to go into Stowmarket quite often to take wheat to the railway station or barley to the maltings. We usually did two journeys a day into Stowmarket; and I always schemed to get the first load loaded up the night before, if I could. Then I got away early in the morning. But sometimes this couldn't be done and we were late starting and late finishing with our second load. When we were taking loads of corn from the farm we got fourpence a day *journey money*. With this you were able to have something in the town with your *bait*. I aimed to have my *elevenses* in town and to have a pint o' beer to go 'long with them. We got no allowance for *loads home*. For instance, when we went empty to Stowmarket to fetch pig-meal or oil-cakes from the station we got nothing. The farmer gave us an allowance only on what he sold. But he were a fair employer, Henry Fairfax Harwood—he were a bachelor. He paid his men thirteen shillings a week; and at that time the usual wage was twelve.'

This farmer had another estate at Tuddenham Hall, a few miles farther east; and an account of the carting jobs between the two holdings of Stowupland and Tuddenham brought out a very ancient agricultural practice. This is the exchange of seed between one type of land and another. Gardeners of the old school in Suffolk rarely buy fresh seed. They grow their own. They pick out a selection of the seed—broad beans or peas, for example—and preserve them as seed for the following year. But they will not do this indefinitely. The stock of seed, they maintain, will deteriorate if sown constantly on the same land. Therefore they have a practice of exchanging seed amongst themselves, preferably with someone in the next parish. Robert Savage, the Blaxhall shepherd, once gave the present writer some gardening advice in his usual direct language, and described the custom incidentally: 'Don't you pick any of your beans off one end of the row. Let a few plants grow and pick the best off 'em for seed about September time. You bin a-dewing that? Right. But you can dew thet too often. You want to farm 'em out next year. You give me some on 'em; and I'll get my Arthur to plant 'em down thar on the heavy land at Farnham. Then he can give you some of the seed back when he's grown a crop. That's how I go on. You can keep the seed up here on this light owd land too long. It goes back. But dew you farm it out now and then on the heavy land, you won't go wrong.'

Similarly, seed-corn was exchanged at the beginning of the century between the farms at Stowupland and Tuddenham for the same reason. 'Seed from the dealers was very expensive. But you could grow your own corn if you didn't keep the same strain on the land all the time; if you exchanged it now and again, it kinda renewed itself.'

Thomas Tusser seems to have known of the practice. Under *August's Husbandry* he has:

> *Once harvest dispatched get wenches and boys*
> *and into the barn afore all other toies;*
> *Choiced seed to be picked and trimly well fy'd*[1]
> *for seed may no longer from threshing abide.*

> *Get seed afore hand in a readiness had*
> *or better provide, if thine own be too bad:*
> *Be careful of seed, or else such as ye sow*
> *be suer at harvest, to reap or to mow.*

And Dorothy Hartley, Tusser's editor, quotes from the thirteenth century *Rules* for the management of a landed estate. These are believed to have been written by Robert Grosseteste, Bishop of Lincoln, but a native of the county of Suffolk:

'Chaunge your seede every yere Myghelmas, for it shall be more advayle for you to seede your londes withe seede that growe on other mennes londis then withe seede that growe on your owne lande.'

John Worlidge,[2] the seventeenth-century writer on husbandry, also commends the practice:

'For we perceive that in the same Land one sort of Seed will thrive where another will not, according to the Proverb, *One Mans Meat is anothers Poison;* and that any sort of Grain or Seed will in time extract and diminish such Nutriment that it most delights in. Which is the cause that our Husbandmen do find so great an Advantage and Improvement by changing their Seed, especially from that Land which is so often tilled which they call *Hook-land* into Land newly broken; and from dry, barren and Hungry Land to rich and fat

[1] i.e. dressed.   [2] *Systema Agriculturae*, 1681.

Land; also from Land inclining to the South, to Land inclining to the North & *e contra*; all which produce a good Improvement.

'As Cattle that are taken out of short, soure, and bad Pasture, and put into good sweet Pasture, thrive better than such that are not so exchanged. After the same manner it is with Trees removed out of bad Ground into good; all which are manifest signs, there there is some particular thing, wherein each Seed delights: which if we did but understand, we might properly apply it, and gain Riches and Honor to ourselves; but because we are ignorant thereof, and are content so to remain, we will make use of such Soils, Dungs, Composts and other Preparations and Ways of Advancement of the Growth of Vegetables, as are already discovered and made use of. . . .'

But Robert Bakewell, the eighteenth century Leicestershire breeder, quoted an incident of a kind that may have induced farmers to exchange seed among themselves: 'I will not dispute with you on the propriety of changing seed neither do I profess myself to have had much Experience in that Business, but I have been told a Person sold his Barley to a merchant about 20 miles from the Place where it grew and made a practice for many years of having a small quantity from the said merchant by way of change—the Farmer attended the putting up of his own Barley and lost his sleeve Button, in sowing what he had from the merchant the Button was found—Excellent Change.'[1]

Arthur Chaplin recalls taking loads of seed for exchange on many occasions: 'Whenever I had this job I had to get up at three o'clock in the morning. As the horses were going on the high-road they had to have a proper grooming: they had to be *braided up*, the mane and the tail plaited with *bast*[2] and coloured ribbon. I'd be away from the farm as soon as I could; and I'd be at Barham Sorrel Horse by half-past six—twenty-to-seven time, and I'd have a pint and some bait. Then I'd be off again without much loitering. It was the dark time o' the year usually, and I had to have the old candle-lamps; but as soon as I left the Horse and got off the high-road into the side lanes, I put out the old lamps and bunged 'em into the back o' the wagon. We

[1] H. Cecil Pawson, *Robert Bakewell*, Crosby Lockwood, p. 142.
[2] The inner bark of the lime tree.

carried on then in the dark: no one was about. We come back loaded up and reached hoom about six-thirty at night. It were slow going. The road were the old stoon roads, made up with flints that they'd picked off the fields; and you had to be some careful if something passed you and you pulled into the side. If you had a big load and you pulled in too close to the hedge, like as not you wouldn't be able to get out. It were a long day, but we got two shillings extra for this special job o' "changing seed".'

One other ancient practice that was kept up at Stowupland until recent years was the payment of glove-money at harvest. Arthur Chaplin has recounted that an item of the harvest contract between the farmer and his workers, before the 1914–18 war, was *Glove-money 2s. 6d.* Its purpose was to pay for the gloves that the reapers wore to protect their hands from the thistles in the corn. Tusser recommended that the Harvest Lord and his reapers should be similarly gloved. But at that time the farmer actually presented the gloves to the reapers; and even at the end of the eighteenth century this present had not yet been commuted for a money payment. Sir John Cullum of Hawstead recorded in 1784:[1]

'The agreement between the farmers and the hired harvesters is made on Whitson Monday. Harvest Gloves of 7d. a pair are still presented.'

The Sorrel Horse, the inn on the main Ipswich-Norwich road, was a well-known *baiting house* for horse-traffic from the farms. Arthur Gooding (born 1887) spent most of his life there: his father and grandfather were landlords there before him. He recalled that it was a popular stopping place for the farm wagons: 'The horsemen used to have journey-money, and they called in to have a pint. Some on 'em would stop all day and hev a skinful. They didn't hev much money, but it went a long way in those days. You could get a pint o' beer, an ounce of tobacco and a box of matches—and you'd still get some change out of a tanner. We'd hev the horses here for the night; but these were not farm-horses o' course. It cost a tanner for stabling and a tanner for bait. It was all horses along this road at that time o' day. On a market-day you'd see scores of 'em going into Ipswich: I recall

[1] *History of Hawstead* (Suffolk), 2nd edition, p. 259.

a man from Diss, by the name of Middleditch. He'd take a lot of horses into the sales: eight or nine of 'em in a string, tied head to tail.'

As well as being the winning post for the informal trotting races from Ipswich, The Sorrel Horse was also the finish for the organised road trotting contests: 'They'd start from Thwaite Buck's Head,

about twelve miles away, and finish up at The Horse. The stake was around about £10. I recollect two men—Jack Ruffles and Tom Ford—trotting from Stonham Tap to The Horse. The stake: the winner took both horses.'

The village carriers from the outlying villages north of Ipswich also used to call at The Sorrel Horse. At that time most of the bigger villages had a man who ran a carrier's business, either full time, or in conjunction with another business. He took goods and passengers into the town in his wagon and brought out supplies to the village shop, or to families who had given him a direct order. Clifford Race, who was brought up in the village of Stonham Aspal, recalled the carrier for that village: 'He had a two-horse wagon with a hood on it. He left Stonham at nine in the morning—Tuesdays, Thursdays and Saturdays—and got to Ipswich at noon. He left the town at four in the afternoon. In between, the carrier used to chase round Ipswich with a long list of things that people had asked him to get for them. You paid him tuppence—quite a bit o' money at that time o' day— but he'd go all over the town to get what you wanted. He came back to the village at about eight in the evening: the journey back took longer because he'd got more calls to make. This carrier—he were called Bridges—took passengers, too: a shilling return to Ipswich. You sat on a kind o' form, and you'd find your feet resting on any- thing from hens to a side o' bacon. The horse-carrier's business finished just after the 1914–18 war. A man named Ling put his bonus (war-gratuity) into buying a motor-lorry; and he set up a carrier's business. Bridges gave up his horses; and another man took over. He didn't last for long though; and the motor soon had all the business. A real good carrier was a great benefit to a village; but the trouble with some on 'em was they couldn't pass a pub.'

In the days of the old horse-traffic, the high-road seems to have had a quality that, to a great extent, it has since lost. A man with any self- respect would not be seen driving a horse on it unless he himself, the horse and the trap or wagon were looking at their best. Even if the sky threatened to fall or the bottom to drop out of the farm, one had to look well on the high-road. And there was great rivalry between head horsemen on neighbouring farms to see who had the best *turn- out*. Two horsemen, each from nearby farms, sometimes met in a village inn. One mentioned casually during the course of the evening that he was taking a team of horses up to market the following day. 'That's funny,' the other commented, 'I'm taking a team to Ipswich myself.' They both left earlier than their usual time, and rose very early the next morning, between two and three o'clock; and they both spent a couple of hours polishing the harness and grooming and braiding the horses. Each was determined to make sure that his turn- out would be at least as good as his neighbours'. One head horseman kept a set of harness of his own at home in his cottage; and on the occasions when he took a light horse and trap from the farm into market, he made sure the night before that both horse and harness kept up his reputation for having one of the best turn-outs on the Norwich road.

But the old horsemen also liked to have a respectable farm-wagon or tumbril for the horses to pull when they went on to the high-road; and when the wagon or tumbril was freshly painted they were very proud indeed. Some of this general pleasure in seeing, or driving in, a respectable vehicle on the high-road is expressed in the apocryphal story that once circulated in the Stonham Aspal district: A tumbril, used regularly by an old farm-worker, was freshly decorated. He was so proud of it that, when he drove it from the coach-builder's yard, he stopped the horse at the side of the road and got down to see how he looked in it from the ground. At the present time not a horse is to be seen on most days along the stretch of the Norwich-Ipswich road just mentioned. The long tradition of horse-traffic is now almost completely broken: the blacksmiths are all dying out; the harness-makers and the old 'horse' tailors are almost as rare; and the *posting* and *baiting* houses along the road are now hardly distinguishable from ordinary *pubs*. The road bears few signs or little visible evidence—except perhaps here and there a mounting-block or a tethering-post with its ring—of the colourful community that once bowled along it; and even these are gradually being removed.[1] We may get an inkling of the length of this tradition by taking a brief look at a series of records discovered in the city of Norwich. They are *The Journals of John Dernell and John Boys*, two carters at *The Lathes*, a fifty acre estate on the north side of the city. The estate was managed as a home-farm of St Giles's Hospital, a religious body; and the date of John Dernell's diary is 1417, the fifth year of the reign of Henry V. But its purpose was not dissimilar to that of the Ransome's stable diary already quoted.

The carters, in addition to doing jobs about the farm, went on

---

[1] 'Five drinking troughs for horses, now in various parts of Ipswich, are to be removed in the current year.' *East Anglian Daily Times*, 30th April, 1958.

outside jobs for which they were hired by various towns-people. In September of the above year John Dernell made the journey from Norwich to Ipswich. He completed the double journey—about ninety miles—and his business in four days; and spent at least one night on the road. His business was to bring home iron. But here is the full entry:[1]

(6th September)

Die Lune proximo ante Festum Nativitatis beate Marie, Dies Martis yo carte to ʒepeswych warde price xiijs. iiijd. Dies Mercurii, Dies Jovis, comyng homwarde with vj Osmonde Barell price iijs. Dies Veneris rest all day. Dies sabbati ij plowes goyng all day.
Summa receptorum xvjs. iiijd.

For costis to ʒepeswych and homwarde viijs vijd. oƀ. Item v comb draf ij buschels price xjd. Item in hors brede xijd. Item a payr of trayce of vƫi ƌi price viijd. Item a payr selys iijd. Item yo dyʒghtyng of yo traice & yo selys ijd. Item hopyng of a payr carte nawes ijd. Item ijƫi flok jd. oƀ. Item my wage xiiijd. Item Clerk jd. Summa expensarum xiijs jd. Et debit iijs. iijd.

And below in a clearer form:

Monday before the Nativity of the Blessed Mary; Tuesday, the cart to Ipswich. Price 13s. 4d. Wednesday and Thursday, coming homeward with six barrels of iron. Price 3s. Friday, rest all day. Saturday, two ploughs going all day. Total of receipts: 16s. 4d.

Expenses to Ipswich and homeward: 8s. 7½d. *Item* five combs two bushels of *draf* (the refuse of grain) 11d. *Item* for horse fodder: 12d. *Item* a pair of traces weighing 5½ lbs.: price 8d. *Item* a pair of sales (*seals* or *hames*): 3d. *Item* for making ready the traces and sales: 2d. *Item* the banding of a pair of cart naves 2d. *Item* two lbs. of coarse wool 1½d. *Item* my wage 14d. *Item* Clerk 1d.

Total expenses: 13s. 1d. Still owing (has in hand) 3s. 3d.

We can infer from a later entry in the Engrossed Roll of the estate for what purposes the iron was used. The entry occurs under *Expenses of Ploughs and Carts:*[2]

[1] *Original Papers*, Norfolk and Norwich Archaeological Society (1903), Vol. XV, Part II, p. 133.
[2] *ibid.*, p. 159.

In iron & steel bought, with the fixing them upon the shares, coulters, & equipment of 2 ploughs at the Lathes this year (1428–9): 17s. 9d.

But to return to the entry from the carter's diary: there are a number of the items deserving of a note. A comb is still an East Anglian corn measure, equivalent to four bushels, or half a quarter. *Draf* was coarse grain, or what is now known as *tailings*;[1] or it might possibly have been also, the grains of malt left after brewing. The purchase of a pair of traces weighing five and a half pounds brings up some interesting points. A present-day pair of traces for a farm-horse weighs seven pounds, and it is unlikely that had these traces been made of iron they would have been lighter in weight than the modern ones. It is probable they were made of some other material with iron fastenings at either end. For during this period most of the harness for horses and oxen was made of rope: straw or hay-rope. Even traces were made of this material; and horse-harness as we know it today was not generally used in country districts until comparatively recent times when the increasing use of the horse in industry and in the towns (chiefly in the nineteenth century) raised the standard of harness-making.[2] Traces were also made of plaited withes—at least for the teams of oxen. Ffransis Payne[3] obtained this information from a man who had worked one of the last teams of oxen in Sussex at the end of the last century. When he started work in 1893 traces made of withes and hay-rope were used by the teams of oxen at the plough. Mr Payne further quotes the practice of mid-Wales farmers who within living memory kept a holly-plantation where withes were specially grown for making traces, as well as for other uses about the farm: hazel was also favoured for the same purpose.

It seems reasonable to infer that as the amount of money the Norwich carter spent on harness and gear during that particular week was so large, it was made of easily expendable material and that the ninety miles journey made almost complete replacements necessary. The *hames* are the pieces of wood or metal fastened to

[1] *A.F.C.H.*, p. 94.
[2] F. H. Hollis, 'The Horse in Agriculture,' *B.O.H.*, p. 181.
[3] *Y.A.G.*, pp. 150–1.

the collar of a draught-horse. The traces are fixed to the hames, and they have to be robust and fit well on to the collar as they take the full pull of the load. Wooden hames are still to be seen on plough-horses even today; and it is likely that the pair mentioned here were wood also. It is worth noting that they are still referred to as *seals* in one or two districts of Suffolk—notably in the Stowmarket area.

Dighting[1] of the hames and traces probably involved securely fixing one to the other— a job requiring much care and some skill as these two items of the harness took the full strain. The next item, was for metal hoops, made for fixing around the wooden wheel-naves or hubs to prevent them from spreading. The *flock* or coarse wool—a fairly frequent entry in the diary—was perhaps to stuff the horse-collars, ensuring that they would lie comfortably on the neck. But wool would not be the ideal material and would tend to mat easily as the collar absorbed the sweat, thus needing frequent replacement to prevent the horse becoming *collar-proud*—unduly sensitive to the collar.

The carter's wage of fourteen pence a week represents the wage for a seven-day week: like the modern horseman he had also to work on a Sunday, at *baiting* and clearing out the stable. If he had been a day-man he would have been paid a shilling only. If a feast-day happened to fall in a particular week he might be paid two pence or even threepence less; because it appears that a statute of the previous reign (Henry IV: 4, c.14) 'enacted that not only should a labourer receive no wages on feast days, but also only half-pay on the vigils of such days when he did not work after the noon-hour'.[2] But John Dernell received only thirteen pence for a full week's work, not because of lost work through religious feasts or similar reasons, but simply because the steward who audited his accounts was a very just man. Each week he crossed out: *Item Clerk 1d.* For the steward evidently considered that it was the carter's job to keep his own journal and his accounts. If he had not the skill, it was a deficiency that no one could be blamed for but himself; and he himself would have to pay to hire the Clerk who did the writing for him.

[1] M.E.: to make ready.
[2] *Original Papers*, (already cited), p. 123.

This crossed-out penny, the last item in the week's entry, explains the discrepancy between the sum of the separate items and the total of 13s. 1d. The total was written down by the steward, as also was the note: *He owes* (or has in hand) 3s. 3d. This represents the difference between the carter's receipts—the monies paid to him by the people who hired him for the various jobs—and the expenses, including his wages, that were incurred during the week.

The Clerk's curious setting down of the journals, with the dates in Latin and the items in English, is not—one imagines—due to any itch to give his second language an airing. We can offer the more charitable explanation that the device was an attempt to differentiate one part of the diary from the other. As far as the carter was concerned the important part was written in English, perhaps at his own request; for though it was manifestly beyond his powers to write his own language he might well have had enough wit to recognise it. In any case he was probably not much concerned with either language, as it was written down; for commerce with people who do not read very much and who are not greatly overawed by the tyranny of the written —and especially—the printed word and its implied and often specious claim to infallibility, seems to suggest that their real attitude to a document such as this is: 'Words—well, words is just *words*. But figures—*figures* now is different'. And the figures were clear enough to the carter, especially, no doubt, the bitter mutilated figure of one penny that the careful steward invariably denied him.

Two items in the carter's diary a few days before the journey to Ipswich may have had some bearing on the expedition. They are: *whycorde jd* and *ij payr langell*. *Langell*, it is believed, are hopples or fetters for hobbling a horse to prevent him from straying too far. We can assume that the carter spent two nights on the road; and as it was September, and not too far advanced in the year, he probably spent them sleeping in or under his cart while the two horses grazed nearby. This was a practice that was not uncommon up to the beginning of this century. Wagoners and horsemen on long journeys from home were forced to take what comfort they could; and they referred to the practice philosophically as *sleeping rough*. And even where they had adequate journey-money, enough to enable them to take a night's lodging, they often preferred to sleep out and save the money for other uses.

One known instance of this sleeping-out on a long journey has been given by a member of a family from the village of Stonham Aspal which the Norwich carter passed on his road to Ipswich. The Berry family of Stonham, and after them the Races, had a small cottage industry: the making of *whitening rolls* or *balls* from chalk taken from the nearby pits at Claydon. The whitening was used for decorating cottages, 'indoor work', when papering was beyond the means of most rural families. The industry was handed down in the Berry family for generations; and George Race (born 1842) married one of the daughters and learned the trade from his wife. He used to go about the countryside selling whitening at three-halfpence a roll or one stone (four rolls) for sixpence. On these expeditions George Race and his mother-in-law often spent a night away from home with their donkey and cart, sleeping on the side of the road if this were at all possible. On one occasion they went as far as Aldeburgh—a memorable visit for George Race: for though he lived into the late 'twenties of this century it was the only time he saw the sea.

To return for two brief notes to the fifteenth century Norwich carters: The week before he left for Ipswich John Dernell got the Clerk to make this entry:[1] *Dies sabbati, a plow goyng tyll none, after none schod oure hors and dyzght oure harneys*. This, and similar entries in the Journals, confirm that ploughing finished at mid-day even when horses had been substituted for oxen. (There were six horses on the estate to do all the farm-work and the carting). The other entry is from the Journal of John Boys, one of John Darnell's successors. He kept an even more detailed diary, and more than once has an entry such as this:

Item: at after (noon) moked oure hors and mendyd oure carte.[2] *Mucking* or *mucking out* (the horses, cattle, etc.) is still the usual expression in East Anglia for cleaning out the stables; and, along with other instances in these diaries, illustrates what a history of long and uninterrupted usage farming words and phrases have. In fact, the main impression one gets from reading through these diaries is that

[1] *Ibid.*, p. 132.   [2] *Ibid.*, p. 156.

they are not after all—although they are five hundred years old—so alien in temper and content to the old pre-machine farming community that some of the older people in East Anglia remember so well. Yet how alien they seem to us today. Or to make the point in another way: how recently has this old farming continuity—extending back, on the present evidence, at least five hundred years—been broken in almost everything except a residual and apparently quickly disappearing vocabulary.

6

The Horseman's Dress

The old horseman had a traditional love of dressing in a way that was peculiar to his trade or craft. Before the First World War each worker on the farm dressed in the manner accepted for his job; and it was not difficult for the country-wise to pick out the shepherd, the stockman, the horseman and the ordinary day-man from a gathering of farm people at a show or a sale. It would not be easy to do this today, apart from the fact that few working horsemen are left. Clifford Race, a blacksmith who had also worked on farms—chiefly with horses—during the early part of his life, commented on the difference:

'All trades on the farm are jumbled up today, that's how it seems to me. Since the machines they haven't got the same organisation. Anybody on the farm can drive a tractor now, and plough a field. They go into a field with a tractor-plough and as long as they make it look black it doesn't matter. Shut the gate on it. It will do. But that's another matter. But look at the way they dress: nowadays everybody wants to look the same as everybody else. It's the same in the town. You see a carpenter or a painter or any tradesman like that, he won't wear his apron or white coat in the street if he can help it. He doesn't want to look different. But in the old days as soon as a man came into the smithy, for instance, in the morning, the first thing he did was to put on his leather apron. I was proud of my owd leather apron; and if I had to slip outside to post a letter before starting work at the anvil I put on my apron first. At that time o' day no man cared who saw him in his working clothes.'

The ordinary farm-worker, however, had little scope for differentiation in dress. He was, for the most part, in the position of the old

Lincolnshire (Louth area) worker who once told the writer: 'I was earning about one-and-six a day; and I had one spare suit and one spare pair of boots—that was when I was in bed'. The horseman was in a special class among the farm-workers: he did not lose work through bad weather, and he had a number of privileges that gave him a steadier and more comfortable living. These were summarised by a Government report at the end of the last century.[1] 'Horse-keepers and stockmen usually have their cottages on the farm, which are of a much better stamp than those in the open villages; and moreover they often have good gardens attached. In addition they not infrequently get rough firing and occasionally potato-ground. Many horse-keepers are given 6d and some 1s. 0d. for a journey of over 2 miles with a wagon. Also they usually take part in the harvest.'

Charles Bugg of Barking has filled in some of the details of the horseman's role at harvest-time: 'The head horseman was often Lord of the Harvest[2] round about here. He took charge in the field at the cutting, and at the stacking of the corn. This was an important job at that time o' day as the corn had to remain in the stack for some weeks until they thrashed it. The Lord walked round the top of the stack, building up the sides. He was responsible for the stack standing up straight after the corn had settled down; and no one was allowed to touch the outside of the stack except the Lord.

'The stockman was rarely Lord. Like the shepherd it was not usual for him to "go in" the harvest. When the head horseman was Lord, the second horseman "stayed out" to look after the horses.'

The 1895 Report quotes actual figures for horsemen's wages: 'The annual earnings of horse-keepers and cattle-men are easier to estimate because they lose no time in broken weather. . . . On six farms the annual earnings of horse-keepers varied from £43 or 16s. 6½d. a week to £48, or 18s. 5½d. a week. But in those cases the men paid rent from £1 14s. to £4 a year.'

[1] *Royal Commission on Agriculture in England: Report by Mr. A Wilson Fox on the County of Suffolk*, 1895, p. 76.
[2] *A.F.C.H.*, p. 90.

Actual Earnings of Horsekeepers

Annual Cash Earnings	Average per Week	Perquisites	Rent Paid for Cottage and Garden
£36 14 3 (Average of 2 men)	14s. 1½d.	Oven wood; malt at harvest: value 12s.	1s. 10d. per week
£39 13s. 10¼d. (Average of 2 men)	15s. 3d.	Free Cottage and Garden	

These figures show that the horseman's skill was recognised in his wages; and—much more than the ordinary day-man—he was able to indulge that taste for a distinctive dress which appears always to have been possessed by those whose work is in any way connected with horses.

For work the horseman of this period wore a sleeved waist-coat with a velvet front and *cantoon*[1] back and sleeves. This waist-coat had flap-pockets and reached down almost to the knees: it was fastened right up to the neck with horse-shoe buttons, leaving just enough space for the red-spotted muffler or *wrapper* to be seen underneath. The wrapper was usually a very large coloured handkerchief that was wound twice round the neck and tied at one side 'with two ends left a-flapping'. On the legs were cord-breeches and *knee-buskins*. These were similar to the ordinary buskins but extended up beyond the knee: 'They used to flap about as you walked; but they were whoolly useful in bad weather.' On the feet were *home-made* boots with double tongues: 'They were made by the village cobbler and cost fourteen shillings: they'd last about two years if you got them *clumped*[2] at the end of the first year.'

[1] *canton-flannel:* cotton cloth on which a nap was raised in imitation of wool.

[2] A *clump* is a half-sole of leather riveted on to the original sole before this wears through.

Frank Whynes, (born 1891) of Stowmarket, a tailor who once travelled round the villages in that area, has described the horseman's dress in detail:

'I had to make the sleeved *weskit* according to the customer's order. Nearly all of them had a *hare-pocket* on the inside, on the left. If you were wearing one of these weskits you could double up an owd

hare and place it inside and button up; and no one knew anything about it. Some men had this pocket extended right round the back of the weskit. If they wanted the pocket lengthened in this way, I then had to fix eight buttons to fasten the top of the pocket to the lining of the weskit: if I didn't do this, when the pocket were full it would sag below the bottom of the weskit and give the *game* away. Occasionally a man asked me to sew in a gun-loop high up on the left side of the weskit—inside of course. This loop held the barrel of the gun while the butt rested on the bottom of the hare-pocket. With a gun loop and one of those pockets, the owd horseman could walk about as though he were a-taking his leisure and had no concern but to get a proper draw on his owd clay-pipe'.

For walking out and for Sundays he had a cord jacket and cord trousers. But the trousers were no ordinary trousers: they were *whole-falls*, that is, trousers with a flap that let down in front like a sailor's. They were also bell-bottomed, with a sixteen inch knee and a twenty-two inch bottom. The outside of the trouser-leg was trimmed with steel-faced horse-shoe buttons. Some of the more dress-conscious horsemen ordered a special kind of trimming on the leg—an inlet or gusset of black velvet, running from the bottom of the trousers, on the outside, and tapering to a point somewhere near the knee. Four or five horse-shoe buttons were sewn to this gusset as an extra decoration.

The jacket had flap-pockets; and fancy stitching on the jacket was usual. 'They'd have what we called a *vandyck* back and sleeves—a fancy stitch something like waves—on the shoulders and the cuffs. Some of them wanted pint-pots worked in fancy stitch on the back, or maybe a horse's head or even a fox-head. The owd horseman knew what he wanted; and it weren't no use a-tryin' to tell him what to have. Those owd country-bo's had wunnerful good clothes: do you know that? They went in for warmth. They'd have their breeches and leggin's lined with flannelette—lined with *swansdown*, they used to say—or fluffy calico. The cloth for their suits was *cord* (corduroy), as I've told you; but sometimes they went in for a suit of heavy tweed—*staple tweed* it was called; and at that time they made it as hard as a board. It were wunnerful stuff. It never wore up. It lasted them fourteen or fifteen years. The cost? Well, about fifty year ago a suit of staple tweed cost £3 10s. Now today . . . but aside from the cost I couldn't make a suit like that today: I couldn't get the material. Breeches and leggings cost 17s. 6d.

'They dressed warm and comfortable, a style of their own. A big silver chain across the front of the weskit, and a big owd tarnip watch at the end of it. On the head they wore a hard hat with a high crown, or a billy cock with a pheasant's or woodcock's feather tucked into the band at the side. We sometimes made an overcoat for one of those owd country-bo's—a head horseman, for instance. This was always a *melton* overcoat. Melton is a thick, very tightly woven woollen cloth. The weave is so tight, wet will never get through it. Here's a piece of real owd melton, the owd stuff. I keep it specially to remind me what it was like. Feel it. And feel this. Here's a piece of what they make and call melton today. They still *call* it melton; but look at the difference: the heart has gone right out of the cloth. The owd stuff wouldn't wear up. You could hand the overcoat over to your son when you'd finished with it; and he could hand it over to his son.

'And look at this piece of material here—a piece of *glissade*. Have you ever slid your arm into the sleeve of a real well-made owd overcoat? Your arm will slide in the sleeve with no effort at all, no pushing and tugging and looking for your hand to come out of the cuff. The owd coat just glides on. There it is; there's the secret. We lined the sleeves with *glissade*. You can't get the stuff today. The owd horsemen had glissade sleeves in their melton overcoats; and here's a button from one of them. I keep it about just to remind myself: here it is, thick mother o' pearl, as big as half-a-crown. Those owd bo's knew the best, and they'd have it. Some on 'em from out Brettenham way used to say to me: "None o' they owd tin buttons for me this time, Frank. I want the *boon* buttons—boon buttons right through!" Although those owd horsemen didn't have high wages they lived cheap, rent free and a piece of land for growing potatoes; and they also had free faggots for kindling.'

Frank Whynes first helped his father with his business of making clothes for country people about fifty years ago. He cycled eighteen to twenty miles every evening after tea, getting orders from the farm-workers. It was no use his going earlier in the day as the men were at work and unable to break off to discuss anything with him. The usual place of meeting was the village inn: he booked a room and measured up his customers there. He delivered the suit when he next came round that way: there was about a month's interval between his visits to a particular village. His customers were not too fastidious, and rarely demanded a *fitting*. 'Only one man I recollect had a fitting. He were owd Bob Steed, the bell-ringer from Buxhall—dead and gone now these many years.'

Robert Overton (born 1895) worked as a horseman at Baylham Hall. The dress in the Baylham district was slightly different from that already described: the sleeved waistcoat had a cord front, and the back was made of drabbet. The leggings were of cord with buttons up the side. At a slightly earlier period, as Arthur Chaplin has recalled, the leggings had *steels* at the side as a fastening. For walking out and for Sundays the most notable article of dress was a long, tailor-made, black velvet jacket with short revers, and five or six buttons. Robert Overton has kept the last velvet jacket he had made; and the cloth is as hard and as durable as a board, seeming to confirm the claim that 'the real owd stuff niver wore up'.

Harry Mason (born 1876) of Coddenham, was a shepherd for all his working life, but his father, Joyce Mason, was a horseman; and he recalls the dress of an earlier period. There does not appear to be any great variation from the above except that the horsemen sometimes wore *elijahs* or *lanigens* (straps below the knee) instead of leggings. They also wore sealskin caps, and sometimes *billycocks*. A billycock was a high hat with its crown tapering slightly to its rounded top. It was made of soft felt. 'It were just the thing for wet weather. You put the *verge* of your billycock down and it would hang round you like an umbrella. The horseman often put a peacock's feather in the side.'

Confirmation for this popularity of *elijahs* among horsemen comes from a farmer who was continually being asked by his workmen to supply new *top-latches*. A *top-latch* is the leather thong that binds together the top ends of the hames or seals on the horse-collar. When he asked what happened to the old ones, the usual explanation was: 'It got *lorst*,' or, 'It *bruk*'. Therefore he made up his mind to find out what really became of the top-latches. After some unobtrusive investigation he discovered that his horsemen were adapting them to two uses: first as *elijahs*; then again as straps to tie up their *beever-baskets*. These were the small, box-like baskets, made of wicker, they used for carrying their *beevers* or *bait*, which was wrapped up neatly inside in a linen-bag, often referred to as a *nose-bag*. One end of the leather-thong was threaded through the two metal eyes that pierced the lid, thus securely fixing it on the basket. A small loop was made at the other end of the thong, and after thrusting a thumb through this loop the worker carried the basket slung over his shoulder.

One old farm-worker has explained that they used *'lijahs* to keep the bottom of the trousers from dragging in the mud, and he added: 'We were a middling clean lot on that particular farm. Everybody shaved twice a week—on Sunday and on Wednesday night, ready for Thursday. And it was clean boots on Monday morning. If anyone came with dirty boots on a Monday, he heard some pretty straight remarks, and he'd be sure to put a better foot forward the next week'.

But Arthur Pluck (born 1888), a clothier from Stowmarket has given a complementary account of the dress of the horsemen and farm-workers at the beginning of this century. His father was also a clothier in the same town; and just before the autumn or spring sales he sent him, as a lad of sixteen or seventeen, out into the villages:

'He used to tell me: "Now you've made a good breakfast; you can't get any more food into you, so you can take these round". And he gave me a huge pile of sale-bills to distribute round the villages. "You needn't come back here till dark: there'll be a good meal waiting for you then. Here's sixpence for you to get yourself something at mid-day." Those were the days when a bicycle was a luxury, so I had to do my round on shanks's pony.

'About the middle of the day I called in at a country pub with my sixpence. This is what I had: Two penn'orth of bread and cheese. This was made up of a half-loaf and a piece of cheese as big as your fist. And a pat of home-made butter cost another penny. They threw in five or six pickled onions, free. A penny for half a pint of beer. That was the meal; and I used to be very pleased with it; very pleased too with the tuppence change, as I reckoned I'd made tuppence on that deal.

'When my father went out into the country he used to book up a room—the *club* room—in the village inn, book for the evening. The farm-workers came in after work and we fitted them up there. I've often gone into the bar on these occasions when I was a young man and been hailed by one of our customers. He'd be drinking beer out of one of the old stone pint-mugs they used to have in those days. It was the custom then as soon as you saw a friend you'd offer him some of your beer—to drink out of your own mug. It wasn't hygienic, I know—in fact I've often thought about it since—but I've done it scores of times. It wouldn't have done to refuse. The customer would have been greatly offended. So I'd be called on to *help* him finish his beer; perhaps his mug was half-full. But after we'd put the drink away between us, then my turn came. I was expected to buy a new, full pint mug for him, and naturally a pint for myself to keep him company! You couldn't put it past those old country bo's for artfulness!'

'I didn't stay long in the country business. Being young I wanted to go farther afield, to get into a better class of business. I put some time in with John Barker of Kensington. I lived in as an apprentice. That was an experience! I was always hungry at that time. But that's another story. When I returned from London I came here and opened up my own business. But I remember clearly how my father conducted his business in his shop in the square at Stowmarket here about sixty years ago. On a Saturday night after the pubs closed he'd often do more business than he'd done during all the week. But he would never stay open after midnight.

'Some of the old country folk used to come in twice a year, to the spring sale and the sale after harvest—when they'd been paid their harvest-money. Here is an actual sale-bill of that time. It will show you the sort of stuff they came in for:

S. PLUCK'S 17TH ANNUAL SALE

of

CLOTHING HOSIERY BOOTS

on Tuesday, April 14th, 1910

———

400 Pairs Tweed Trousers from 2s. 6d.
150 Pairs Cord Trousers from 3s. 9½d.
10 Pairs White Cord 5s. 11d.

'During the period of the sales my father kept a nine-gallon cask of beer under the counter. It was brewed for us by a local brewery—a thin beer, though very good—and we bought it at three-farthings a pint. Before one of the old country bo's started buying my father gave him a glass of beer. And after he'd wished my father health and drunk the beer, most likely he'd place the glass down on the counter and say: "Aren't you a-going to wet the other eye, maaster?" So the glass was filled up the second time; and then the bargaining started. Every item he bought he paid for, as soon as it was on the counter. He wouldn't have a bill. He wouldn't trust a bill. Perhaps he couldn't understand it; couldn't add up the separate items quickly enough. Some of the labourers came into the town only very rarely in those days; and they were a bit lost and wary when they did come. They were off their home ground, so they were very careful. So he'd have a pair of trousers; and he'd pay for it and put it on one side. And he knew exactly where he was then. He'd then buy a jacket; pay for that; then a pair of boots; pay for those—and so on until he'd got what he wanted.

'Not so long ago a very old man came into my shop and told me what he'd bought from my father at one of the sales nearly fifty years ago. He had a cap, muffler—a square of brightly coloured artificial silk—a shirt, vest, pants, a suit and a pair of boots and he still had some change out of his gold sovereign. And he reckoned he was well clothed. Today, a farm-worker will go on to a field with a tractor; and he'll be wearing, like as not, flannel trousers and a pair of dancing pumps. But in those days they were dressed for the job. They kept warm. Now I remember calling on a farm-worker: I was fitting him for something, I believe. This is what he was wearing: a thick vest, long pants, cords, shirt and muffler, two ordinary waist-coats, a sleeved waistcoat, a cardigan and a jacket. That old boy worked hard enough in the field, if it was only in carrying all that stuff around with him!

'But the ordinary worker's dress for Sunday was a square-cut, long, black velvet jacket with short revers and about six buttons down the front; a very good cord trousers, medium drab in colour; and a bowler hat with a *set* (or straight) brim—the curly brimmed bowler was the wear for the *toffs*, the gentry. The makers of these bowlers always put a peacock's feather on the side of the hat. Every man liked a feather in his hat. Often a new bowler hat had a clay-pipe stuck in the band as well; or even a cigar. You could get a *sure-shot* cigar for tuppence in those days.

'The bowler was made of stiff felt. They also wore a billycock, a tallish hat made of semi-stiff felt with a black band round it just above the brim. The band was made of silk, worked in an oak-leaf pattern. The farmers and sometimes the head horsemen wore a *square-crown* or *half-high* hat made of stiff felt.

'Mention of the clay-pipe, though, reminds me that you won't have a complete picture of the old horseman or farm-worker unless you've got his old clay-pipe in. They were called Dublin clays; they were mostly made in Dublin, I understand; but a tobacconist could have his name and so on stamped on them by the makers. They cost a halfpenny; and they used to sell them, and even give them away, in the pubs. There used to be a kind of competition among the customers to see who had the blackest pipe. This is what they used to do: as soon as they bought a new-clay they'd soak it in their beer. Then when they smoked it the pipe would turn as black as your hat. They'd be unwilling to part with it when it got like that; and if the stem broke they'd smoke it even if it were only an inch long.

'They used a *tuppeny ha'penny shag* in those days—twopence halfpenny an ounce. It was made by Churchman's and was real good stuff. I remember the smell of it as clearly as if I'd been near someone who was smoking it out there on the pavement. I'll tell you why. One morning when I was a young man I got up about four o'clock to cycle to Capel St. Mary; and on the way there it was just getting light —a fine morning with the sun coming up and dew on the grass— when I got behind three or four farm-workers on their way to work. They all had their old clay-pipes going; and the aroma—I've never forgotten it—it was better than any cigar you'd like to mention.

'Another thing that's tied up with the clay-pipe is the old *Ha'penny Screw*. This was a halfpenny-in-the-slot machine. It was made of brass, about eight inches square. It's a collector's piece now, and would fetch a lot of money. You'd find them on the counter in the pubs. You put in a half-penny and you'd get out a *screw* of tobacco, about enough for three pipes.

'But we were talking about the dress. There were only two or three kinds of shirt on the market then—white and black-and-white, that is a white shirt with a thin black stripe. The working man never bought a shirt with a collar—there wasn't one made in fact. They wore leather collars with their shirts—no tie. These leather collars were about an inch-and-a-half deep, and had a patent leather surface on the outside. This patent leather was decorated with vertical, coloured stripes—usually black and white. The big advantage of these collars was that they were easily washed. The wearer had only to wipe the surface with a wet flannel to have a clean collar—at least on the outside.'

But it appears that the farm-worker of that period paid great attention to the type of corduroy he chose for his everyday clothes, and especially for his walking-out dress. There were many kinds of corduroy on the market to satisfy him. The *cords* were chiefly made by the Lancashire mills; and a firm from Peterborough—Brown and Son—distributed large quantities over East Anglia. Some of their chief varieties were: *Pheasant-Eye, Genoa, Thick Sett, Doncaster, Fine Reed, Nine Shift* and *Partridge*. Arthur Pluck has added a note about two of these: 'In the *Pheasant-Eye* cord they copied the colours of the pheasant's eye: it was a brownish cord patterned with "eyes" that stood up a bit redder. But the *Doncaster Cord* was in many ways the most interesting. It was woven to represent a field that had been horse-ploughed in the old narrow stetches. You'd have a band of ribs together to represent the furrows in a stetch; then a small gap to show the water-furrows between the stetches. Often times when I was going into the country after orders and so on in the autumn, I'd look at a field that had been freshly ploughed up after the harvest; and I'd think to myself how much like a piece of *Doncaster Cord* it was—colour, straight lines and everything.'

The concern of horsemen for the way they dressed was, as has already been stated, in a very long tradition. Why this is so, it is not easy to discover, unless the hard and varied nature of the job made clothing of a more durable quality than was usual an unquestioned necessity. And once the norm had been passed in one direction it was easier to branch out in another, and with the extra shillings of their wages, to have clothes that had an individual cut and mark and even an individuality of invention. Yet it is unlikely that any of the horsemen of the period we are concerned with—nor yet any of their masters—would have fallen prey to this newspaper advertisement, printed in the reputedly reasonable eighteenth century:

PATENT VENTILATING BREECHES

John Tomkins of Woodstock, Leather-Cutter &c. having Philosophically considered the Causes of Galling in Riding, and found it to proceed merely from Heat; has, after long Study, contrived Leather Breeches with Valves so adapted as to suffer Air to pass in freely; but to let none pass out. This having a double Advantage both in Point of Coolness and Sweetness, he hopes it will meet with the Approbation of all Gentlemen, who ride during the Hot Weather. N.B. Allowance made to Postillions and Out-Riders who take a Number. Letters directed as above will be duly attended to, by his Customers most obedient humble Servant,

JOHN TOMKINS.

Part Two

THE FARMER

7

Arthur Biddell

One of the most noticeable features of the county of Suffolk —at least to the outsider—is its strong links with the past; not only in the more obvious instances of surviving old buildings and old institutions but in the manner the rural people have preserved their continuity up to recent times: first, by tending to remain in one village or in one part of the county; and again, by persisting in the occupation traditional to their family. These tendencies are natural to any rural, and especially agricultural, community; but they survived in East Anglia—in Norfolk and Suffolk and to a lesser extent in Cambridgeshire—later than in other comparable regions; and this leads one to suppose that they were due not so much to a conscious individual or family choice, or to any inherent disposition to remain rooted while people in the rest of the country moved about, as to certain social forces that operated in the whole region to a more or less equal extent. To inquire what these forces were and what were their origins is beyond the scope of the present work; but it would be safe to say that the history, the traditional economy and the geography of the area have all combined to make them operate. And the geography of East Anglia may well have been the strongest single influence. For it lies off the main north-south route that has been so important throughout history, and that was doubly so during the nineteenth century when the rate of change reached its first great peak.

If a generic name were needed for these forces in East Anglia one could risk calling them, without making any value-judgment, the passive force of inertia—the resistance to basic change inherent in any purely agricultural community, strengthened here by its natural advantage of being removed from change's strongest foci. A people—that is, families as opposed to individuals—does not move, especially from a rural area where links to soil, place and community are very tenacious, unless the force of economic change is powerful enough to uproot them. Although farming had many ups and downs during the nineteenth century and many of the more vigorous members of rural families emigrated or moved into the towns, notably during the depression at the end of the last century and the beginning of this, yet there was no great dissolution of the rural community, none of that great quickening that had already come to many of those country districts contiguous to the great industries that had sprung up during the century. The First World War, and the internal combustion engine that it effectively established, were the first real solvents: it was during this time that those fixed social relations were broken down, relations compounded of class and immemorial custom which perhaps more than anything else had kept the rural community in Suffolk in a state where change, although operating, had up to that time no real effect on the basic structure.

Until 1914 most of the smaller Suffolk villages appear to have been comparatively undisturbed and to have had the air of an earlier epoch circulating about them; and even today one can sometimes find a village where one or two families outnumber the rest of the community. These are the families that have been in the village for generations, from the time when movement beyond the immediate district or even beyond the parish or village itself was rare enough to make it a memorable occasion. The surname of Ling, for instance, in the small Suffolk village of Blaxhall, is so frequent that it often causes the postman difficulties: but the difficulties of the postman before the First World War were greater still. For at that time the family was so numerous in the village and the christian names of the men so often duplicated that nick-names became an essential means of identification. *Skilly* Ling, *Mory* Ling, *Ludy* Ling, *Croppy* Ling, *Rook* Ling, *Straight* Ling, *Wag* Ling, *Pessy* Ling, *Finny* Ling and *Nacker* Ling became better known by their acquired names than their baptismal ones; and the newcomer to the village, wishing to be polite, had to be very careful not to make a mistake of strategic dimension by calling Jim Ling *Mr Rook* and thus having the whole clan deploy in determined action against him.

The practice of handing down the trade of the father to one, at least, of the sons was the keystone of the old rural community; and it was strictly followed wherever a body of closely guarded craft skills and secrets was involved. Centuries ago this practice became enshrined in the surname which described accurately the trade of the man who bore it: Smith, Baxter, Forster, Farmer, Wright, Fowler and so on. But these occupational surnames have long ago ceased to have any relation to the jobs of the people who hold them; and it would be difficult, if not impossible, to find a family whose occupation had always remained the same from the time it was first used to give them a descriptive surname. Were a search to be made it would have more chance of success if it were confined to the remoter areas of East Anglia where there are families who have been tied to the land for centuries. Such a family would be the Grooms of the Claydon district of Suffolk. William Groom (born 1884) a small farmer, started his career as a horseman. His father, grandfather and great-grandfather had all been horsemen on farms in the surrounding district; and family tradition says that the Grooms had always been connected with horses: 'Groom by name, and groom by calling', as William Groom put it. His two brothers were also horsemen on farms, not very far away at Needham Market.

But it is among the families of farmers in Suffolk that this continuity of occupation is most common—as one would expect; because the physical nature of inheritance of land, buildings and stock is a strong inducement to a son's carrying on the farm, and keeping the property intact in the family; and the argument from sentiment, aptitude and even real love for the land could usually be addressed with a force backed by the tacit consent of the whole community to any son whose wavering tended to make a break in the traditional family calling. Moreover, the care with which marriages were made among Suffolk farmers tended to keep this continuity, and it would be no exaggeration to characterise many of these as *marriages of conservation*—conservation of real property and also the more imponderable but equally real conservation of cherished family traditions.

But this continuity was noticed some time ago by an American visitor. He came over here about 1875 to buy Suffolk horses. He had high praise for the breed, and also for the quality of the farming in East Anglia:[1] ' "No wonder," said he, "you are such capital farmers; you make your sons farmers—you have been farming for generations." '

It is proposed to treat of one of these farming families, the Biddell family of Playford, near Ipswich; not because the family is typical—it was one of the most outstanding farming families in Suffolk during the nineteenth century—but for other reasons: the family has left fairly copious records of its farming during the last century; and again, one of its members, Herman Biddell, did more than anyone else to raise the Suffolk breed of horse to an excellence that is acknowledged wherever the heavy breed of horse is known.

There were Biddells or Bedells in Suffolk as far back as the sixteenth century, but the branch we are concerned with had its growth from Arthur Biddell who was born in 1783. When he was a young man he moved from Rougham, near Bury St Edmunds, and rented a farm at Playford from the Marquis of Bristol. Arthur Biddell stayed at Hill Farm, Playford until his death in 1860. It was about 250 acres in extent, but the size of the home-farm is no indication of the extent even of his farming activities; for Herman, one of his sons, wrote:[2] 'At one time my father must have rented a thousand acres. Shortly before his death he told me he had been present and paid his rent at a hundred and one half-yearly audits without missing a single audit. As churchwarden he signed the warden's book forty-four years in succession; and after his death I held office for exactly the same period.'

Arthur Biddell married Jane Ransome, daughter of Robert Ransome already noted as the founder of the firm of agricultural engineers. Jane Ransome appears to have been a woman of some culture —two manuscript books of her verses are extant—and a good working partner for her husband. But Arthur Biddell's name is linked with the Ransome's in another way: he invented and designed two agri-

[1] Herman Biddell, 'A History and Register of the County Breed of Cart Horses,' *The Suffolk Stud Book*, 1880, Vol. I, p. 611.
[2] *Thomas Clarkson and Playford Hall* (MS monograph by Herman Biddell. Deposited at Ipswich Borough Library).

cultural implements which J. Allen Ransome described in 1843: 'With the harrows are intimately connected the scarifiers. They approach so closely in their character that it is not easy to draw the line of distinction: indeed, the last mentioned implements may, with equal propriety, be classed with the scarifiers. These latter were the production of an age of considerable agricultural advancement. It

was only after the poorer soils had, by the necessities of mankind, been forced into cultivation, and the less valuable lands had become infested with couch-grass and other weeds which tenant long-culti-vated poorer descriptions of arable land, that the necessity was generally felt of a more powerful implement of bringing to the surface the roots of the stubborn weeds thus growing; hence arose the first attempted variation from the form and principle of the common harrow, and finally the invention of the now highly useful class of scarifiers, scufflers and extirpators.'[1]

[1] J. Allen Ransome, *The Implements of Agriculture*, pp. 73 and 75.

Arthur Biddell became well-known for his scarifier. This is how Ransome describes it: '*Biddell's Scarifier;* the invention of Arthur Biddell of Playford, first made under his direction but thirty years ago, with a framing of wood and tines of wrought iron . . . during the last few years it has been made principally of cast iron and generally introduced.'

Also '*Biddell's Extirpating Harrow:* similar to the scarifier which bears Arthur Biddell's name. It is used for breaking up land when it is too hard for the heaviest harrows, and for bringing winter fallows into a state of fine tillage. In working summer lands it is calculated by the shape of its teeth to bring to the surface all grass and rubbish.'

Arthur Biddell was also a land-surveyor during the whole of the time he was at Playford; and during the early part of the century, principally in the 'thirties, he did a great deal of work in connection with the *Tithe Commutation* surveys. Farmers of that period who employed Arthur Biddell to survey land for them were accustomed to speak of his skill by saying: 'He could measure a bush-faggot under water.' That he was a man of strong 'commonsense' is clear from a letter of his that survives. He wrote it in answer to a Mr Alexander of Yarmouth. This man was acting on behalf of two ladies who were offering their services as 'assistant friends' to the Biddell's—just beginning their family of four sons and six daughters. Arthur Biddell kept a copy of this letter which is undated; but it appears to have been written about 1817, when the beginnings of the post-war depression in agriculture would tend to make a farmer act with a little more than his usual native caution:[1]

'My dear friend,

Many thanks for your kindness and attention to my letter. I shall be happy to find any opportunity of returning the obligation I feel under to you. I only had your communication today & 'tis too late for me to get this letter to Ipswich in time for Post. Your letter was delayed at Woodbridge & then forwarded to our Post Town (Ipswich).

My wife is poorly and gone to my Brother's near Bury for a little

[1] *The Biddell Papers*, Ipswich Borough Archives.

change. In her absence I am sure I may say you have her esteem and thanks. I am sorry that my anticipations respecting the young Ladies you mention are realized by your information. Their qualification and merit justify their looking for a more lucrative and better situation than we can offer them.

I am on that account pretty confident that were Mrs Biddell at home she would decline giving Miss M.A. the trouble of a conference on the Subject. Framlingham is within an hour & a half of Playford & the ride there wd. be agreeable to Mrs B. or to have given Miss A. an invitation to see our Family as a visitor if there had been a probability of their wishing to form part of that family with a moderate Salary.

Now you will say, if there be a probability of Miss M. A.'s suiting you, what is the object (objection?) of 8 or 9£ a year in Salary? I can answer, very little if taken by itself. But 'tis similar to the difference in the cost price between Gay Plates and White Ware which is trifling—if taken by itself—to mention. But to be consistent; if you have Gay Plates you require Silver Spoons set at every corner of your table, Glasses instead of Black and White Mugs—a clean cloth and nice knives and forks—a servant with a different dress, to that she wore an hour before dinner, to wait at table. The carpet which 6 or 7 children had trod upon since breakfast, which would do with White Plates, would not be consistent with Gay ones. The Viands, the Wine, the Desert—must go hand in hand with your Plates, which if really good must be followed by real China Tea Things, a Silver Cream Jug and Plated Pot. The whole appearing better by Candle Light induces you to put off Tea till a late hour. Bed Time is consequently deferred—late rising follows as a matter of course—your appearance out should correspond with appearances at home & your Tailor's Bill is swelled by the use of Blue and White Plates instead of Plain ones—Now any of these things separately considered would be trifling, yet in an establishment of 12 in the Parlor and 5 in the Kitchen it makes 150£ a year between Plain White Ware and Gay Plates. You can bear testimony as to which we use, and we never had but one sort. I do not know that you will read thus far—your time is valuable and I ought to apologise for trespassing upon you with so

long a letter and such a round about comparison to justify my wife
declining the interview which you proposed at Framlingham.

I again thank you, my kind Friend—you have just to deliver a
handsome Message to the Ladies you spoke to and say that the salary
we have been giving to our assistant friends is not equal to what Miss
A. will probably obtain elsewhere. I am, my Dear Friend, faithfully
yours,

Arthur Biddell.'

It is interesting to compare Arthur Biddell's attitude—implicit in
this letter—to the scale and manner of housekeeping best suited to a
farmer and his wife, with some observations on the farmers of
Suffolk made at the other end of the century when agriculture was
in the middle of another, like depression. Royal Commissions follow
depressions like a pack of none too lively hounds stalking a destruc-
tive, smelly but elusive old dog-fox; and the following excerpts are
taken from the report of the 1895 Royal Commission already referred
to. A wave of Scottish farmers, attracted by the prospect of a better
price for milk and by the low rents of farms that the natives themselves were loath to take on owing to the unpromising state of the
times, had moved south into East Anglia five or six years before the
Commission sat. One of the Scots who held a 300 acre farm in Suffolk
reported to the Assistant Commissioner: 'All the Scotch farmers,
their wives and their daughters work hard. The Suffolk women do
nothing. I cannot understand how the Suffolk farmers pay for
servants.' And the Assistant Commissioner confirmed: 'They (the
Scots) and their families work immensely hard and live hard. The
Scotch women certainly undertake work which no Suffolk woman
would dream of doing. The latter would think it socially beneath
them, and farther that the work was too arduous and not suitable
for them. Even in the North of England, where the wives and
daughters of small farmers work very hard at cheese- and butter-
making, feeding the calves and sometimes milking, I have never seen
them mucking out sheds and pig-styes as I am informed that some of
the Scotch farmers' wives and daughters do in Suffolk.'

Many of the Scots had undoubtedly been accustomed to 'family' or subsistence farming; and while their activities in home and cowshed were evidence of an uncorrupted native industry, the comparison with the Suffolk wives of the time was perhaps a little harsh. For the Scottish wives when they first came into Suffolk were merely continuing to act in a way that had the sanction of the community they had just left; but the grandmothers of the Suffolk wives had long before this fallen victims to the fashion that Arthur Biddell at first attempted to resist. This was the fashion satirised by many writers in the early nineteenth century and given its well-known pithy expression in some verses written in 1843 and quoted by G. M. Trevelyan:[1]

OLD STYLE

Man, to the plough;
Wife, to the cow;
Girl, to the yarn;
Boy, to the barn,
And your rent will be netted.

NEW STYLE

Man, Tally Ho;
Miss, piano;
Wife, silk and satin;
Boy, Greek and Latin,
And you'll all be Gazetted.

But even at the very beginning of Arthur Biddell's career farming in Suffolk had long moved away from the subsistence level of an earlier period. The high prices the farmers obtained for their produce during the Napoleonic Wars (the average price of wheat for 1812 was 126s. 6d. a quarter) had set up many of the East Anglian farmers; and though prices went down sharply even before the end of the war the expenses of a visit to London, made by Arthur Biddell on January 12th, 1816, a few months after Napoleon's defeat, show that he was

[1] *English Social History*, Longmans; 1944, p. 472.

not yet affected by this downward trend (wheat was 78s. 6d. in 1816). His purchases also show that his interests were far wider than the average working farmer, most of whose energies were absorbed in cultivating his land.

Visit to London

£

5 & 5 One Pound Notes

Jan. 12th In Hand	£11	os.	od.
Silver		11	o
Coach Hire: Coachman and Guard on Mail			
to London	2	2	o
Bill at The Bull		9	6
Coach Hire in Town		2	o
Servants		2	o
Expences in Town & on Road		6	o
Coach Hire to Ipswich		16	o

Coachments to London   £3 17s. 6d.

Paid into Bruce & Co's Bank, No. 2	£98	os.	od.
Bartholomew Lane, to be forwarded to the			
Sunderland Bank for Booth & Co.			
Nicholson's Dic.ᵗ ʸ of Chemistry		9	6
Memoirs of Kotzebue		2	o
Voltaire's		5	o
Fables & another Book		3	6
Seeing the Spoils of Bonarparte & 2 Books			
about them		4	ꞌ6
Travelling Trunk	1	4	o
Cash in Hand: Silver		15	6
Brass			6
Notes	19	o	o
An Ivory leaf (?)			9
Down as Memorandum	£135	13s.	9d.
Deduct Money on top	11	11	o
	£124	2s.	9d.

An old mail and stage-coach time-table (*Cary's New Itinerary*, 1815) helps to illumine Arthur Biddell's journey. The *itinerary* or route from Ipswich to London is not very different from that followed by the railway: Copdock, Bentley, Stratford St Mary, Colchester, Marks Tey, Witham, Chelmsford, Shenfield, Romford, Ilford, Stratford; and most of the inns that were the London termini for the East Anglian coaches were not far from the present railway terminus at Liverpool Street. Two or three of these inns were actually in Bishopsgate.

Without a doubt there were then many places along this route where Arthur Biddell felt much safer, with £100 or so in his pocket or under the seat, knowing the hired guard was sitting alongside the coachman. One wonders whether it was this fear of attack that prompted him to take none of his money in gold. Or were gold sovereigns not available at that time owing to a post-war inflation? He had a further reason for the extra guard if he travelled on the night *Mail*. This coach, *The Royal Mail* plying between London and Yarmouth, began its return journey from The Duke's Head, Yarmouth at 2 p.m. (*Dep. 2 aft.*): it called at Ipswich, leaving The Bear and Crown[1] (now 'The Oriental Cafe') at 9.30 p.m. and arriving at The Saracens Head, in Aldgate Street at 8 o'clock the next morning. *The Post Coach*, the fastest coach of the day, left The Golden Lion on Cornhill, Ipswich, in the morning (*Dep. 7 and 8 morn.*) and arrived at $\frac{1}{2}$ *past 5 aft.* Yet another coach had its headquarters at The Bull Inn, Bishopsgate; and as Arthur Biddell put up at The Bull he may well have used the term *Mail* loosely and actually travelled on this coach. But The Bull Inn, Whitechapel was also the starting point for yet another East Anglian coach.

The Kotzebue book, one of Arthur Biddell's purchases, was written by the elder Kotzebue (August F. F. von), the German dramatist and novelist who had spent much of his life in the Russian civil service: he was assassinated three years later at Mannheim by a student. His son, Otto von Kotzebue, was a navigator who made an attempt to discover the North East Passage (1815–1818) He was also a writer;

[1] Leonard P. Thompson, *Old Inns of Suffolk*, Harrison, Ipswich, 1946.

but the English translation of his adventures did not appear until 1821.

The Biddells must have got together a fair-sized collection of books some of which they lent to their friends: Arthur records the loans in his Day Books:

> '*Nov*. 1820: Lent Mrs Walford. Manfred—Vol. of Byron & Wolsoncrofts Rights of Women
> Jane Blencowe:
> > *Child Harold* & Mrs Blencowe *Don Juan*
> > G. Ely has Condorcet'

It is amusing to note that the mother went off with *Don Juan* and not the daughter. Byron appears to have been the Biddells' favourite poet: in fact, they called their first child, Manfred.

When Arthur Biddell took his trip to London he did not seem to have paid much regard to the impending 'recession' in agriculture; yet within the next two years he began to be a little anxious. Here is his analysis of his accounts for one year with a revealing note at the end:

Memorandum of Expences between Oct. 11, 1818 & *Oct.* 11, 1819
Collected and Arranged under the following Heads:

1st	Implements, Blacksmiths, Wheelwrights, Collar Makers Bills & Things relating to them	£76	16s.	3d.
2nd	Workmen & Servants	577	3	1
	(No 3rd Head included)			
4th	Repairs	165	7	11
5th	Cloaths, Doctors, Farriers Bill. Expences of all sorts when necessarily incurred	98	12	6
6th	Furniture, Coopers Bills, House Linnen and things used in Dairy, Backhouse & House	51	10	0
	Rates, Tythe, Rent, Taxes	394	1	11
	(This item unnumbered)			
7th	Superfluous Expences	76	18	4
	(add Investments, Charity, etc.)			
8th	Housekeeping	440	0	0
		£1880	9s.	2d.

N.B. add rent of Bransons Land without Cottages
    to Rent, Rates and Tythe   50   0   0

Add also to superfluous expences Horse given to
Case and accounted for in farming expences   9   0   0

                 Total Expenditure   £1939 9s. 2d.

From which the Superfluous Head should be
deducted as not being connected with farming
(£76 18s. 4d. & £9 for the horse)   85 18   4

                             £1843 10s. 10d.

Clearly Sold from the farm as pr Farming Accts.   £1616   0   10

              Lost by Farming   £237 10s. 0d.

Considering Housekeeping expences equal to re-
muneration for Personal attendance to business—
but the whole interest of Capital employed is sunk.

The phrase *Lost by Farming* has a familiar ring; but it was too stark
a phrase to describe Arthur Biddell's real position. It appears from
the above that he and his family were getting a fair living from the
land, but just at that time the whole capital he had sunk in the farms
(the *Bransons Land* referred to was an *off-hand* holding) was not
giving him the return it would have done if invested elsewhere. But
he weathered the storm, though he had much lee-way to make up
when in the late 'thirties agriculture began once more to be comparatively prosperous. He had to do without *frills*, and governesses
for his children; yet in many ways he suffered very little compared
with farmers in other parts of the country.[1] As one writer has pointed
out, the men farming the lighter soils of East Anglia, as Arthur
Biddell was, were to a large extent insulated against the depression
by their progressive and enthusiastic application of the Norfolk four-
course system of cropping, and by the general high excellence of
their farming.

We have a record of how excellent Arthur Biddell's farming practices were, both from the testimony of his sons and the impartial
evidence of his *Day Books* and *Work Books*—farm journals which he

[1] *E.F.P.P.*, p. 348.

kept regularly and scrupulously from the early 'twenties right up to his death.

But before going on to look at the Day Books, the dates at the head of the previous accounts are worth a comment. As most farmers still do, Arthur Biddell made up his accounts from Michaelmas to Michaelmas. But he was still using the date of the old Michaelmas[1]— October 11th and not September 29th, as it is today and was officially at the time of his entry. Although the Gregorian Calendar had been introduced into England over sixty years before this (1752) yet he still used the old Julian Calendar known to his forefathers. At this time, too, and later in the century—so family memories tell us—two Christmas festivals were celebrated in Suffolk: the modern one and the old Christmas, occurring twelve days later on January 6th. Such was the tenacious clinging to old usages—a tendency that still survives in Suffolk in spite of the revolutionary changes of the past few years.

[1] The old date, October 11th, is still used by many Suffolk farmers.

8

Arthur Biddell's Day Books

A farmer's Day Books were his diary of events on the farm—what he sowed, where he sowed, what money he received when he sold his crop, what payments he made when he bought his seed-corn, his oil-cake or had his wagons repaired and his horses shod, and so on. As already indicated by the previous excerpts Arthur Biddell included in his Day Books a detailed account of his personal expenditure; and, what is just as valuable, he included details of the various experiments he carried out in connection with his farming. These diaries were also called *field-books* because their chief purpose was to preserve a record of cropping: a very important function at a time when the East Anglian farmers kept to the old Norfolk four-course system with the zeal of a religious sect adhering scrupulously to the letter of its creed. For convenience, however, Arthur Biddell made his Schedule of Cropping a supplement to his field books; and it is contained in four large sheets: it listed all the arable fields in Hill Farm, Playford, and the off-hand farm, Bransons, from 18c7 until his death, after which the list was kept by one of his sons until the year 1870.

The past tense is here used in discussing field-books because it appears that present-day farmers in the county rarely keep such detailed records of their cropping. It is only farmers of the old school—men brought up under the old system to regard field-books as *implements* of cultivation almost as important as the seed-drill—who still continue the old practice of detailed recording. One of these is a Blaxhall farmer, Robert Sherwood (born 1885) whose father farmed the next holding to the Biddells' at Playford—S. A. Sherwood and Herman Biddell, Arthur's son, were contemporaries and although they were close neighbours they often used to conduct arguments on farming matters through the columns of the local newspaper— Robert Sherwood has kept up the practice of scrupulous recording into an age whose temper it is to live from year to year and to regard the land as something that has a shorter memory than even the people who farm it. The new farmer—many of the old school maintain—no longer relies on his field-books but on his fertilisers; and he expects these faithfully to cover up his mistakes and bolster his short-comings. Cultivation is no longer by rule or by rote but by formula; and the modern fashion is to ignore the living quality of the land and to look upon it merely as a rather complicated chemical whose rhythms can be effectively controlled from the laboratory.

'The Norfolk four-course has gone by the board today,' Robert Sherwood said; 'It's barley following barley and all manner of things that would make men like my father and Herman Biddell turn in their graves. Farming is not ruled by the same factors today. It's get what you can.' An old farm-worker also expressed himself on this, relying more on his instinct than on his ability to give a reasoned statement of the facts: 'In time they won't grow as much corn on the land as they're doing today. Chemicals are not putting back into the land everything the crops are taking out. It's not recovering like it should. The land will go back. It won't happen in my time, maybe; but later it will happen.'

To Arthur Biddell, as to many of the farmers of his day, his own farm was his laboratory; and one of the first experiments he conducted was to discover accurately what advantages he could gain by *salting* his hay and clover. This old practice is still followed today by some farmers in Suffolk, Robert Sherwood among them: 'If I cart hay that is a little on the *rare*[1] side I get the men to sprinkle a pail or two of salt on the stack—every two loads. It keeps the stack cool and lessens the risk of its catching fire.' A horseman has also described how they used to salt chaff on the farm where he worked: 'The salt kept the chaff moist and sweet. After we'd cut the chaff we shot it into a deep bay in the barn and kept a-sowing a little salt on every layer. It

---

[1] *rare*—not quite *made*; *rare* meat is underdone meat (*Shorter Oxford Dict.*)

kept the chaff fresh. A hundred-weight of salt was enough for a whole stack. But nowadays they don't even make chaff, let alone salt it: they feed the hay long. Though there wouldn't be so many stack-fires if they used salt today.'

Arthur Biddell, however, set out to find what exactly in terms of weight he gained by salting his hay or clover. His first experiment was entered under *December* 1821:

'*Memorandum* 37
May 24th   *Measured of Salted Clover*
Stover from the Middle of a stack 34¾ cubit feet which weighed 342 lbs or about 10 lbs a foot—this had been on two sides exposed to the Sun 3 weeks—suppose the next trusses below would have been heavier & those above considerably lighter. On the whole I think the stack wd. weigh 9 lbs to the foot allowing for shaving off.'

'Some time previous to the above experiment I weighed from the bottom of a Hay Stack near two years old some Hay that weighed abt. 12 lbs to the foot. It had been salted.'

June 25, 1822: *on Salted Hay*
'The Meralds (?) Meadow was mown on Saturday, 22nd June, was not strawed—had two showers of rain upon it. On Tuesday, June 25th, the Swathes were turned in the morning and the afternoon. The Hay was weighed off the Meadow containing 2A. 2R. OP. (except where the Hay Stacks stood which part was not measured). The Hay was coarse & from not being Strawn (or Shaked) was irregularly made. Half of it, weighing net 372 Stones or 46½ Cwt, was stacked nearest to the Garden without Salt. The other Half of the Hay was stacked near to the other but nearer to the Gate and Salted with 56 lbs of Common Salt which was added to the 372 Stones of Hay, making this Stack with the Hay weigh altogether 372 Stones *with the* Salt.'

'*Memo on Hay Salted June 25th*, 1822
The Stacks before mentioned were both carried up together and weighed with Scales, about 2 Cwt at a time—and 3 weighings put upon one Stack & then 3 Weighings on the other.'

'*May* 14*th*, 1823: Measured the two little Stacks. The Salted Hay nearest the Gate, circ. 39 ft, 6 ft high, contained 726 Feet Cube; weighed 35 cwt 61 lbs or 5 lb $7\frac{1}{2}$ ozs to the foot.

The unsalted stack 38 ft in circ., $6\frac{1}{2}$ ft high, 741 ft Cube weighed 35 cwt 6 bls or 5 $\frac{28}{100}$ lbs or 5 lb $4\frac{3}{4}$ ozs to a foot.

The above Hay was weighed in very warm, dry weather—full sun. The other Experiment some years back was made in Damp weather in the months of Sept. & the Hay had always been shaded & this may account for there having been more difference then than in the experiment above related'.

Although the above experiments do not seem to be conclusive, this experience did not stop his zeal for recording and trying out his theories. In the same year as he started the above he made a record of his sowing of wheat. He experimented on one field, *dibbling*[1] part and drilling the rest.

'*Wheat Sowing, 1821:*
Finished in Home Barn field Nov. 23rd. The 1st Dibbled Stetch nearest the Gate is of Wheat from Mr Fullers. The next (2nd) Dibbled Stetch of Wheat is from Scotch Wheat or North Country from Ely's; the third Dibbled Stetch is of North Country Wheat (such as a coomb is left). The 4th Dibbled Stetch is wheat of my own growth. All the rest of the feild is Drilled. The further side with Wheat from the North—such as on the 2nd Dibbled Stetch. About 2 Acres on this side is Drilled with such as 3rd Dibbled Stetch. The Headlands all round the feild is rather mixed.'

At this period there was a healthy spirit among farmers in Suffolk to experiment[2] with various strains of corn. Almost at the same time as Arthur Biddell was carrying out the above experiments another farmer of similar turn of mind stumbled across an unusual strain of barley: out of this accident developed one of the most famous barleys of the nineteenth century. The story is quoted in the Report of the 1895 Commission already discussed:

[1] *A.F.C.H.*, p. 119.
[2] Arthur Young's *A Course of Experimental Agriculture*, London, 1770, probably had a lot to do with this.

'About the year 1820 John Andrews, a labourer of Mr Edward Dove of Ulverston Hall, Debenham (Suffolk) had been threshing barley; and on his return home at night complained of his feet being uneasy; and on taking off his shoes he discovered in one of them part of a very fine ear of barley—it struck him as being particularly so—and he was careful to have it preserved. He afterwards planted the few grains from it in his garden; and the following year Dr & Mrs Charles Chevallier, coming to Andrews's dwelling to inspect some repairs going on in the cottage (belonging to the doctor) saw three or four ears of the barley growing. He requested it might be kept for him when ripe. The doctor sowed a small ridge with the produce he thus obtained; and kept it by itself until he grew sufficient to plant an acre; and from this acre the produce was $11\frac{1}{2}$ combs (about the year 1825 or 1826). This was again planted and from the increase thence arising he began to dispose of it; and from that time it has been gradually getting into repute. It is now well-known in most of the corn markets of the kingdom, and also in many parts of the Continent America etc. and is called Chevallier barley.'[1]

Arthur Biddell's observations on his corn crop during another year are worth transcribing for more than one reason:

'*On the Crop of Corn Grown in 1824*
Memorandum

Wheat never was so Stout on the Ground. There was generally 2 to three large loads Pr Acre. No Crop that I ever grew yeilded so little corn in proportion to the Straw, and it yeilded best where the land had been worst treated.

From the *New Lay* after Tares, the Tares self-sown after Tares on about $6\frac{1}{2}$ Acres, the land worked like Summer-land, and thinly mucked about 15 Loads Pr Acre. This yielded 53 C. 2 Bushels, or nearly 8 C. Pr Acre, contrary to every expectation. The other Part of the Field treated just the same but sown with Barley. The Crop was poor—about 7 or 8 Pr. Acre.

'*Alescroft:* $5\frac{1}{2}$ Acres is a very high State of Culture after White

[1] From the MS *History of Debenham, 1845:* now in Debenham Parish Chest: quoted in 1895 Report, p. 14.

Clover, fed with Sheep, mucked with Town Muck. The Wheat very Stout, but only yeilded 40.3 or about 7 C. Pr Acre—expected 10.

In Former Years I had always estimated my Wheat Crop very near its actual quantity. This year I was greatly deceived from its stout appearance.

The Barley Crop averaged upwards of 12½ C. per Acre, there being 416 C. 3B. from 32½ Acres.'

This memorandum had somehow got into Arthur Biddell's *Work* (or Wages) *Book* for that year: it was his usual practice to write his notes in the field-books.

Mention of town-muck in this note is a reminder of the old practice of farmers near big towns undertaking to collect night-soil for use on their land. It appears from a passage in *The Autobiography of a Farm Labourer* (see p. 44) that the farmer allowed the labourer seven shillings a load for the night-soil he collected from Ipswich. Presumably at that time, owing to the demand, householders and stable-keepers were able to sell their night-soil and stable-manure; and the seven shillings paid to the labourer were not all for his labours but were partly to re-imburse him for the money he had already paid out to obtain his load. It would be satisfactory to record that this practice of collecting town-muck or night-soil in Suffolk towns has already died out; but like many bad customs this shows a greater tenacity to survive than the good ones whose falling away are so often lamented. District or Urban Councils without a comprehensive drainage scheme still have a system of 'collecting buckets' in some towns; and as the disposal of the material tends to be costly, throwing a great burden on the rates, some of them gladly get rid of it to any farmer who is willing to use it on his land. Ashes[1] were similarly collected for dressing fields; and the scale on which ashes and night-soil were used in Arthur Biddell's time may be gathered from the *Stock Taking* of 1820. It is quoted in full since it gives some idea of the type of farming he practised:

[1] cf. Virgil's *Georgics*, I. 79:
  Sed tamen alternis facilis labor, arida tantum
  Ne saturare fimo pingui pudeat sola neve
  Effetos cinerem immundum iactare per agros.

'*Stock Taken, Oct. 11th, 1820*

32 *Cows*, including Black Heifer, at £9 10s. &
   The Ley (which was cut in the beginning of
   Sept.) in all 33 at £9 10s. od.   £316 10s. od.

Horses: Jolly 23, Bumper 22
         Dragon 7, Dodman 12
         Diamond 16, Proctor 16, Smiler 5,
         Jack 26, Boney 25, Old Rider 7.
         Riding Colt £16 5s. 6d.: Horse at Diss 30   223   5   0

Pigs & Hogs

24 Small Pigs at 16s.	£19	4s.
1 Fat Pig	2	5
1 Young Brawn	2	2
1 Old do.	1	10
4 Sows & 8 Pigs each	16	16
2 Old & Young Hewet	7	10
5 Young Sows	8	0
1 Cossett Sow	3	0
2 Sows Tollgate & Hasketon	7	10
1 Leg Hog	2	0
2 Sows	5	0

                                                £74   7s. od.

2 Bush. Peas   18   0
56 Coombs Oats in Granary ⎫
 4   Do. lent Clarkson at 10 ⎭   30   0   0
5 Coombs Beans   4   10   0
2 tons 10 cwts Hay lent Manning ⎫
2 „ 13 „   Old Do. in Stackyard ⎭   17   10   0
1 Coomb Old Wheat at Mr Manby's   1   5   0
9½ C. Wheat at 30s.   14   5   0
Ashes bought since last Michs. & Manure laid
on for Wheat etc. for which no profit is yet
derived   30   0   0
92 Cheeses weighed 2483 lbs. at 2d.   19   4   6

(Best Cheese 41 lbs. at 6d. [This item is erased]	(1	0	6)

Entered to House Expences)

add to Stock of Cheeses the Cheeses owed for in
Jane's Book

1	13	11

£733 8 5

Flax Broken	£10		
Do. Whole	5	}	16 0 0
Hemp Broken	1		

£749   8s.   5d.

His list of stock shows that Arthur Biddell farmed a mixed farm
with a bigger herd of cattle than was later usual in this part of Suffolk;
and for a number of years after this his stock-lists were of roughly
similar composition. But this may well have been a transition period
between the old farming economy and the new bias which later made
the area almost completely arable. For in the sixteenth and seventeenth centuries Suffolk cheese and butter had been famous; and
though later they were not much heard of outside the county, some
farmers evidently continued to make butter and cheese in very large
amounts. But Arthur Biddell had a ready market in the nearby town
of Ipswich; and this would be a natural inducement to his carrying on
the old methods without changing over entirely to arable farming as
most of the Suffolk farmers—including his sons—did later. By the
second half of the nineteenth century, the classical period of the
Norfolk system, the four-course became the orthodox practice; and
this did not leave much room for dairy-farming. As Robert Sherwood
commented: 'Under the old farming of Herman Biddell's and my
father's time they never kept cows to any extent. If a farmer started
to keep a dairy-herd, his friends would shake their heads and say he
was going down-hill. Cows were not part of the system. With cows,
they said, you took more substance from the land than you put back.'

The cheap cheese, listed in the stock at 2d. a pound, was undoubtedly the maligned *Suffolk Bang*, a skimmed milk cheese that
got itself a bad reputation for hardness. A later entry in the Day
Book for 1829 shows on what scale Arthur Biddell sold butter and
cheese in the town:

Feb. 14th

Abbot for Butter sent before Michs.—		
18 Firkins	£32 14s.	8d.
Do for Cheese 4120 at 48s.	10 7	6
before Michs.		

A note underneath this entry is typical of his hard, commonsense in recording even his mistakes in the hope that these will profit him later on:

Memo:

'Remember that the above is a Lesson not to trust any Grocer with Butter and Cheese to be kept for their use & to allow what they please for it. I lost by the above goods 5£ or 6£ in trusting to Abbot.'

But Arthur Biddell appears to have learned another lesson before the above: *catch-as-catch-can.* An entry for January 5th, 1825 reads:

'For the Leg[1] Bullock	£6 os. od.
sold to Mrs Newson	
Of Mrs Newson, change given by mistake to me	
in Paying, a five Pound note instead of a 1£	
—This she had evidently taken for a 1£ & she	
cheated me of 10s. in the Bull Leg above & I	
am not disposed to tell her of her mistake unless	
I find she had taken the note for five pounds	4 0 0
Put to no Account	

The first entry relating to cows may require explanation: the farmer appears to have allowed £9 10s.—the price of one cow—for the amount of food that is left on *The Ley* or meadow, after it had been cut in September. It was probably a clover-ley; for often in this month, clover was cut and harvested for seed.

Clarkson, the man Arthur Biddell records as having borrowed

---

[1] Possibly *Seg*. The Raynbirds wrote (*A.O.S.*, p. 298): '*Seg*—any animal emasculated when fully grown; a bull-seg.' This animal is also called a *stag*. When killed its meat was tough; hence the low price.

some oats, was Thomas Clarkson, the slavery abolitionist who lived
at Playford Hall. Herman Biddell described him in a monograph he
wrote later in the century: and Jane, Arthur's wife, dedicated at least
one of her poems to the cause of negro emancipation.

The listing of the stock of flax and hemp gives a clue to an industry
which was carried on in the cottages at this time. An entry in the
work- or wages-book for the following year (1821) confirms this. It is
against a workman called *Jno. Garrod, Senr*. But it should first be
explained that Arthur Biddell had two columns in his wages-book:
one debit and the other credit. The debit column records the amount
he paid to his workers either in kind or in money; the credit column
records the amount the worker earned either in wages or for piece-
work. But here is the full entry:

Jno. Garrod, Senr.

1820		Dr.	Cr.
Feb.	More coming to him on Dibbling		1 6
1821			
March 16	Cash	10 0	
	To Surveyor's account		7 0
	2 Days Setting behind		
	Plantation at the Cottage. This		3 0
	was his last work, being taken ill		
	and died, April 1821		
	Flax had with view of selling the		
	same in cords when worked—		
	28 lbs. at 1½—but say 1s. 6d. to		
	make it even	1 6	
		11 6	11 6

The very odd arithmetic, 'say 1s. 6d. to make it even,' is a very
human touch, balancing the dead man's account. Yet later in the year
when another of his workmen died, owing him much more than the
few pence he had crossed off in the above instance, Arthur Biddell
felt that it required something more than a brief comment and a
stroke of the pen. The debt of £1 19s. 7d.—he had probably let the

man have a pig out of his stock—was a large one; and to console himself he took a leaf out of his wife's book and had recourse to verses. Here again is the full entry:

Wm. Wright (Smith)

1820   Dr.

To Balance from Page 107 in Old Book   £1 19s. 7d.
Memo

Gristley Death with a Tyrant's Sway
Cancelled this Debt, but Nothing did Pay.
The Spirit of Wright, having no Controul
Over an Act which seemed so foul,
Took its flight, from the Body Driven,
To settle his Earthly Accounts in Heaven.

(Died the Summer of 1821)

But to return to flax and hemp: there was a large amount of hemp grown in Suffolk at this period, as Arthur Young notes. The great hemp-growing district extended from Eye to Beccles. Much flax was also grown in the county; and as Robert Reyce noted[1] in the seventeenth century part of the process of working the raw material into cloth and cord was carried on in the home: 'in other parts (of Suffolk) where the meaner sort doe practise spinning of thread linnen'.

Tusser also advised:

Good flax and good hemp, to have of her own
in May a good huswife will see it be sown;
And afterwards trim it, to serve at a need
the fimble to spin and the karl for her seed.

Fimble is the female hemp used—as Arthur Young recorded—for making shirts, sheets, table-linen and huckabacks. *Karl* is the coarse seed-hemp used for making ropes. The process of preparing flax for

[1] *The Breviary of Suffolk*, 1618: With notes by Lord Francis Hervey, Murray (1902), p. 57.

spinning involved breaking and *scutching*[1] or pounding. After *retting* or soaking in water, hemp was broken up into serviceable lengths on a hand-driven hemp-breaking machine[2] as one of the steps preliminary to *heckling*, combing with a hackle until it reached the fluffy condition ready for spinning. Traces of the industry are still left in the county: first of all, as often happens, in the name of an inn—there is at least one Scutchers' Arms in the county;[3] again, though cotton has long ago ousted linen, housewives in out of the way Suffolk villages still refer to their clothes-line as their *linen-line*, and the prop as the *linen-prop*. In recent years flax was grown occasionally for the linseed—for instance, at Broad Green Farm, Henley (Suffolk) which was at one time a horse-breeding farm: the linseed was used for feeding the horses.

The *Pigs and Hogs* in the list require a note. Although *hog* is still heard in Suffolk as a generic name for all kinds of pigs, it appears to be used here in its specific sense of a castrated male swine. A *brawn* is a boar, and the word was used in the dialect until recent years. A *cossett* is a pig that has been brought up by hand—the *pitman*, the weakest pig in the litter. In spite of a long search no success was met in finding the significance of *hewet*. Walter Dunnett (born 1888) who was pig-man for sixty years at Hill Farm, many of these years during the Biddells' occupation, had not heard of the term.

The horses on the list are about the number one would expect for a farm of this size. The name *Dodman* was probably descriptive: *dodman* (more often *hodman* or *hodmedod*) is the dialect for a snail. But Dodman at £12 could not have been very slow as he was by no means the lowest in valuation. This place was reserved for *Smiler* who seems to have accepted it philosophically. *Boney* is, naturally, not descriptive, but merely an echo of the late troubles in which 'Boney the Warrior' figured largely.

By 1828 Arthur Biddell's stock of horses had increased considerably. They were:

[1] A *scutch*—a wooden implement for dressing flax or hemp.
[2] Allan Jobson, *Household and Country Crafts*, Elek, p. 198.
[3] In the village of Long Melford.

1 Riding Mare	£20 0s.
1 Mare—lamed	18 0
1 4 yr old Gig Mare	24 0
1 2 yr old Black Riding Colt	30 0
2 yearling Riding Colts	38 0
1 Black Smolensko, 5 yrs old (Dragon)	25 0
2—Jack 25£ Dodman 6	31 0
2—Bumper 8, Jolly 5	13 0
1 Black Horse (Tinker)	32 0
Lavenham Horse	8 0
Windbroken (Sharper)	8 0
1 Chestnut Colt, 3 yrs old (Smiler)	32 0

Peggy 18	Depper 15	
Tye 30	Darby 28	126 0
Mumper 7	Tinker 28	

£387 0s.

The increase appears mainly to be in riding and trap-horses—a definite indication that Arthur Biddell, unlike many farmers of the period, had not been forced to 'put down his chaises and his nags': on the contrary, he had acquired more.

It has probably been noticed that there were no sheep on the 1820 list of stock. Nine years later, however, Arthur Biddell had moved nearer the 'four course' practice of sheep as an essential part of the corn husbandry of this part of East Anglia. He wrote:

October 11th, 1829:

Wool from last yr. 1085 Fleeces—supposed
worth 6d. pr lb. 3 lbs. to a fleece   £81   7s.   6d.
about 480 fleeces this yr at 1s. 6d.   £36   0   0

Here, to end, are a few entries—from the same Day Book—relating to horses:

August 29th, 1821

For Shoeing Horse at Woodbridge   1   6

October 20th, 1821

Mr Mickelborough for 15 sets of whipple-trees   £5   17   6

March 5th, 1822

Agreed with Mr Haggar to shoe the 9 cart horses at 7s. 6d. each for a year. to be left in good order; & to put them in good shoes. I agreed to pay him for 14 new Shoes although only 3 were off.'

Arthur Biddell's interest in the buying and selling of horses remained right to the end of his life. He was an enthusiastic breeder of Suffolks, chiefly of the Shadingfield strain; and four days before his death he bought a mare from his eldest son.

This entry—one of the last he made—reads:

'*May 21st, 1860*

3 yr old Mare of Manfred   £30 os.

There were only two more entries after this; and these were in a hand that was much less firm than when he had first started his diaries, over forty years before. Then followed an entry in another person's handwriting, probably that of his son Manfred:

A Biddell died May 25th, 1860.

9

Arthur Biddell's Work Books

These wages-books have already been quoted. Apart from an occasional entry that seems to have strayed from the field-books, they contained the lists of jobs allocated to people employed on the farm, and the amount of wages due to them. The Work Books offer us a great deal of information about farming methods at this time; and a comparison of some of these with the practices recalled by the old Suffolk farmers and farm-workers of the present-day show that these methods continued into very recent times.

Before discussing these, however, it would be useful to comment on the phrase *To Surveyor's Account* in the Jno. Garrod entry already quoted.[1] The Surveyor was Arthur Biddell's co-officer in the parish of Playford; and his full title was Surveyor of the Highways. He was sometimes known as a *Way-warden* or *Stone-warden* and was appointed by the justices at their special Highway Sessions. Stone-warden is a good description of his main function which was to see that the bad places on the highway were duly filled in with stones. These stones were normally obtained from farmers in the parish: in Playford they were flints picked up from the fields. An early entry from the Day Books explains what happened:

'*April 15th, 1815:* 7 horses and 2 men carting stone from Mr Cutting's warren into loads beyond the Church. One horse miss ¼ day. 11 loads. The man that fetched the loads of stone is down to Parish day work.

Say Recd. for the above work   £1 4s. 0d.'

We can assume that Arthur Biddell later claimed this amount from

the Surveyor of the Highways. An entry from an early Work Book
shows how he was connected with the parish in yet another way:

'*Jan. 9th, 1821:*

Thrashing 47 C. Wheat sent to Dowsing		}		£4 4s. 9d.
9 C. 2 B. Dross in Granary				

Allowed by Parish on account of 3 men being in
a Barn instead of using Thrashing Machine—
4d. pr Coomb to Mr Galls — 18 10

Screening the above; extra ½d. pr Coomb — 2 4

3 | £5 5s. 11d.

each £1 15s. 3½d.

Between Wooby, Sam Robinson and Ben Clover.'

This entry shows how the Overseer of the Poor, another parish
officer, had arranged with Arthur Biddell to allow three men to thrash
in the barn using a flail, in order that their full maintenance and that
of their families would not fall to the expense of the parish. For by
this time the threshing machine, invented during the latter half of
the eighteenth century, was beginning to displace a great deal of
farm-labour that had formerly been engaged during the slack winter
months in hand-thrashing in the barn. This caused an amount of
distress; and in some districts of England the farm-workers' resent-
ment had turned against the machines, and there had been out-
breaks of machine-wrecking. Therefore, by compounding with the
Overseer of the Poor to employ three men, who would otherwise be
without work if all his corn were thrashed by machine, Arthur Biddell
was keeping his workmen in good heart and at the same time helping
to keep down the poor-rate—a real concern of his as one of the
principal holders of land in the parish.[1]

An entry for November 1st, 1821 has:

'Filling and Spreading and unloading a Hill of
35 Rods on the top of Thistley Feild   £2 16s. 3d.'

This entry can best be explained by reference to the practice carried

[1] See G. E. Fussell, *The English Rural Labourer*, Batchworth, p. 96.

'*Nov. 31st, 1820: Between Sam and Clover*
½ day each, thrashing Carrot seed
½ day Sam, sowing Wheat, & job .... I 9

Dec. 8th: Threshing 19 Bushels Radish Seed at
3s. 6d. .... £3 6s. 6d.
.... 2 | £3 10s. od.

Sam Robinson & B. Clover: each' .... £1 15s. od.

The entry for a threshing job, done in January by the same two men and a third to help them, was given in the previous chapter.[1]

'*Feb 9th, 1821:* Thrashing White Clover began Wednes., Feb. 7th.

23rd Memo.: began to Thrash on Wednes. Feb. 20th
Laying down Frame[2]
Finished Thrashing Saturday, Mar. 17th

March 23rd: Thrashing 28 B. Best Seed } at 9s. £15 19s. 6d.
7 B. Dross

March 30th: Thrashing 8½ Bus Trefoil Seed at
3s. 6d. £1 9 9
Breame's share 7s. 5d., Garrod with Boy 12s. 11d.,
Dickn. 9s. 5d.'

'*March 30th, 1821:* Cutting & Tying up 33½ Rods
of Bushes: 10d. .... I 7 II
Cutting (without faggoting) 23½ Rods; 5d. 9 10
.... 2 | £1 17s. 9d.
Between Wooby & Sam' 18s. 10½d

[1] p. 116.
[2] This probably refers to a rectangular frame used for sifting th[e] clover-seed after the cobs had been threshed. A fine meshed siev[e] containing the seed was slid backwards and forwards in the fram[e] until the seed fell through, leaving the husks etc. in the sieve.

on in Suffolk until just before the last war. It has already been mentioned in a previous chapter[1] but Arthur Chaplin has described it in detail:

'In the respite between haysel and harvest, about the second week in June, we cleaned out the stockyards and made hills or *hales*[2] as we called them in the fields that were due to be mucked. Some of these hills had as many as 200 loads in them; and they were properly made.

You chose your spot then you *kicked up* your load of muck—you took the *toe-stick* out of the front of the tumbril and it would tip up.

'Then you *spreed* out the muck to form the bottom of your hill. Then as you tipped more loads the hill began to shape up, and you made a ramp at one end to get on top of it with your tumbril; and a ramp at the other end to get down. You'd have two, or even three, horses in your tumbril to take it up the ramp as the hill got higher. The hill went down as tight as a road with the tumbrils and the horses going over it; but after it was up about six feet high we *squared-up* the farther end—the ramp we used to take the tumbril back down. By now the top of the hill was wide enough to turn the tumbril after the trace-horse had been unloosed, so you could get

[1] p. 46.
[2] A *hale* is also a *clamp*—e.g. a hale of turnips—in the dialect.

back down the first ramp. When we had flattened the top, we squared up the first ramp to finish the hill off. With the hill of muck down tight like this it wouldn't heat up too much and lose all its goodness —the ammonia and so on wouldn't go off into the air.'

The hill was then left until just before the winter ploughing, usually sometime in October: 'When we loaded the muck to *spreed* it in the autumn, we backed the tumbril against the hill—*setting the cart* we used to call it; we took a *kench*,[1] a section of the hill, and worked down to the bottom—from one end. Then you *bottomed up* or cleaned the surface and took out another *kench*. We carted the muck into the field and put it down in heaps at definite intervals—seven yards from heap to heap and nine yards from row to row. There were seven heaps to a load and ten loads to an acre, the usual amount for corn. We usually worked three *fellers* (fillers) to a hill; and the three of us were expected to fill sixty loads a day. Twenty loads was a man's *standard*; and as soon as he had finished his standard he could stable his horses and go back home. We could get done quicker if only two of us were working: there wasn't so much waiting about as with three—you didn't have to wait to set your cart.

'We usually *took* the job—did it on piece-work—at two shillings an acre. You could do an acre in a day comfortably. If you managed a bit over you might earn 2s. 3d. But you wouldn't try to earn half-a-crown otherwise the farmer would say that he was setting the rate too high! The amount of muck for each field was fixed: ten loads an acre for corn, fifteen if the land was very poor, and up to twenty for beans. If we *spreed* fifteen loads we got three bob an acre.'

Arthur Biddell refers to these hills in other parts of his diaries as *compost-hills*; and it was the old theory that muck so composted was better for the land than if it had been carted direct from the stock-yards and spread on the fields. Tusser refers to it as *compas* and a verse from his *August Husbandry* shows that the making of muck-hills was a common practice in the sixteenth century:

> *Or ever thou ride with thy servantes compound*
> *to carry thy muck-hilles on thy barley ground:*

[1] Also *canch*: that part of a hay-stack or heap *in cut*.

'*March 4th, 1825:* Ditching 42½ Rods between
  Bransons Meadows and Mr Clarkson's at 1s. 0d. 2 2 6
  1 Day P. Cooke, Brushing Brambles   1 6

            4 |£2 4s. 0d.

  Between Cooke, Dickenson, Ben Garrod &
  Webb'   11s. 0d.

April 20th, 1821
  Sawing 1020 feet of Ash, poplar and Willow
  Boards at ¾   2 |£1 14s. 0d.
    Between Wooby and Fuller   17s. 0d.

May 4th, 1821: Hoeing 6 Acres Jolly's Wheat £1 4 0d.
  Cash to Warner to divide between Cooke,
  Dickenson & himself'

June 14th, 1822:
  Reaping 3¼ Acres Turnip Seed in Westrups
  at 4s. pr Acre   13s. 0d.
  1 Day & 1 hour each for 5 men Jobbing 8 6½
  Mowing Common field Clover 11 Acres⎫ at
   „ Barn field   „ 1¾ ⎬ 1s. 9d. 1 2 6
  Allowance for beer in mowing   2 6

  Between Bacon, Wooby, County, Cooke
  and Dickenson   5 |£2 6s. 4½d.
              9s. 3½d.

'*July 6th, 1821: To Mowing Account: Jas. Bacon & Co.*
  1½ Day for one man & 4 hours for 1 man
  helping after Clover & Hay   3s. 6d.
13th Mowing 21½ Acres of Grass in the
  Bridge Meadow'   £2 8s. 4½d.

Aug. 3rd, 1821: Thrashing 6 Coombs & 1½ Bus.
  Wheat at 1s. 6d.   2 |9s. 7d.
    Between Cooke & Hagger'   4s. 9½d.

But most of the months of August and September would naturally be spent in the corn-harvest. Arthur Biddell made a full note each year of the harvest and the salient details of the harvest contract; but the actual contract itself was no doubt entered on a separate sheet which the company of men would witness. None of these full contracts seems to have survived; but details of a harvest contract made later in the century are given elsewhere.[1]

A note given by an old farm-worker may help to illuminate the above details. It appears that when a farmer and his men discussed a job that he had decided to have done by a company there was a more-or-less set formula for the actual proposal. After details had been gone into, the farmer finally said: 'Well, I'll put the job out to you.' The worker, acting either for himself or the company agreed upon, responded: 'I'll take it.' It was natural that the men should discuss the agreements among themselves afterwards, comparing the rates and the conditions with those they had received and experienced on previous occasions. If after stating the rate he had contracted for a job a worker capped his account by saying: 'I took it,' sometimes his mates, critical of his bargain, chaffed him and retaliated: 'You took it! You mean it *took you*!'

The above treatment of *taken-work* implies that it was of very early origin and was common in Suffolk farms during the early nineteenth century: oral evidence also suggests that it was so right throughout the century up to recent times. If all this is true, it may appear that any generalisation about farm-wages during the last century in this part of Suffolk is bound to be very provisional; as the money a worker could earn would seem to depend on the generosity or carefulness of the individual farmer. Yet in spite of the frequency of contract work there is evidence to show that most farmers saw to it that their men got no more—and usually no less—than the average wage. This tendency is shown in an entry in the Biddell wages-books. It was made by William Biddell, another of Arthur's sons, who became member of parliament for West Suffolk:

'*1847: Memorandum:* The day wages of the men previous to Jan. 1847 were 1s. 6d. per day. They were then increased to 1s. 9d. per

[1] *A.F.C.H.*, pp. 85–6.

day, and so continued until Michaelmas 1847. The Horsemen's (wages) were proportionally increased. The *taken-work* was also put out on a much higher scale than commonly, purposely so as the men could earn from 12 to 14s. per week. This was done because of the great rise that took place at this time in the price of Flour and provisions. The price of Flour having in April reached 4s. 1d. per Stone, though the previous Michaelmas it was little if any more than 2s. 0d. per Stone—before and after it fell rapidly so that now the price is only abt. 2s. 0d. per Stone as (?) it was last October.'

March, 1848.   Wm. B.'

Before leaving this subject it is worthy of note that the method used by Arthur Biddell for paying his company of men for ditching or draining—by so much a rod (5½ yards), quoted on page 121—lasted until recent years, if not up to the present. William Cobbold was a skilled drainer and this, he related, was the usual method of payment. He won many certificates for proficiency in pipe-draining at the beginning of this century, and has described the work as it was then carried on at Loose Hall, Hitcham:

'Gangs of men—five usually, sometimes more—worked together on the draining. The drains, perforated earthenware pipes, were laid in the land nine yards apart and a yard deep. For laying pipes a yard deep—*yard-work*, as it was called—we were paid seven shillings *a score rod*—110 (20 x 5½) yards of pipes laid. A team averaged two score a week and had to work very hard to do that, as they had to dig out the drain, pipe it and fill it in. The ordinary pipes or *eyes* were two inches in diameter; the mains three inches. We laid the mains at the lowest level of the field and fitted the drains obliquely into them. At first we had to bore holes in the mains to admit the side-drains; but later the farmer hired a brick-kiln at Wattisham and had his own pipes made with holes already made in the mains. For fitting a *neck*, as this join was called, we got threepence extra. No cement was used at the join; little pieces of pipe were fitted into the join to keep it firm and the whole covered with a piece of clay. We dug the ditches with a draining-spade: this had a tapered blade, eighteen inches long for ordinary drains, twenty-two inches for the mains. We laid the

pipes in the ditch with an L shaped tool—I used to make them myself:
just a wooden handle and a piece of iron bent at right angles fitted
into it. The art was to make sure that you dug the bottom of the ditch
out level: you could then lay the pipes so accurately that they'd all
appear to be one pipe without a single join.'

Arthur Chaplin has recalled that at Stowupland they were paid five
shillings a score-rod for pipe-laying; but the drains there were only
thirty inches deep. He also recalled using a tool called a *bass spade*—
with a tapering blade similar to the ordinary draining spade, but with
two long pieces taken out of the centre to make the blade lighter and
easier to work in clay.

An entry in the Work Books related to the above demands a note
owing to the unusual term contained in it:

Jan. 22nd, 1829:   *Isaac Maltster*
   39 Rods *Delf digging* in Luck's Meadow (8d.)   £1 6s. 0d.
   6 Do. at 3d.   1 6

Delf—sometimes *delfin*—is a Dutch word probably introduced into
English by Vermuyden and his seventeenth century compatriots who
reclaimed so much land in East Anglia. It still survives in the Suffolk
dialect and it denotes a deep sort of trench or ditch. The town Delf
or Delft in Holland was so called from the *delf* (delve) or ditch—still
the name for the chief canal in the town.[1]

[1] Joseph Wright, *The English Dialect Dictionary*, London, 1898.
A. O. D. Claxton, *The Suffolk Dialect of the Twentieth Century*,
Adlard, Ipswich.

10

Methods of Cultivation

One of the most pervasive and intractable elements—almost as intractable as man himself—that the historian has to handle is time. Everything he studies is part of a development in time; and he is forced to *isolate* phases of this development before he can properly begin his study. 'Time must have a stop,' is more than a mere catch-phrase protesting at the relentless onward movement of events, it is of necessity the first device in the historian's technique. He must stop the movement and make arbitrary divisions in time in order to ask his questions. He must assume, for his purpose, that history is not a process and he must immobilise events before he can study them. The trouble begins when the historian's 'arrested' and provisional picture of the past is taken for the reality itself, when it becomes something like a multi-coloured tapestry of events tapering back into time, and is cut into convenient lengths in order to study the design and interpret the posturings of the figures woven into it.

The study of agricultural history, in many ways, is a good corrective to this tendency to ignore the provisional nature of these isolates in time, a tendency endowing them with a reality they never possessed. For in no part of history is its organic nature more emphasised than that which treats of the way the land has been cultivated: how social organisation, customs, beliefs and usages are closely bound up with the actual methods of cultivation. The old agricultural, village community has always been to a large degree resistant to the pressure of outside change. Changes of dynasties, changes of government, it is true, affected it, sometimes profoundly; and the change in the tenure of land—the replacement of the open-field by the individual enclosed holding—put a great strain on its framework. Yet it preserved its continuity from early times right up to the present century, because in essentials the methods of cultivation had remained the same. From earliest times up to the period studied here, the farmer has relied on draught animals to cultivate his land. Whatever changes have come about have been due in a large degree to the improvement in the efficiency with which he used these animals and harnessed them to a gradually improving machinery: these were the instruments that any change in methods of cultivation relied on; and therefore the amount of change was necessarily limited. But during the last fifty years a new type of machinery altogether has been evolved—the internal combustion engine, that has its own propulsive power and in addition an apparently hidden potential not only to make revolutionary changes in methods of cultivation but also to make the biggest break in continuity that the old rural, agricultural community has yet experienced in its long history.

Viewed from this standpoint the date 1485 is of comparatively little significance: from a narrowly political standpoint it was the beginning of the end of the Middle Ages; but it can be stated with equal force that, as far as agriculture and the countryside are concerned, the true end of the Middle Ages is not the accession of the Tudors but the introduction of the internal combustion engine. There is obviously more evidence for this statement in some parts of Great Britain than in others. For the regions of countries, as well as countries themselves, appear to be affected by the law of unequal development; and even in a comparatively small area like the British Isles it is possible to find one district, in many aspects of its living, centuries behind another. Recently, for instance, it was stated:[1] 'There were no horses on Fair Isle (between the Orkneys and the Shetlands): it was not until 1951 that the last of the bullocks which drew the plough were superseded by small tractors.' And while the exceptional nature of this instance would not perhaps strengthen the argument unduly, the evidence here in Suffolk is that the Middle Ages—albeit in vestigial form—has persisted right up to the last two generations who saw the introduction of the internal combustion engine to the farmlands. The agricultural historian or the folklorist working in a

[1] Seaton Gordon, *The Times*, 10th May, 1958.

rural community in this part of England can put no retrospective limit to his inquiries: his backward view will extend, as far as farming is concerned, at least to the time when the three-field system was the typical background of cultivation; and an inquiry into the beliefs of the rural community and some of the customs that are as closely bound up with the land as the methods of cultivation themselves will take him back much farther still—to the days before Christianity became the dominant religion of these islands.

But before proceeding to actual cultivation, mention must first be made of an aspect of the social organisation of some Suffolk villages that has brought out comments such as this: 'Such-and-such a village is feudal;' and this was said of at least one village until as recently as ten years ago. 'What the lord-of-the-manor said, was absolute law; and if you dared to question it you were out—on your way, and in most cases not knowing where that way would take you.' Although *feudal* in this sense was used loosely for undue dependence upon the whim of one powerful person, the temper of the governors in a number of Suffolk villages, and—it must be said—the attitude of the governed themselves, were little different from those which obtained under absolute serfdom. In the 'closed village', until quite recent years *adscripti glebae* (or *adscripti casellis*, which amounts to the same thing) was a true description of the status of most of the villagers: they were tied to the land and the cottages and were at the mercy of the squire; and if they criticised him in any way they did not stay in their cottages longer than it took to get the machinery of ejection working. That the lord or squire in most cases exercised a benevolent regard for their tenants did in no way alter the fact that this precarious status was indeed feudal. The attitude of some of the governing class about a hundred years ago can be illustrated by a story[1] about the wife of the squire of the village of Playford. An old servant 'who would have gone through fire and water to serve her mistress' asked her for a holiday. She got the peremptory answer: 'Holiday? Why you had two days last year!' And this lady was the wife of Thomas Clarkson, the abolitionist, who devoted the greater part of his life to the emancipation of the negro slaves. The observation of a man of

[1] Herman Biddell, *Thomas Clarkson and Playford Hall*, p. 53.

sixty-five about the social life of the Suffolk village at the first part of this century shows that this attitude died very hard indeed: 'At that time o' day you had no peak to your cap, like as not: it were all wore up a-touching on it to the gentry.'

One or two instances of the above-mentioned continuity have already been quoted: another is concealed in the term *summer-land*[1] which occurs in Arthur Biddell's 1824 crop memorandum.[2] A summer-land is a fallow; and although the Norfolk four-course system, in the main, did away with the necessity of leaving land bare for a period in order that it could recover, this rotation of crops did not abolish the clean (*dead* or *naked*) fallow entirely. As Arthur Young noted at the transition time, at the end of the eighteenth century: 'There is no question of the merit of fallowing, when compared with bad courses of crops. If the husbandry is not correct in this respect, the fallowist will certainly be a much better farmer than his neighbour; but there are courses which will clean the foulest land as well as any summer fallow by means of plants which admit all the tillage of a summer fallow. Cabbages planted before June or July; winter tares admit three months tillage if tillage be wanted; beans, well cultivated, will preserve land clean which has been cleaned by cabbage. And, in any case, two successive hoeing crops are effective in giving positive clean-ness. These observations are not theory, they are practice; and it is high time that mankind should be well persuaded that the right quantity of cattle and sheep cannot be kept on a farm if the fallows of the old system are not made to contribute to their support.'[3]

As a vigorous advocate of the new farming, what Arthur Young is saying is that a farmer had better stick to the old method of having a long, clean fallow if he is not sufficiently conversant with the new system of rotating the crops; but he will not farm his land as he should do until he has learned to forgo the practice of occasionally having part of his land quite unproductive. But Arthur Biddell continued to use the old system, alongside the new, at least thirty years after this; and in 1849 the Raynbirds could observe: that in spite of the

---

[1] *summerling* in the dialect.   [2] see p. 105.
[3] *G.V.A.C.S.*, p. 49.

adoption of the four-course rotation on the heavy land of Suffolk:[1] The recurrence, on the average, of a long fallow once in eight years is considered absolutely necessary by the best farmers for the cleaning and amelioration of stiff land by repeated ploughings and pulverizations; and there are a few who consider a clean fallow is necessary every four years.'

A study of Arthur Biddell's cropping schedule shows that during the early part of the century this was in fact his practice. He had a clean fallow every four years on some of his fields; and it was only later in the century he followed the new approved course of growing tares, beet or turnips on the land that required resting before a corn crop. On the eleven-acre field the *New Lay*, already mentioned in the *memorandum*, he had a summer-land or clean fallow every fourth year between 1823 and 1840: but after this he rested the land in the fourth year by growing Swedish turnips, turnips, beetroot, beet, Swedes, white turnips, etc.

The Raynbirds described the method of preparing a long fallow or long summer-land over a hundred years ago. But William Cobbold of Battisford has recently described how he used this essentially medieval method of clean fallowing, until about twenty years ago, on the heavy land of this area:

'We sowed rye and Italian grass on a field in the spring and left it to stand until the following spring. Then we *fed* the land with sheep—the lambs that had been born that year had their first feed off this. Then we treated the land with five *earths*.'

The word *earth* as used here gives a clue to the antiquity of the practice. The *Rectitudines Singularum Personarum* (Services Due from Various Persons),[2] a Latin translation of a Saxon manuscript, probably of the tenth century, records that one of the services of a *villanus* or *gebur*—an owner of about thirty acres of land—was to plough and sow a *gafol-yrth*, or three acres of land, for his lord. *Yrth*[3] is the Saxon word for a ploughing and *gafol-yrth* was a tribute or 'rent' ploughing. The word earth has exactly the same meaning of *a*

---

[1] *A.O.S.*, p.9.
[2] Quoted by Seebohm, *E.V.C.*, p. 129.
[3] *yrth:* O.E. *erian*—to ear or plough: Lat.: *arare;* Welsh: *aredig.*

ploughing when it is used like this, as it often is, in Suffolk even today. Tusser uses the word also:

> '*Such land as ye breake up for barlie to sowe,*
> *two earthes at the least or ye sowe it bestowe.*'

And Cullum of Hawstead says:

'To *ear* is to plough; so used in the English translation of the Bible and other contemporary writings. *Earable*, in this lease, is the same as arable: from the Latin.'

'The *first earth*,' as William Cobbold recorded, 'was the first ploughing. For the *second earth* you turned back the furrows, ploughed them back until you were as you were before. For the *third earth* you *crossed* it: that means you ploughed it across or *overwart* (overthwart) as we called it: you ploughed at right angles to the first furrows you made. After the *third earth* you let the land lie for a while. It would be very rough, great old clods of soil and stuff, but the elements would get to work on it and help to pull it down. You then harrowed and rolled it and kept it moving. Most of the old spear-grass would come to the surface after the second ploughing: the harrowings would bring it out for you to burn. At the *four' earth* you ploughed it back—turned it so you were *as you were* once again. Then you came to the *five earth*—the really skilled part of the whole job—when you stetched up the land for your crop of corn. Winter wheat usually, about November. The first-baiter was the one who did this. He measured the stetch with his nine-foot stetch-pole and he took a stick from the hedge, peeled off its bark so that it stood up white for a guide for his first furrow.

'They don't seem to take as much care today. There're still ploughmen and *ploughmen* of course; but today most on 'em aim to keep in the field, and that's about all. In the old days it was con-sidered very important that you ploughed every square inch of your work: nowadays it seems to be *cut and cover*. But at that time they used to teach 'em to plough. It was a hard school, I can tell you: I've heard my father tell a story about a lad who was ploughing. The plough came out of the furrow so the lad kicked over the soil with his foot, saying: "Oh, that won't be seen!" But the farmer who happened to be on the other side of the hedge heard him. He came into the field and said: "Take off your coat, boy." Then he took his stick and gave the boy two or three cuts across his back: "Now do you put your coat on again: that won't be seen either!" '

Although this seems more like a cautionary tale than a true one, it appears that some farmers in the old days were not beyond correcting a learner with stronger means than either word or good example afforded. Nor were fads or foibles regarded:

'Uncle Bill was *living in* and the farmer went into Stowmarket—this would be between eighty and ninety year ago—to the market; and as he came away he thought he'd take some sprats hoom. His wife cooked the sprats and gave some of them to the men to eat. The next time she see my grandmother she say to har:

' "Your boy William, he fare not to eat the *hids* of the sprats or the *boons*. He shan't hev any agen!"

' "Well, he moight not stop for you to offer him any!"

'Sure enough, Uncle Bill left after that. He went up to London and he settled down up thar comfortable. And in later years he used to say if it warn't for sprats' *hids* and *boons* he'd still be on the farm down in Silly[1] Suffolk.'

To revert to *summer-land* for an additional note: Against the field called *New Lay*, Arthur Biddell wrote in his cropping schedule for 1823: 'Tares self-sown and made Bastard Summer-land.' This is referred to in the memorandum made in the following year and already given.[2] A bastard summer-land is so called to distinguish from a true summer-land or long fallow. The term is still used, as Robert Sherwood of Blaxhall has stated, although not in connection with a partially clean fallow as Arthur Biddell appears to have used it: 'A bastard summer-land is one that is broken up before the usual time. As soon as the ley-crop is taken off in June the land is *busted-up* and a *catch-and-grab* crop of turnips is sown in July.' Robert Savage of the same village also recalled: 'They used to let the land lie *falley* in the heavy-land parts where it was too heavy to fold sheep. They'd leave a

[1] From O.E. *Saelig*—happy, or perhaps holy, referring to the number of religious establishments once in the country.
[2] p. 105.

THE FARMER

field *falley* every four year. They'd keep a-turning on it over the whole fore-part of the year to kill all the weeds and grasses; then they'd sow wheat in the autumn. This were under the four-course. But in this light land here they didn't follow the four-course strict. You could get a catch-crop chance-times: if you put your seed in right quick in between, you could get an extra crop.'

The cultivation of carrots, already referred to as a feature of the light-land districts, extends at least to the time of John Norden, the Tudor topographer, as Arthur Young pointed out. And the method of cultivating beans was until recently similar to that described by Young over 160 years ago; although in his time the beans were either sown broadcast or dibbled.[1] 'Beans have been dibbled in a row on every *flag* (furrow-slice), by others on every other flag. Dibbling is the best and most effective method of cultivating beans.' Certainly, dibbling was more effective than the broadcast sowing; but by the middle of the nineteenth century 'ploughing in' beans was the general method of planting. A small wooden hopper or container mounted on a wheel about sixteen inches in diameter was fixed behind a plough: as the plough turned the furrow the beans dropped into it. The beans could be regulated by a screw device that varied the width of the aperture at the bottom of the hopper through which they fell into the furrow, thus varying the rate of sowing. Two ploughs usually worked at the sowing of beans—'one drilling and one covering up': one plough with the attached hopper opening the furrow and dropping in the seed, the other following behind opening another one, or sometimes two furrows, and at the same time covering up the seed. The interval between the rows of seed was eighteen inches (every other furrow of nine-inch width) or twenty-seven inches (every third furrow). No instance has been recalled of beans being sown in every furrow as they were in Young's time.

In the farm where Arthur Chaplin spent most of his working life every other furrow was the rule: 'But if the land was *foul* (full of weeds) we drilled every third furrow—though the beans were sown a bit thicker then. One coomb an acre was the average rate of sowing bean-seed; though when I were a lad they couldn't afford to sow at

[1] *G.V.A.C.S.*, p. 78.

that rate: they put on only half as much—two bushels an acre.' (This was the rate in Arthur Young's time). 'If you wanted to check up on whether you were sowing at the right rate, you stood with your two feet along the furrow with a space of a yard between them. You counted the beans you could see between your feet. If there were twenty-three or twenty-four you knew you weren't far wrong and sowing would be coming out at about a coomb an acre. We used the beans to fatten bullocks and we also fed them to the horses. You weren't a farmer in those days unless you could grow a good crop of beans.'

William Cobbold always sowed beans in rows twenty-seven inches apart. He drilled using a single (Ransome's Y.L.) plough and followed with a double (Bantall) plough: 'As it was all stetch-work, we couldn't finish with a double plough—not by the standards we had at that time o' day—so we left a four-furrow *baulk* and shut up the stetch later with the single plough.'

A further note[1] quoted by Arthur Young, about the cultivation of beans, shows that the three-furrow interval was used specifically for cleaning the land: 'They should be drilled at thirty inches distance and ploughed between; if any *quickens*[2] are found or remain two or three ploughings in spring for barley will eradicate them.' This method of *ploughin' 'tween beans* was used in Suffolk until recently. The breast of the plough was first removed and the ploughing was done with the share only: a similar method was adopted in cattle-beet cultivation.

But Arthur Biddell did not find that Young's recommendation in regard to bean cultivation worked out in practice, as the following entry shows; and it was perhaps one of the reasons why he held so long to the old method of a *dead* fallow in order to clean his land. The entry is also from the 1824 memorandum in the *Work Books*: '*Net House*[3] *Peice*: 10 A. Wheat After Potatoes and after Beans. The land after Beans was so foul of Speare Grass that I had it taken up by Forks before the Wheat Sowing at an expence of 15 or 20 shillings p. Acre. (The Potatoes Previous to the Wheat were an amazing Heavy

[1] *G.V.A.C.S.*, p. 33.
[2] Variously called, *quitch*, *couch*, *twitch* or *spear* grass; but a bane to farmers and gardeners under whatever name.
[3] Usually *Nettus* in Suffolk: the neat- or cow-house.

Crop) mucked lightly for Potatoes and Wheat too—not for Beans but after them for Wheat—this yeild to 77 Co. or 7C. 3B. Pr Acre.'

Before leaving the cultivation of beans two old processes connected with their harvesting are worth recording. The beans were stored in the barn and most of them were threshed by machine; but the beans the farmer kept for seed were 'knocked out' with the flail. The flail did not bruise the seed as the machine did, and there was thus a much higher percentage of germination. Rider Haggard wrote at the beginning of the century:[1] 'On a farm belonging to Mr Edgar (near Preston, Suffolk) I noted a man using a flail to thrash out beans in a barn—a very unusual sight now-a-days.' After the beans had been threshed they were put through a *cavings-sieve*—a round sieve with a wicker-plaited bottom. It was called a cavings-sieve from its use with the corn: it separated the *cavings* or bits of straw from the grain. Arthur Chaplin recalled: 'As you shook it the corn fell through and the cavings or straw-stuff stayed in. You then threw this onto a heap at the side.—It were hard work using a cavings-sieve, shaking it full o' corn or beans out there on front of you. So we invented a *sifting-horse* to make it easier. This was a T-shaped frame made of wood and about eighteen inches from the ground: we used to make them on the farm. You sat at one end—the bottom of the T—rested the sieve full of corn or beans on the long arm of the frame; and slid the sieve back'ard and forrard in front on you until the seed fell through. When you wanted to fill your sieve, you rested it on the cross-piece. With beans, naturally, you had a sieve with much wider mesh.'

A farmer recalls: 'My owd father was very particular about sifting the beans: he wouldn't have any half-beans in the seed. They were no use: we sifted them out with the stalks and so on. It took us half a day to sift a coomb of beans on the owd sifting-horse; and you didn't *cop* (throw) the beans into the bushel-measure you had 'long side you until they were done properly.'

Some of the old bean drills are still to be seen lying about in farm sheds and barns: here and there they are still in use. A farmer from the Southend district of Essex, seeing an old drill at the exhibition of

[1] *Rural England* (2 Vols.) 2, Longmans Green, 1902.

old farm-tools at the Royal Show at Norwich (1957) said that he still used one on his farm, as also did one of his neighbours.

The cultivation of cattle-beet or mangel-wurzels as practised generally until twenty or thirty years ago, and by an occasional farmer until the present time, is another old method it will be of interest to record. Mangels were first cultivated as a farm crop during the latter half of the eighteenth century—that period of enthusiasm for better farming that Arthur Young and Thomas Coke did so much to promote, and which farmers like Arthur Biddell carried on well into the next century. The method of cultivation does not appear to have changed much since Young's time: certainly it is not very different from that described by the Raynbirds in 1849. William Cobbold's description summarises the method as practised on most farms in this area:

'If it was a dry season we ploughed up the land directly after harvest and let it stand like that for most of the winter. Then in the spring we *ridged* the land *overwart*[1]—worked it at right angles to the furrows. The first step in ridging was to mark out the land, with a measuring-pole and peeled sticks, into thirty-one inch strips. We then started at the side of the field and drew a furrow: we then came back down the same furrow and threw the land the other way. We then carried on turning furrows to meet one another, thus forming an arch or ridge. You'll notice that when you are ridging up like this you are ploughing up and down the furrow and not round and round as you do when you're stetching: in other words you are turning your furrows on to unploughed land. You are not *cutting into* all the land—that part in the centre of your work hasn't been touched. But we come to that later. Next the ridges were *tommed-up*: we went through the furrows with a *double-tom* or *tom-plough*—a plough with two breasts—heaping up the ridges still further.

'We then mucked the land. A tumbril full of muck gave six heaps, nine yards apart. When the tumbril was tipped it was not allowed to go right over: it was held by a *lock-chain* at an angle so the *toes*[2] of the

[1] Virgil's *in obliquum:* see *Georgics*, 1. 97.
[2] A *toe-stick* held the body of the tumbril to the shafts. A *lock-chain* was also used on a wagon with a *slade* or shoe that was placed under one wheel as the wagon went down-hill.

tumbril—the two pieces of wood sticking out at the back—didn't go
right down on to the land and disturb the ridges.

'We made the ridges exactly thirty-one inches apart for this
reason: the tumbril wheels were set sixty-two inches apart so when
the tumbril of muck went on to the land, the wheels travelled in the
outside two of a group of three furrows while the horse walked in the

centre one. In this way neither horse-hoof nor wheel disturbed the
work. We next spread the muck.

'Then the job was to *split the ridges:* we opened a furrow down the
centre of each ridge, throwing back the soil and covering all the muck.
When we split the ridges, as you can see, we were really coming back
to the land we had not cut into when we first ridged up. Now the land
was ready for a light *roll*, and after rolling, for the drill. The drill we
used was a *two-coulter* Garrett drill specially kept for the purpose.

'When the beet came up we put the *scoop* on 'em. The *beet-scoop* was fitted to the plough-beam; and we went down the rows pulling the ridges down with the scoop so the space between the rows would be level. Then came the time for *chopping-out* the beet with a six-inch hoe; and after this the women and children *singled* the plants out. The more soil you got away from the beet at this stage the better it liked it: and as it grew each beet would be soon standing up like a gate-post.

'When the season was wet we couldn't follow this method just as I've described it: we had to wait until the land was dry enough to go on, and then do the best we could. Some farmers used to split the ridges and then give them an extra *earth* in February; but this was a mistake on heavy land: the land would usually take harm at this time.'

Charles Bugg of College Farm, Barking (Suffolk) has this year (1958) ridged beet by the old method, using a horse-plough and a two-coulter drill made by Murton Turner of Kenninghall in Norfolk. This is an old style horse-drawn drill that can be set for ridges varying in width up to thirty inches. There are two hoppers—one above each coulter—to hold the seed; and in front of each coulter is a large capstan-shaped roller, made to fit the top of the ridge. In the centre of each of these rollers is a metal sleeve which makes a miniature furrow along which the coulter deposits the seed right in the centre of the ridge. Behind each coulter is a small cylindrical roller which rolls out this small groove or furrow and thus covers the seed deposited in it.

Two or three instances have already been given of the great respect accorded to the land, under the old system of farming, after it had been got ready for the crop. Nothing must travel on the stetch once it had been prepared; and after the crop was sown the seed-bed was considered almost sacred—to be disturbed by neither hoof nor wheel. The plain reason for this, especially on heavy land, was the danger of *hard pan*: as a vehicle or horse went over a prepared seed-bed the hoofs and the wheels put down the land and formed a *hard pan*[1], a layer of hard mud that the seedling would scarcely penetrate. There-

---

[1] This dialect phrase was taken to the U.S.A. by early English settlers. It is still used by American farmers. See Deeraff and Haystead, *The Business of Farming*, University of Oklahoma Press, 1948.

fore horse and wheel were so managed as to travel invariably in the furrows between the stetches or the ridges. In no process is this care better demonstrated than in the old farmers' method of drilling. In drilling the twelve-furrow (nine feet) stetch, for instance, neither horse nor wheel touched the actual seed-bed. If a whole or nine-foot drill was used, six horses drew the implement. The horses were harnessed *at length*, three in each furrow; that is, each horse walked behind the other, three each side of the stetch. Six horses drawing a nine-foot drill for sowing wheat on heavy land was usual in the Raynbirds' time. But four horses were the number with the smaller drills and for drilling spring corn, when the coulters were set to bite into the land not quite as deeply as they did when wheat was sown. But even at that time the *half-stetch* drill was being more generally used for twelve-furrow work than was the whole drill, probably because the draught was lighter and the drill could be used with two horses.

The principal makers of the half-stetch drill in Suffolk were the pioneer firm of James Smyth and Son of Peasenhall. Their technical problem in the early years, apart from those problems connected with the actual design of the drill, was to make a drill robust enough to stand up to stetch-work. As one of their catalogues (c. 1878) stated: 'No class of Drill requires more care in its construction than does that used for drilling on land ploughed in stetches. What with deep furrows and general heaviness of soil it is essentially necessary that the Drills should be not only well and strongly made but also of good seasoned material.' The firm may be said to have succeeded in its object, for there is at least one Smyth drill—made about 1850—that is still in use after more than a century's continual handling.

The half-stetch drill, as the name implies, drilled only half the stetch at a time, thus reducing the draught considerably. Two horses were used to draw this drill—a *filler* and a trace-horse. On very heavy land three horses were sometimes needed. Whatever number was used the horses were harnessed *at length* and walked in *one furrow*. To enable them to do this the shafts of the drill were *set on the quarter*—that is, they fitted on one side of the drill frame; at the other end of the drill was a shackle and to this a chain was attached and coupled at the other end to the trace horse, thus ensuring that the drill moved forward in a straight line. The frame was fitted with a *sliding* or *false* axle that could be extended beyond the width of the drill. In twelve-furrow work this axle was extended to the full nine feet, allowing both wheels of the drill to run in the furrows.

The half-stetch drill was a *hind-swing steerage* drill: two handles were fitted behind, and the man operating the drill used these for setting the coulters transversely, when completing the second half of the stetch, to ensure that all the rows of corn were sown at uniform intervals. Arthur Chaplin has supplied a note about the half-stetch drill: 'The drill operator walked behind and by pressing on the two handles he kept the coulters in the land. We often hung pieces of old iron on these steerage handles to give them extra weight. We drilled fourteen rows in the twelve-furrow stetch when we were drilling barley and thirteen when we drilled wheat. As there were seven coulters to the drill, with wheat we had to block one of the coulters when we drilled one half of the stetch. Our rule was: *Up six and down seven.* We blocked a coulter when we went up one side of the stetch and there were only six working; on the way down the second half of the stetch we let the blocked coulter run. Some of us used to call the half-stetch drill "the owd *block-drill*". We were paid a penny an acre extra for drilling, and you were expected to drill ten acres a day. You went on until you'd done your ten acres, too. Sometimes I've seen the horses shivering and their chains (traces) shaking with tiredness but they had to go on until the ten acres were finished. Our rate of sowing was two bushels[1] of wheat to an acre and ten pecks of barley.

'When the corn came up and if we found that we'd had a *block* in drill that we didn't know about (showing by a bare patch in the growing corn) we'd lose the penny for that acre.'

Mistakes in drilling figure in the folklore of the Middleton district

[1] cf. *E.V.C.*, p. 157, A tenant who held land in villenage in the manor of Tidenham (Gloucester) during the reign of Edward 1. —1306—had to do certain *precariae* (bene- or *boon-works*—work done for the lord of the manor). One of these was sowing corn: 'He made 1 *precaria* called "cherched" and he ploughed and harrowed a half-acre for corn, and sowed it with 1 bushel of corn from his own seed.' Two bushels an acre was, therefore, a truly traditional rate of sowing.

of North East Suffolk. There is a superstition in that parish that if a worker misses part of his stetch in drilling and a tell-tale blank shows in the corn, there will soon be a death. Conversely, if—as sometimes happens—part of a stetch is inadvertently drilled twice, there will soon be a birth in the parish.

On much of the land, however, stetch drills were not used. William Cobbold used a 'six-and-a-half foot drill' that was drawn across the furrows and not along them. He describes the preliminaries to the drilling: 'As we ploughed the field a *comb-harrow* followed the plough. Next the comb-harrow went *overwart* the furrows. The two harrowings broke up the land, flattened it out to a certain extent; but it didn't fill in the furrows altogether: you could see them quite easily as you drilled. We saw to it that the drill went *plumb overwart* each furrow: both wheels had to cross the furrow at exactly the same time. In this way we were sure that the *counters* bit into the land at an equal depth for the whole width of the drill.'

Horse-hoeing was also touched on: 'When the corn was about two inches high we hoed it with the horse-hoe. This hoe had nine whole hoes and two half-hoes—one half-hoe at each end. The reason for the half-hoe was this: You took your hoe up the *ringes*[1] and as you came back to hoe the piece of land alongside, at one end of the hoe you'd be hoeing between the same two ringes of corn as you'd already done. If there was a full hoe like as not you'd be cutting into the corn and harming it. We called the row between the two runs of the horse-hoe the *closen-ringe*. You had a *closen-ringe*, too, when you were drilling *overwart*: the drill operator had to estimate the interval between the two runs of his drill so it would be the same as the set intervals on the drill itself. Often times the drilling would have been done so accurately and the closen-ringe was so much like the fixed intervals made by the drill that it was a puzzle to pick it out when we came to the horse-hoeing. A man using a horse-hoe had to mind his business and he wanted a good man with him a-leading his horse.'

It is worth noting that the horse-hoes and rollers used in twelve-furrow work were also fitted with sliding-axles enabling both wheels to travel in the furrows. The *twin-rolls* on heavy land were often fitted

[1] Rows of corn.

with a smaller, metal-banded, wooden roll something like an elon-
gated barrel. This was called a *pup-roll* or *follower*. This last name
describes its function: it followed behind the twin-roll accounting for
the little strip of land that was left between the two rollers.

One thing, at least, stands out from the foregoing account of the old
farmers' method of cultivation: this is the necessity of being accurate
to the inch; and this accuracy had to be combined with a degree of
finish in working the land that would have done justice to the most
exacting craftsman in any rural trade—like the carpenter, the wheel-
wright or the smith. But all these have had the social approbation and
esteem that seems to have been denied—as it were, traditionally
denied—to the farm-worker. Not so long ago the farm-worker—along
with the coal-miner—was the pariah of British labour; and yet both
were the very base and buttress of industry in this country. But the
farm-worker was never accredited with skill: he was hardly accredited
with sense; and it took two wars to induce society to give him even a
modicum of the recognition he deserves, and a wage comparable to
that of skilled workers in other national industries.

A townsman going into the country today is impressed by the
amount of machinery he sees in a field; and he admits to himself,
however grudgingly, that farming must require *some* skill if it is only
the handling of all those intricate-looking machines. But it is probable
that the old farm-worker had more real and more differentiated skills
than the average worker who today tills the land with machines.
Today differentiation is no longer in the worker but in the machine
itself. The machine is not an extension of his own skill as the old
tools and horse-machines were: he is merely the activator of the
machine and to a great degree a 'passive' one at that.—So it appears
to some of the old school who watch the present-day farm-worker
'goo a-ripping and a-roaring' across the field on a tractor. Perhaps the
old school see the farm-worker today getting somewhere near the
status he deserves; and they are rather bitter that they in their time
were persistently denied it. Yet one of them spoke for the farm-
workers, old and new, when he said: 'They talk about a bricklayer and
a carpenter and a plumber and so on being skilled men. Good luck to
'em. But the farm-worker is as skilled as any on 'em. It takes years to

learn your trade on the farm—the same as anywhere else. To prove it you've only got to get some 'un fresh and put him to do the simplest job on the land—you'd have to close the gate on him right quick to keep him in the field.'

Some methods of cultivation are hinted at in the old gnomic sayings that have been the vehicles for traditional farming lore and practices ever since the time of Hesiod; and a kind of primitive animism in talking of the land is still usual in country districts, no doubt expressing a half-conscious belief that the land is more akin to a living animal than to unquickened matter like a stone or a piece of rock. Poor land is *hungry land*. *Kind land* will give good crops, and so will land that is *fat*; and in the very word *yield* is the figure of the soil clinging to its concealed riches and only releasing them after the farmer has struggled with it in the sweat of his brow.[1]

One saying that contains a piece of old farming lore is quoted by W. A. Peek, a Blaxhall farmer: it refers to the breaking up of new ground:

> *To plough rushes is copper;*
> *To plough heather is silver;*
> *But to plough bracken is gold.*

Another of his sayings is: *Drunk or sober sow wheat in October*. He also quotes a rhyme to show that in farming, as in most enterprises, the temper and morale of the business is set by the man at the top:

> *Trim tram:*
> *Such as master,*
> *Such as man.*

And if a farmer is going to run his place on the philosophy, '*It's a poor owd farm thet can't keep one lazy man on it*,' his workers are likely to take their tempo from him: the whole business will then gradually slip down-hill and he will soon find himself in the mire.

Another saying from the heavy land district seems at first sight to be the sort of advice an old crone gives to a young mother nursing her first baby; but it is in fact a piece of sound farming lore: *Keep its top*

[1] cf. Virgil's *Georgics: infelix tellus; ager ille malus;* and *occultas vires terrae.*

clean and its bottom dry. In other words: Keep your land free from weeds and see that it is well drained.

A frequently quoted mnemonic saying among the old school of farmers was: *A man's wages is equal to the price of a sack (or comb) of corn.* Raymond Keer, a Bealings farmer, has given the saying its full significance. The wages before the First World War were:

	Per Week
The *worker* had the equivalent of a sack (a comb or 12 stones) of oats:	12s. 0d.
The *horseman* had the equivalent of a sack (a comb or 16 stones) of barley:	14s. 0d.
The *head-horseman* or *foreman* had the equivalent of a sack (a comb or 18 stones) of wheat:	18s. 0d.

It is sometimes said of a farmer:

> *He is getting on a bit queer in a place where the bottom is too near the top.*

A note from Arthur Young can again enlighten us on this:[1] 'By *bottom* is not meant an unstirred sterile subsoil, but the lower portion of that surface which has been stirred by the plough.' The philosophy of the hard-fisted small farmer is contained in the following:

> *I don't spend threepence until I can see fourpence back.*
> *If I get a shilling I keep it: if I see a sovereign I go after it.*
> *Any man's my friend if I can make a shilling out of him.*
> *Don't you fry him for a fule, dew (if you do) yew'll waste your fat.*
> *I've got a saying of my own: If I say to myself: 'The man's a fule'*
> *I know it's I'm the fule for thinking so.*

This view-point is also expressed in the cautionary saying that is held up as an awful judgment on the captious: '*The owd fule! He backed his hoss into the ditch hid fust.*'

The man who does not love a horse cannot love a woman.

Multiply the number of the loads by three: This cryptic saying is a mnemonic used by an old farm foreman: 'Supposing the farmer wanted all the corn from a field put into one stack, and he estimated it

---

[1] *G.V.A.C.S.*, p. 79.

would come to fifteen loads. To find out the size of your stack your sum was: 15×3; and that would give you the area of your stack bottom—45 square yards. That meant your stack would be 9 yards by 5. If you had twenty loads to put in a stack, your sum would be 20×3, giving 60 square yards. Now you could have a stack with either of two measurements: 10×6 or 12×5. You chose which size stack you'd have according to the state of the corn. If the corn was a bit on the damp side when it was carted, you'd have a stack of five yards width. This was the minimum: it wouldn't do to have a stack under this measurement as it wouldn't be safe.'

I could do everything on a farm bar make eggs: an old farm-worker boasting of his versatility.

If you lay an egg, though it be a gowd 'un, don't caackle.
Here are three old farming rhymes from north Suffolk:

> *Dry March, wet May:*
> *Plenty of corn, plenty of hay.*
> *Wet March, dry May:*
> *Little corn, little hay.*

> *By St Valentine's day:*
> *Half your beet, and half your hay.*

(By the 14th February you should have used half your winter stock of cattle-beet—mangel-wurzels—and half your hay.)

> *February waan:*
> *Sow peas and baan.*

(When the February moon begins to wane sow your peas and beans.)

And the last saying was both advice and a test of skill under the old farming:

> *Farm in front of your rubbish.*

'A good farmer sowed his seed so he could take his crop of corn before the rubbish (the weeds) came on. You had to be a good farmer to do that—a good practical farmer. And you wouldn't get the knowledge out of a book. There was no short cut: farming was an art and few men had it unless they'd come by it the hard way. Out of the gentle-men who came into farming at that time (before mechanisation etc.) only about one in twenty could make it go: the others had to have a skilled man to manage the farm for 'em. *But the skill has gone out of farming now.* Today, if a man takes over a farm and gets into a muddle, he has the fertilisers, the sprays and the weedkillers—the whole lot—to get him out of it.'

Part Three

THE HORSE

11

Historical Sketch of the Suffolk Horse

The heavy- or farm-horse in Suffolk is primarily the horse of the Suffolk breed that has evolved in the county of its name. Since earliest times provinces or areas of certain countries have been well known for their breeding of horses: Epirus and Mycenae in classical times, and Central Arabia and Libya even before this. It is likely that qualities of soil, grass and climate combined to make a given area suitable in the first place; and that later, tradition and acquired skill in the breeding, rearing and feeding of horses tended to perpetuate the initial advantage. For instance, the Bedouin tribes living in the Nejd district of Central Arabia—an area which is elevated and mountainous and possessed of water running off limestone and thus suitable for the formation of bone—were in the right place to breed horses; and down the centuries, when horses and their pedigrees were handed from father to son as their most precious possessions, the advantage was consciously exploited.

In the development of the heavy breeds of horse in Britain Suffolk appears to have been differentiated relatively early as a county suitable for evolving its own breed of horse; and the fact that it reached perfection in the *Sandlings*—the coastal strip of East Suffolk—argues that certain properties of soil and water in that area had at least some effect on the original location of the breed. For most of the principal studs in the history of the Suffolk horse, before the foundation of the Suffolk Stud-Book Association, were situated in the *Sands*: Butley, Sudbourne, Rendlesham, Newbourn and Melton; and even in later years when the breed became more widely known, and successful studs were founded all over the country, the *Sands* studs continued to hold their own and turn out their quota of 'winners'.

Robert Reyce the Suffolk Chronicler, writing at the beginning of the seventeenth century, implies that the process of evolving a horse peculiar to the county had already started some time before. He states: 'Among the many ornaments of this shire, I may not omitt to speake here of the horse, for the breeding whereof this country hath many apt places of most profittable use.' Suffolk, Reyce went on to complain, had not paid enough attention to breeding the horse for military purposes: 'butt such is our slothfulness in this respect that for the most part we rather desire to bee furnisht from our dear faires with the refuse of other countries, though after our long labour and great cost wee commonly meet with pampered counterfeit, or deceipt. Now for our horses of burden, or draught, experience of long time teacheth us, how uncertaine this proofe is of that which wee pay so dear for at others hands, causeth us to esteeme our owne home bred the more, which every way proveth so well for our owne use and profitt, that our husbandmen may justly compare in this respect with any other country whatsoever albeit they often complain that many vain sports, and idle occasions did never in any age consume more good horses than this age doth, which otherwise might prove of great use to them and the common wealth.'[1]

In the phrase 'the refuse of other countries' Reyce is no doubt referring to the efforts of Henry VIII to increase the size of the English horse. Much of the farming stock in England appears to have dwindled in size during the fifteenth century, the horse particularly. During the next century attempts were made to improve the breeds: for this purpose Henry imported foreign horses and in a Statute of 1541[2] enacted: 'That no person shall put in any forest, chase, moor or heath, common or waste (where mares and fillies are used to be kept) any stoned horse above the age of two years, not being fifteen hands high, within the shires and territories of Norfolk, Suffolk, Cambridge, Buckingham, Huntingdon, Essex, Kent, South Hampshire, North Wilts, etc. . . . ; nor under fourteen hands in any other county on pain of forfeiting the same.'

[1] Robert Reyce, *The Breviary of Suffolk*, 1618, John Murray, 1902, p. 42.
[2] 32 Henry VII c. 13.

But the danger of undersized or ill-bred stallions 'running in' with the mares on communal or 'stinted' pastures had become considerably less in Suffolk by Reyce's time, as much of the county, as he himself states,[1] had already been enclosed; and individual owners would have been able to keep their stock apart and breed as they desired, thus escaping the risks of a merry mating of 'nobody's son with every-body's daughter'. Reyce's account is of special significance as it indicates that the first enclosures were in the eastern part of the county where the Suffolk breed of horse was chiefly evolved.[2]

The early enclosures in Suffolk must have been favourable in an-other way to the differentiation of the heavy breed of horse, for the enclosures enabled the farmers to change over from the ox teams, or mixed teams of oxen and horses, to the teams made up solely of horses. Communal ownership was the key-note of the plough-team in the 'open-field'; but when the enclosures began it became desirable for farmers to work their own teams. The horse was more suitable for this style of 'several' farming for the compelling reason that it was more speedy at the plough than the ox; and as individual farmers were now paying day-men to do their ploughing the saving on the wages-bill would be an inducement to change-over as quickly as pos-sible. Just as today, even those farmers who would like to keep their horses have discarded them in favour of the tractor, chiefly because it does the job more quickly. The invention of lighter ploughs also helped the change-over from oxen to horses. Moreover, owing to the discovery of gunpowder and the decreasing use of heavy armour in battle, the 'great—or military-horse' was being released at this period for what the farmers, as Reyce states, considered his proper use.

But this tendency to use horses solely appears to have started much earlier than this in East Anglia, as we have seen in the Norwich records already quoted; and the region was spared that later battle with custom and tradition that handicapped other areas at a critical time in the later development of farming. What a favoured start East Anglia had in this respect can be gathered from the experience of

[1] *Breviary of Suffolk*, p. 27.
[2] See also W. E. Tate, 'A Handlist of Suffolk Enclosure Acts and Awards,' *Proceedings of the Suffolk Institute of Archaeology*, Vol. XXV (1952), p. 225.

Coke of Holkham when he went into Gloucestershire: 'seeing a team of six oxen attended by a man and a boy at work in a field (he) decided he would show local farmers that such work could be done efficiently and even more quickly by employing two horses and a man. The demonstration did nothing to remove the prejudice from the horse and the affection for oxen.'[1]

In the early part of the nineteenth century Robert Bloomfield could write, referring to his own region: 'No groaning ox is doomed to labour there'; and the present-day oral tradition in Suffolk can confidently state: 'The *Sheres*[2] never dropped bullocks as soon as we did' —in spite of the fact that there were isolated examples of ox-teams in this county (for instance, Robert Makens of Ringshall) right into the present century.

The Reverend Sir John Cullum, writing about the Suffolk parish of Hawstead in 1784, stated: 'When the constant use of oxen was discontinued and only horses were employed by the farmers here I cannot say. Oxen are not mentioned in the leases of the reign of Elizabeth; for then when the landlords reserved to themselves the power of coming upon the farms to carry away timber, mention is made of carts and horses only, for that purpose. Yet from several passages in Tusser, who was a Suffolk farmer early in that reign, if not the preceding one, it should seem as if they were then used in some parts, at least, of this county.'[3]

By Cullum's time the Suffolk horse had developed into a recognisable type, already well-defined and known to a certain extent outside East Anglia for his strength in *drawing* heavy loads; and the county became famous for its *drawing matches*. These matches have been described elsewhere,[4] but the passage where Cullum delineates the Suffolk Punch should be quoted here:

'Having mentioned horses I must take this opportunity of doing justice to a most useful breed of that noble animal, not indeed peculiar to this parish, but I believe to the county. The breed is well known by the name of Suffolk Punches. They are generally about fifteen hands

[1] F. H. Hollis, 'The Horse in Agriculture,' *B.O.H.*, p. 174.
[2] *A.F.C.H.*, p. 78.
[3] Sir John Cullum, *History of Hawstead*, 2nd edition, 1813, p. 256.
[4] *A.F.C.H.*, p. 125.

high, of a remarkably short and compact make; their legs bony and their shoulders loaded with flesh. Their colour is often of a light sorrel, which is as much remembered in some distant parts of the kingdom as their form. They are not made to indulge the rapid impatience of this posting generation; but for draught they are perhaps unrivalled as for their gentle and tractable temper; and to exhibit proofs of their great power. . . . An acre of our strong wheat land ploughed by a pair of them in one day, and that not an unusual task, is an achievement that bespeaks their worth, and which is scarcely credited in many other counties. These natives of a province varied with only the slightest irregularities of surface yet when carried into mountainous regions they seem born for that service. With wonder and gratitude have I seen them with the most spirited executions unsolicited by the whip, and indignant as it were at the obstacles that opposed them, drawing my carriage up the rocky and precipitous roads of Denbigh and Caernarvonshire. But truth obliges me to add, though not to the credit of my compatriots, that these creatures, formed so well by nature, are almost always disfigured by art. Because their long tails might, in dirty seasons, be something inconvenient, they are therefore cut off infrequently to within four inches of the rump so that they scarcely afford hold for a crupper, and as absurdity never knows where to stop even the poor remaining stump has often half its hair clipped off. In a provincial paper, a few years ago, one of these mutilated animals was expressively enough described as having a short mane, and *a very short bung'd dock*.'

Arthur Young, writing in 1797, when he was fifty-six, recalled that there was considerable rivalry among farmers in the *Sandlings* in breeding the best horses, even forty years before when he was a young man:[1] 'I remember seeing many of the old breed which were very famous, and in some respects an uglier horse could not be viewed; sorrel-colour, very low in the fore-end, a large ill-shaped head with slouching heavy ears, a great carcass and short legs, but short backed and more of the *punch* than the Leicestershire breeders will allow. These horses could only walk and draw; they could trot no better than a cow. But their drawing power was very considerable.

[1] *G.V.A.C.S.*, p. 217.

Of late years by aiming at coach-horses the breed is much changed to a handsome, lighter and more active horse. . . . A spirited and attentive breeder upon a farm of 1,000 or 1,500 acres of various soils that would admit two or three stallions and thirty or forty capital mares, might by breeding in and in, with close attention to the improvements wanted, advance this breed to a very high perfection, and render it a national object.'

Young, in spite of being a Suffolk man, did not let local sentiment cloud his estimate of the old breed. Although it had been to a certain extent improved by the time he was writing, he admitted the Suffolk still had many faults left; but, like a good practical man, he suggested a way to correct them. The Leicester breeder he had chiefly in mind was Robert Bakewell of Dishley. Bakewell (1725–1795) had made revolutionary improvements in stock-breeding through experiments on his own farm; and his methods are basically those still in use today. He had paid much attention to improving the Black Horse of the Midlands, and by eschewing out-breeding and breeding in-and-in had produced stallions that travelled and became famous all over the country. Bakewell corresponded with Arthur Young, the best known agricultural writer of his time and later the first Secretary of the Board of Agriculture; and in some of his letters we can detect a note of asperity, a disapproval of Young's 'cocksureness' which he deemed, as another letter shows, to be a fault of many Suffolk farmers. He writes of 'Mr A. Y.': (8th Feb. 1787)[1] 'Perhaps he thinks every Person who writes has as much time on his hands as he has which I believe with men of business is seldom the case. I have just heard his Account of your publication and Account he gives of his Journey to this place and on the whole considering what hands we have been in I think we have escaped pretty well. I think he has great merit as an Author but if he was less severe and sarcastical in his expressions he would not disgust so many of his Readers and his very useful Performance would still do greater good.'

The position appears to have been that Bakewell, as a scientific breeder with an international reputation, was peeved to find that the Suffolk horse breeders were resistant to his 'empire' and still per-

[1] H. Cecil Pawson, *Robert Bakewell*, Crosby Lockwood, 1957, p. 106.

sisted with typical stubbornness in the empirical methods they probably claimed were at least as good as his. In the following letter we
can see the beginning of that rivalry of the breeds that so enlivened
the agricultural shows and sales of the next century. Punctuation, as
the reader will have gathered, was not Robert Bakewell's strong point
as a letter-writer: the letter is dated, 8th May, 1789; and was written,
as was the previous one, to his farmer friend, George Culley:

'I am obliged to you for the favorable account of Ed. Porter and his
Horse which think will in time remove those objections that are too
frequently made to all black Horses and that a usefull Farmers Horse
may be under a black Skin—on Monday last I was at Ipswich Fair
where was a large Shew of Stallions, many of them of the true Suffolk
kind which the Bigotry and Prejudice of the Farmers in that Country
lead them to believe and roundly to assert are the best in the World
and a few days past I saw one advertisement in a Welch Paper offering
a Premium of 20 Gs. for He that should shew the best Stallion the
preference would be given to a Suffolk Punch but a Certificate must
be produced that he was of that kind, this advertisement surely was
drawn up on the other side of the Water or why prefer Blood to form
or action? from hearing what they said at Ipswich I proposed a Mode
of examining their Stallions venturing to give it as my Opionon that a
Horse either for figure or use, particularly the former, should have his
fore end so formed that his Ears when is is shewn to advantage be as
nearly as may be over his fore feet, that measuring a Horse from the
fore part of his shoulder points to a little below the Tail and divide
that measure in to three parts that from the Shoulders to the Hip
should not be the longest and when a Horse is shewn as Stallions
commonly are he should be wider over the ribs than from Shoulder
to Hip, this Doctrine was new to them but I rather think will have
some effect I forgot your description of a Horse or probably might
have availed myself of it.'[1]

One wonders whether the early preference the Welsh seem to have
shown for Suffolk stallions came through observing the Punches
owned by eighteenth century travellers in search of the picturesque;
and particularly the way those two horses of Sir John Cullum drew

[1] *Ibid.*, p. 138.

his reverend bulk, making little of the frightening gradients of the native roads. Yet one thing emerges out of the controversy between Bakewell and the Suffolk breeders: Arthur Young paid him the sincerest compliment in advocating Bakewell's own methods of breeding in-and-in. Undoubtedly Bakewell's discoveries had a great influence on the methods followed in the Suffolk studs during the nineteenth century and was partly the reason for their early successes. In fact Young made the handsome acknowledgment: 'Years after Bakewell's death his system was established with such completeness that men forgot not only the existence of any different conditions, but even the very name of the most active pioneer of the change.'[1]

Yet in the very year that Young was urging Suffolk horse-breeders to the new policy, the Government in a panic burst of taxation to meet the cost of the war, placed a tax on all horses. The relevant parts of the Statute[2] are:

Schedule C: A Schedule of Rates and Duties payable for all *Horses*, *Mares* and *Geldings* kept and used by any Person or Persons for the Purpose of riding or for the Purpose of drawing any Carriage chargeable with Duty by this Act—

For one such Horse, Mare or Gelding and
no more and so on to: £1   4s. 0d.

For twenty such Horses, Mares or Geldings
or upwards   £2 15s. 0d.

Schedule D: A Schedule of the Rates and Duties payable for Horses, Mares and Geldings, not charged with any Duty, according to Schedule C and also Mules:

For each Horse, Mare or Gelding kept by any
Person and not charged with any Duty   6s. 0d.

It may, or may not, be some consolation to farmers to know that their ancestors a century and a half ago were not spared the necessity of wrestling with *Schedules*. But Schedule D was of a nature no one

[1] *Ibid.*, p. 45.   [2] 38 George III c, 41.

cares to meet—'All the fish we've not caught in the other net, we'll make sure of with this'—and for the farmers it meant that even the horses used in husbandry were brought in as well. The purpose of the tax, apart from the revenue accruing from it, may have been to divert as many horses as possible from civilian to military service; but the effect on the farmer or landowner interested enough to breed horses and to attempt to improve his stock must have been disastrous. For however real a farmer's enthusiasm for improving the breed, it could not be unimpaired by the insult to his pocket and the rebuff to his public spirit that the tax seemed to offer. A note in the second edition (1813) of Cullum's *History of Hawstead*[1] shows that the first, at least, was quite considerable:

'The duty paid for horses used in husbandry in the parish of Hawstead for one year from 6th April 1801 to 5th April 1802 (including one small farm in the extra-parochial place of Hardwick) was 44£.'[2]

To sum up: the state of development of the Suffolk horse up to this time was briefly as follows. At first he was 'a very plain made horse', to use a euphemism of the time; and even the most partisan advocates of the old breed had to admit he was no oil-painting. But his looks belied his true qualities, and during his hey-day looks, in any case, were not at a premium; for competition was not by parade or exhibition in the show ring but by actual proof of a horse's strength in drawing heavy loads of sand or stones. In this, the low position of the old Suffolk's shoulders gave him a tremendous advantage. The old breed had been improved by the end of the eighteenth century as we have seen from Young's testimony, and Bakewell's testiness when he realised that his cherished Black Horse—the ancestor of the modern Shire—had a rival. Yet during the next forty years, in spite of the war and the discouragement of the horse-tax, the breed was so improved as to become one of the finest in the country. A Suffolk took the prize for 'the best horse for agricultural purposes' at the first meeting

[1] p. 253.
[2] The Statute does not appear to have been amended until 1874. The *Ipswich Journal* 21st April comments on the Budget of that year: 'The remission of the Horse Duties will assist the agricultural interest in so far as it will, undoubtedly, stimulate the demand for horses.'

of the newly formed Royal Agricultural Society of England at Oxford in 1839; and for the first twenty-three years of its existence a total of fifteen first prizes went to Suffolk horses. How was the improvement effected?

Herman Biddell in the *Suffolk Stud Book: Volume One:* A History and Register of the County Breed of Cart Horses (1880), examined this confused but formative period of the breed and picked out five main families of the horse whose breed eventually became stabilised in one. This was the family of *Thomas Crisp's Horse of Ufford* 404[1] foaled in the year 1768. This horse was advertised five years later as 'able to get good stock for coach or road' and was described as 'a fine bright *chesnut*[2] horse full 15½ hands'. Herman Biddell wrote of him:[3]'We must make up our picture of Crisp's old horse as of low fore-end, large carcase, short legs and bent hocks, and perhaps a less inelegant head than most of his contemporaries.' The next family was the *Blake tribe*, so called because its members were descended from a horse named Farmer 174, owned by Andrew Blake, and introduced into the county in 1764. Blake's Farmer was a trotting stallion brought from Lincolnshire. The third considerable tribe at this stage in the history of the breed was that descended from a horse named Farmer's Glory 1396 owned by John Wright of Attleborough in Norfolk, and was known as the *Attleborough tribe*. Farmer's Glory was foaled about 1796 and was reputed to have similar provenance to Blake's Farmer, and like this horse also infused a good deal of his blood into the Suffolks of that period. The fourth tribe stemmed from another fresh strain of blood introduced about the same time. This was the *Shadingfield stock* and was distinguished by being chiefly dark chestnuts. The tribe came out of one stallion, Barber's Proctor 58, a horse foaled about 1793. His colour was bay although he came from a chesnut Suffolk mare. The fifth tribe was listed by Herman Biddell as being distinct and deserving of separate notice, more out of the need for absolute accuracy than out of any conviction that it was a family stemming from outside blood. It was called the *Samsons* and

[1] The number in the Stud Book.
[2] This spelling is the traditional rendering wherever the word is linked with the Suffolk horse.
[3] *S.H.S.B.*, Vol. 1, p. 39.

its sire was Samson 324, a horse bought in the south-west corner of Suffolk.

But the important thing as far as the later stabilisation of the breed is concerned is this: by 1880 Herman Biddell could write that the first family—that coming from Crisp's Horse of Ufford,[1] a descendant of the old breed of Suffolks—had succeeded in establishing itself over the other strains of imported blood; and it was from this stock that all, except a handful, of the stallions of that time were descended. The new blood had improved the old indigenous stock; but this, although admitting modification, was too tenacious to relinquish the main-stream through which the best characteristics of the old breed had come down. And by 1952 this process had gone further: the outside blood had been completely absorbed; and Raymond Keer, the present Secretary of the Suffolk Horse Society, could write that 'every animal now in existence traces its descent in the direct male line to Crisp's Horse of Ufford.'

But what are the main characteristics of the Suffolk breed of horse? The first and obvious one is the clearly defined colour. The colour of the old breed was distinguished by the now obsolete term sorrel[2]—a name which still remains in many Suffolk inns. The colour today is chestnut; but there are seven shades of chestnut: the red; the golden; the lemon or yellow; the light, mealy chestnut; the dark; the dull-dark, and lastly the bright chestnut. The bright chestnut is considered the most characteristic colour and, all other things being equal, the one to be preferred.

The Suffolk's head is big with a broad forehead, and often with a star on it or a *shim*[3] or *blaze* down the face; the neck deep in the collar and tapering to a graceful setting of the head; the shoulders long and muscular and thrown well back at the withers. The well rounded rib —the barrel chest that has helped to give the Suffolk the name of Punch—is a distinctive feature, as is the deep carcase. This last is one

[1] 'From this animal are descended, with the exception of less than half-a-dozen, *all the Suffolk horses now (1880) at stud.*' S.H.S.B., Vol. I, p. 21.

[2] *Sorrel* was the name of the horse that tripped over a mole-hill and fatally threw William III.

[3] *shim*: a white mark, a dialect word from O.E. *scima*—brightness or splendour.

of the first essentials of a true Suffolk; for it was bred for use on the farm, and for use on the Suffolk farms in particular, where it was the custom—as we have already seen—for the horses to work a long day from 6.30 a.m. to 2.30 p.m. without nosebag or any break for rations. An ample *bread-basket* was thus indispensable to the Suffolk; and this

characteristic—emphasised by selective breeding—is another example of the inspired fusion of breed, local custom and use that has gained East Anglian farmers such a deserved reputation as stock-raisers.

The shapely outline of back loin and quarters is as noticeable as the deep carcase. 'Feet, joints and legs—the legs should be straight with fair, sloping pasterns, big knees and long clean hocks on short cannon bones, free from coarse hair; the feet should have plenty of size with circular form protecting the frog; walk, smart and true; trot—well balanced all round with good action. If one were asked the question, what are the four chief characteristics of the Suffolk Horse? the answer would certainly be—colour, quality, compactness and hardy constitution.'[1]

These, the present day characteristics of the Suffolk, began to merge in their main outline during the obscure but important formative period of the breed in the early part of the nineteenth century. Farmers at that time were stimulated by an atmosphere of experiment in agriculture; and Suffolk farmers in particular saw the results that had already been obtained in improving local breeds: and their enthusiasm, even though it appears to have been backed by nothing more than traditional, trial-and-error methods, did wonders. But as early as 1840, shortly after the Suffolk breed of horse came into the picture through his early successes at the Royal Shows, a local farmer pointed out that if the Suffolk was to continue to deserve the name they would have to compile an accurate registry of pedigrees. Had there been men with the resources and opportunity to follow Arthur Young's advice earlier in the century, it is probable that the Suffolk would have attained an earlier perfection. For if the main responsibility of improving the breed had been concentrated in the hands of a few breeders who knew exactly what they were aiming at, without doubt a stud book would have been started at that time.

It was only when these conditions had evolved, later in the century, and breeding was concentrated chiefly in the hands of three outstanding studs that there followed the real stimulus to set up an organised society to sponsor the making of a stud book. These studs were Cretingham Rookery (Nathaniel Barthropp); Butley Abbey (Thomas Catlin; and Thomas Crisp, after 1855); and Newbourn Hall (Samuel Wolton). Herman Biddell summed up the influence of this handful of breeders by saying about Catlin what he could have said, equally well, about the others: 'But in Suffolk of late there has been a Bakewell abroad.'

The Suffolk Stud-Book Association, later to become the Suffolk

[1] Raymond Keer, 'The Suffolk Horse,' *M & B Veterinary Review*, Vol. 4, No. 2, November, 1952.

Horse Society, was founded in 1877; and the first volume of the stud book was published in 1880. But even at this date it is likely that the project would have fallen far short of the founders' intentions had not a man like Herman Biddell been at hand with the energy and determination to carry it through. For, ideally, it was a job that should have been started at least thirty years before; and only a man of Herman Biddell's temper would not have been daunted by the task of going back into the obscure period above mentioned and laboriously picking up and unravelling the many threads that had become tangled long before by time and death's haphazard handling.

12

Herman Biddell and Volume One

Afriend of the Biddell's at the end of the last century stated that the record of the family was of such a kind as to lead their contemporaries to look for great things of anyone bearing the name. There was 'a strong intellectual and moral fibre' running right through the Biddell's; and Arthur Biddell's sons certainly confirmed this judgment. Manfred, the eldest, was a very successful farmer and breeder of horses; he became the first treasurer of the Suffolk Stud-Book Association and has left a series of interesting and informative letters written to his friend Thomas Crisp of Chillesford Lodge, another Suffolk farmer and horse-breeder. George Arthur Biddell was an engineer who started his career with Ransome's, as already stated; he became well-known all over England for his inventions not only in agriculture but in the wider field of civil engineering. William Biddell, the third son, became Member of Parliament for West Suffolk during the 'seventies; he was known as 'The Tenant Farmers' M.P.' and did a great deal at Westminster towards forwarding their interests. But Herman was in many respects the most outstanding of the four brothers. He was a man of great strength and versatility of mind. He had all of the Biddell family's strain of commonsense and practical application; was a rare judge of a horse and an authority on all aspects of farming. But in addition he was an artist of 'no mean execution' and an accomplished and ready writer with a blunt, sinewy style and the gift to coin, on occasion, a particularly memorable phrase. Also, in the words of a contemporary: 'he was a speaker of such power of illustration and readiness one feels at times that he ought to quit all other callings and take himself to the platform.'

All this seems the more remarkable when it is stated that the only formal education the four brothers received was that given at a little school at the nearby village of Grundisburgh. George Biddell, in later life, stated that they had obtained a good elementary grounding at the Grundisburgh school, but his one regret was that he had not been trained in the higher mathematics as this subject would have considerably eased his early efforts to make way in his profession.

Herman followed his father and two of his brothers as a farmer; and this was his chief occupation throughout his life: farming was his true calling in spite of his many other pre-occupations. He first set up on his own when he was twenty-one years of age; and the opening entry of his first Day Books shows him marshalling his assets like a young soldier who was about to enter a stiff but not unexhilarating engagement. The A.B. referred to is undoubtedly his father; and it was from him that he had learned the practice of making a frank avowal, at least on paper, of his resources:

October 1853: I this Michaelmas Take the Grundisburgh Farm of my Brother William and set off with a Capital of something like £1310 in business for myself. The money I have become possessed of has come in this way as near as I can remember:

The six Shares which I own in the Ipswich Gas Light Company were bought with the Legacy left me by Mr Dociora, sundry gifts from my late Uncle George, gifts from other Relatives etc., and are now worth about	£96	0s.	0d.
1 Share in the Great Northern Railway bought with gifts chiefly from A. B.	14	12	0
Sundry Articles of my own Clothing, little pieces of furniture, Books etc.—say	8	15	0
Share of my late Uncle George's Legacy clear of Legacy Duty—paid by the Executors	1158	0	0
Interest received for Money left with Mr Shepherd who bought cottages of me	7	10	0
Profit on Cook's Cottages sold to Shepherd	10	0	0
Interest on 600£ Note of Hand with A. B.	11	13	0
Interest for Money kept at Alexanders'	4	10	0

At this time the Money as described on opposite page (as above) is placed or invested something pretty nearly as follows:

	£	s.	d.
The six Gas Shares	96	0	0
G. Northern R. W. Share	14	12	0
Clothing, Books, Furniture, etc. etc.	8	15	0
With A. Biddell in a Note of Hand	600	0	0
At Alexanders' Bank as a running Acct.	420	2	0
Stock bought for the Grundisburgh Farm, etc. up to the Present Time	171	11	0
	1311	0	0

Herman Biddell
November 22nd, 1853
Playford,
Suffolk.

He married in 1870, having taken over Hill House farm in 1860 soon after his father's death in that year. His interest in the Suffolk horse showed itself early in his career; and he could see, even as a young man, that the Suffolk would not continue the successes he had already won unless the more or less haphazard, or at best 'intuitional', methods of breeding were changed. A register of breeding was essential not only to consolidate the gains already made but to prevent deterioration and to fix the breed along the chosen lines as consciously and as scientifically as possible. Before Herman Biddell's time two of the old breeders—Shawe and Barthropp—had advocated a stud book, and about 1850 Barthropp had actually started on one; later, however, he was compelled to lay the manuscript aside. Then in 1862 Herman Biddell, realising that many of the facts that would be basic to an accurate stud book had never been written down and would soon be lost irretrievably unless they were then taken from the men who knew them, called together at Hill House a meeting of the oldest and best informed *leaders* in Suffolk.

A horse-leader is a groom who during the *season* (early spring) is responsible for leading a stallion to serve the mares in a chosen district. Herman Biddell knew it was from these grooms he was likely to get the most accurate record of the various horses that had been prominent in the county during the first fifty or sixty years of the century. He was not mistaken: 'The torrents of fact which the party poured forth was a history in itself.' The meetings at Hill House were repeated, and fresh history was garnered on every occasion; but it was fifteen years later before it could be written down in the manner that had been planned so long before.

The delay would have discouraged a less determined man than Herman Biddell; but he was more than equal to the job of persuading his fellow farmers of the need for a register; and, moreover, of later carrying the difficult work through. A description of him at a later stage of his life was no doubt almost equally appropriate to this time: 'He was a man of strong personality, stood six feet three inches high, weighed eighteen to twenty stones, a born fighter with a strong face surmounted by a thick crop of iron grey hair.'[1] A story, recalled by Robert Sherwood, illustrates his temper: He had been, as he himself confessed, churchwarden at Playford for forty-four years—in sole command as it later turned out. But along came a new bishop and tactfully pointed out that according to church law there should be *two* churchwardens in any one parish. But Herman Biddell would have none of this:[2] the churchwardenship was too narrow a deck on which to share the command with anyone; and as a special faculty was not forthcoming he immediately ceased to be churchwarden, content merely to equal his father's record and not to surpass it.

The founding of the Suffolk Stud Book Association in 1877 for the specific purpose of compiling a register was, as far as Herman Biddell was concerned, the end of a long campaign. It was also the beginning of a shorter one, but one that was infinitely more arduous; which was to take up most of his working and waking moments for the next three years until the initial work was completed and Volume One was published. For he was made editor, and he realised from the start that he was working under the greatest disability that could have

[1] The Suffolk Agricultural Association, *A Century Review, 1831–1931*, by Cordy S. Wolton.

[2] *Playford Churchwardens' Book:* Parish Meeting Minutes, April 11th, 1904: 'Mr. Herman Biddell announced that as the Vicar had decided to have two churchwardens, he should decline to act.'

hindered an editor in a task of this nature: '*We commenced too late*', as he himself well knew, twenty or thirty years after the groundwork should have been completed. Yet he went into the job with good heart, and could write at the end of it: 'In conclusion let me add, that it was in no blind ignorance of the magnitude of the undertaking that I accepted the responsibility of editing the Suffolk Stud-Book. The sacrifice it required at my hand was a call on almost the entire time of two years and a half; but I look back with something more than satisfaction at the days I devoted to the object we had in view. The work was ever a labour of love; it never became a burden, and as each sheet had been revised for the press—as each day brought my task nearer to its end, the regret would come—that there would soon be no more of its work to do. I would that another year's labour at the Stud-Book was before me—one more year to have filled the blanks— one more year to have fetched up the lost threads in the tangled skein which had given me such pleasure to unravel.'[1]

He met indifference and suspicion from many who could have made his task easier, but this did not deter him: he was sure he could salvage much and enshrine in Volume One a record of the patient efforts of breeders, both known and unknown, reaching back into the previous century. Volume One is a monument to his dogged persistence, and to his belief that he was not engaged on a work merely of the hour: the Suffolk, he believed, was an animal that would be not only a pride and use to the county but—as Arthur Young had stated many years before—an asset and an ornament to the nation.

The sources of information at his disposal when he began his search were varied: advertisements of the horses by their owners— these were either printed on special cards or in the columns of newspapers; catalogues of sales and of Shows; oral information from breeders, owners, dealers and leaders. These last—some of the men Herman Biddell had gathered together at Playford—supplied him with the bulk of the information on which he built the first volume.

An advertisement in the *Ipswich Journal* for Saturday, April 11th, 1801 will give an idea of the type of material in which he searched and will indicate how much checking and cross-checking would have to be

done to identify the horse advertised. This particular horse is probably 1117 in the stud book:

'To Cover This Season

At William Spinke's, Eyke

A Bright Chesnut CART HORSE at 15s. 6d. each Mare. To pay the
Man at the time of Covering. He is 16 hands 1 inch high, short
leg'd and large boned. He will be at Alderton Swan on Tuesday, at
Bealings Admiral's Head on Wednesday mornings, from 9 to 11;
at Woodbridge White Horse same day; and at home that night; at
Saxmundham Bell on Thursdays; and Bramfield Queen's Head on
Fridays; at Framlingham Crown on Saturdays; at Parham-Hacheston
Queen's Head that night; and at home on Mondays. Such mares as
were not stinted last season may be covered at 8s. 6d. each.'

The above helps to elucidate the phrase so often used in connection
with a leader: 'He travelled a horse in such-and-such a district,' that is,
he led the stallion round to the farms or to agreed points in the area
where the mares were brought to him. A very valuable stallion rarely
travelled: he would be advertised as *standing at stud* and he rarely left
his own farm except on his prize-winning tour of the shows. About
this time another horse-breeder, who also figured in Volume One,[1]
advertised in the same paper; but the advertisement is not directly
about a horse:

'FIFTY POUNDS REWARD

The Cramp put in the Mouth

Whereas Mr William Smith of Helmingham has lately, at a public
house in Ipswich, before some respectable persons, made use of
many unguarded expressions, as well as very false ones, endeavour-
ing to injure the character of Pells Kersey of Framsden, by telling the
company he was a rogue, all which things Mr Smith will be found
unable to prove; a reward of 50£ will be paid by Mr James Hayward
of St Clement's parish, Ipswich, to Mr. William Smith, or to any

[1] *S.S.B.*, Vol. 1, p. 245.

surgeon, or any other person whomsoever, that will procure any medicine, or give any other assistance to Mr Smith, so that the cramp may be removed so far from his mouth, or to give liberty to his tongue, so as to prove any one thing which he has said against the said Pells Kersey, or to prove one dishonest thing ever done by the said Pells Kersey, to any man from the day he was born to the present moment.—I was lately at a Nobleman's who had the cramp set on one of his legs; to prevent it going into his thigh, a small cord was tied below the knee; but when the cramp is set in the mouth, the cord must be tied below the chin, to prevent the disorder getting to the heart, from whence this cramp first proceeded. An evil heart ought to be guarded against.

PELLS KERSEY'

Nov. 23, 1801

Herman Biddell's researches took him all over the county of Suffolk and often into the adjoining ones; and the trouble he took to be exact in the registering of every horse included was endless and equalled the highest discipline of academic scholarship. He realised from the start that the stud book would be useless unless it was accurate to the last degree. For in addition to being a record it was also to be a guide to action. This, indeed, was its main purpose: a blue-print for the breed and a guarantee that known horses would breed as near to an agreed type as human judgment and knowledge between them could devise. Once the stud book was completed it would be comparatively easy, for there was little disagreement about the type they were aiming at: they were breeding a horse for agricultural purposes; they were not raising one as an agricultural product; he was primarily for use *on the farm*, not for sale *off the farm* as a dray horse to be used in general transport.

He was also scrupulously accurate in recording any infusion of out-side blood; and he did not attempt to conceal—as in the case of Catlin's Duke 296, one of the most famous of the nineteenth century stallions—his belief that in the best of horses, as in the best of men, purity of breed is only relative. But what he did claim, and the sub-sequent history of the breed has borne him out, was that the old

169

native stock was strong enough ultimately to absorb any stem that was grafted on to it. Blake's tribe, for instance, the most vigorous of the importations, flourished widely at the beginning of the last century. Yet, although the new stock was for a time so numerous, they soon began to fall off, and animals descended directly from the old breed again became the prevailing line in the county. It was as though a freshet had suddenly poured into a slow, broad-flowing river, altering its appearance and making it sparkle in the sunlight, but without altering its main course one jot.

In addition to the value arising out of the completion of its main purpose, Volume One can claim to be an important historical document if only for the glimpses it gives of farming in Suffolk during the middle of the last century. One of these concerns Thomas Crisp, a noted breeder of Suffolks:

'The marvellous stories of his shipments for abroad are amply testified by the porters at the railway station. One day every horse box within call would be telegraphed for to Wickham (Market), for a consignment of Suffolk horses to one of the colonies; the next week a whole menagerie of animals would be sent off to Prussia; and then the pleasant rumour would go forth to the county breeders that Mr Crisp was buying up all the decent two-years-old colts in the county, as some German Baron wanted six of a certain hue. Again, a visitor at Butley would be startled by the sight of a row of wheat stacks at some off-hand occupation, the growth of a year long since forgotten by any miller in the county; and strange tales are told of incredible clips of wool which had seen every shade of variation from 10d. to 2s. 6d. a-pound. Curious grasses of rapid growth and an enormous yield would be raised from seed sent direct from some unknown region in the Wallachian Provinces. Another season, when flock-masters were starving under sunny skies and dewless nights, strange tales would go from market to market telling how the poorest, dryest and most wretched walks on the Tangham farm were knee deep in sheep feed, a luxurious herbage, the very name of which not one in ten had ever heard of as an agricultural product. It is said that it was no uncommon thing for Mr Crisp to have as many as three thousand sheep feeding away from home; flocks that had never seen Butley, nor

been within ten miles of it—a branch in the trade none but those of
the serenest of tempers and most untiring energy should ever attempt.
His losses from 'dropped' sheep—death from natural causes and
common casualties—amounted to one-a-day, 365 a year; we had this
from his own lips. He must have farmed not less than four thousand
acres, and what with reapers, haymakers, horse hoes, and well
chosen over-lookers few occupations of a hundred acres could present a better face than did the whole of the land under his cultivation.
Perhaps no figure in all Suffolk was so familiar to the agricultural
community in the county as the late Mr Crisp; no one was better
known or more respected, and his sudden death (in 1869) in the hunt-
ing field spread a gloom over the whole county, and carried grief into
many a household besides those of his own family.'[1]

The practice of sending flocks of sheep out from a farm is mentioned in Arthur Biddell's Day Books where he refers to it as *keeping
sheep*; and there are occasional entries showing how he fed so many
sheep at so much a head for a certain period. The custom is also re-
miniscent of the foldcourse system practised in Norfolk and some
parts of Suffolk during the sixteenth and seventeenth centuries:[2] this
system was associated with the sheep-corn husbandry of the light,
sandy soils of East Anglia. Sheep were folded on arable land, and thus
mucked the soil preparatory to corn crops. It is likely that a practice
described by a present-day Trimley farmer is traditional to this light-
soiled district of Suffolk: 'After sheep we ploughed lightly with a
Ransome's three-furrow paring plough—a pair of horses could
plough about two acres in a day—and then we sowed oats right into
the sheep-muck. We had some of the heaviest crops one could hope
to get when we did this.'

A foldcourse was an area over which a manorial lord could feed
his sheep at certain times of the year. It included, as well as his own
demesne lands, the strips of certain of his tenants in the open-field,
as well as part of the adjoining heathland. The sheep usually fed on
the strips from which the corn or hay had been taken, and the
tathing or fertilising properties of the flock were considered sufficient

[1] *S.H.S.B.*, Vol. I, p. 633.
[2] *The Agricultural History Review*, Vol. V, Part 1, 1957.

payment for the privilege. Most tenants, in fact, paid the lord for this benefit of *tathe*, though many tenants possessed a 'cullet right'—the privilege of turning in a fixed number of their own sheep with the manorial flock. Feeding sheep on land from which a crop has been harvested is called *shacking*: the term is still used in Suffolk today. There were two kinds of shacking: *Lammas shack*, the feeding of sheep on meadow-land after the hay had been taken; and *Michaelmas shack*, stubble-feeding after the corn harvest. An old map[1] of Bury St Edmunds, now in Moyses Hall in that town, shows that a fold-course system was once in existence there; and some of the fields are characterised thus: 'Several Sheep Shackage to Holderness alias East Gate Barn's Flock; Several Sheep Shackage to Eldo Flock; and Inter-Common Sheep Shackage.'

Herman Biddell's description of one of these occasions when sheep were 'on the move' is quoted below both for its value as a farming picture and for its portrait of old Boon, the Butley shepherd, and his typically East Anglian reaction to a curious stranger: the story is put into the mouth of Kersey Cooper, the Duke of Grafton's agent:[2]

' "First I met a drove of colts—thirty, forty, fifty, I should think —more than I could count. Then came a hundred beasts—cows, lean bullocks, young things; foot sore, tired and hungry as they could be; followed by the biggest flock of sheep I ever met in a road in my life. They were like the flocks of Abraham. At last came old Boon,. leading a pony and cart with half-a-dozen skins and two lame sheep.

'Boon was a tall man—six feet one, and stooped a good deal, or rather leaned forward and plunged along in a slop[3] down to his shoes like a man with sore feet on flint stones, and always walked with his eyes on his boots.

' "Well, my good man, and whose, in the name of goodness, are all these things you've got here?"

'Boon pulled up, took his eyes off the ground and said very slowly:
' "Well, they belong to my marstar."
' "But who is your master?"

[1] *A Survey of Bury St. Edmunds*, 1791.
[2] *S.H.S.B.*, Vol. 1, p. 643.
[3] Suffolk dialect for smock.

' "My marstar, sar? Why, the gentleman that own all these couts and ship and things!"

' "Well, where are you going with these 'ship and things'?"

' "I'm a-going arter some feed my marstar ha' bowt for 'em."

' "And where are you going tonight—you can't lie on the road, can you?"

' "Oh dear, no sar—there's too many on 'em to lay i' the rud—I can't lodge 'em i' the rud."

' "Well, well shepherd, as long as they are not going to mine I don't know that I've any business with it—good night."

' "Good night, sar—but I was just a-going to say *pra-ay could you tell me where Mistar Karsay Cooper live some where in these parts?* I was to go to him for a night's lodging."

'The most abject apology followed, and profuse were the explanations that he "hadn't the la-est idea who I was a-speaking tu, but you know, sar, my marstar al'ays tell me not to know nothing when anybody ax me about my business. He said he thowt you had a *little middar close to the house that 'ud du nicely'*." And in the "little middar" the mixed multitude lodged, and little was left but the soil when they passed on the next day for another stage.'

Passages like the above help to make Volume One a classic of its kind. The book, too, is memorable for the language in it, the curious phrases to describe horses and their destination: 'a good horse—all over a gentleman', 'a very catching-looking colt', 'he was sold to go into Westmoreland', 'Boxer 299 was sold in 1844 to go, as one of the Butley Abbey men informed me, into "the Sheres", an indefinite region to which Southampton Briton 301 was consigned sometime before.' 'Of the true Suffolk breed and a good drawer,' 'an out-sized horse and a good mover but had little of the Suffolk character about him.' Duke 68 was 'a savage brute—not much used as a sire: sold by Mr Grout, kicked out the end of the box on the railway and was shipped for the Continent to diffuse the cranky temper of his maternal grandsire among the German mares.' A particular horse was '*own* brother to Catlin's Duke 296' *Own* signifies that the horse had the same dam as well as the same sire. 'Captain, alias Ripshawe 294: A heavy horse with bent hind legs and a bad temper. Was first at

Ipswich (Show) in 1850. The cognomen of *Ripshawe* comes from the hasty temper and pugilistic disposition which a former governor of the county gaol at Ipswich, of that name, was wont to exhibit when put out of his way.' 'He was then in bad condition, lousy, but turned out a good horse; he had an in-and-out shim on his face.'

At one point in his absorbing reminiscences of horses and horse-breeders, Herman Biddell digressed[1] to tell the story of an Essex farmer who was an enthusiastic stock-breeder. He had in his possession a painting by Cuyp, the seventeenth century Dutch landscape artist; but he did not approve of the conformation of one of Cuyp's cows—'The brute was deformed—no ribs, no anything—he could not have a cow like that in his dining room'—therefore he got a painter down from Chelsea to paint a straight-backed Hereford over the offending animal.

But the writer's finest descriptive powers were naturally reserved for the horses themselves; and some of them, like Catlin's Duke 296, Biddell's Major 153 and Garrett's Cupbearer 3rd 566, figure in the book almost as characters in their own right. To the grooms and leaders, as to the farmers and breeders, horses were their life; and they treated the show horses like monarchs, letting them want for nothing in comfort, food or attention. Like monarchs, too, they had to be treated with respect, as the following story shows: A groom at a well-known Suffolk stud in the *Sands* was mucking out the stall of one of the show horses; and he called out to him cheerfully: 'Come over, Buttercup' (or some such name as that). The farmer happened to be passing at the time. No true Suffolk had ever held up his head under the name of *Buttercup*. The reaction was immediate: 'Look, I can't have you calling my horses fancy names. Do you leave on Friday!'— a decision that was revoked when tempers had cooled off and outraged honour had been appeased.

The stable kings of the last seventy years have been equally as outstanding as those celebrated in Volume One; and names like Wedgewood 1749, Eclipse 2627, Sudbourne Beau-Brocade 4235, Bawdsey Harvester 3076, Sudbourne Peter 3955, Sudbourne Premier 4963, and Shotley Counterpart 4903, are worthy members of the old dynasty.

[1] *S.H.S.B.*, Vol. 1, p. 625.

13

Herman Biddell and the Oral Tradition

The oral tradition has been much discussed within the past few years; and the importance, especially at this time, of taking account of the lore that has been handed down from one generation to another is becoming more widely recognised. It is certain that no satisfactory history of any country region of the British Isles can be written solely from books, documents and physical evidence in the field; and if the historian ignores the oral tradition in his particular area of study, he is cutting himself off from a vital and valuable source of historical fact—and what is more important—of historical enlightenment and perspective. For there is enough evidence to show that in addition to the surface and popularly accepted culture of the countryside there has always been a much older, submerged culture that has been displaced, or to a large extent driven underground, by the newer one. In many ways it is antithetical and even antagonistic to this historically more recent culture; and it has an inherent toughness that has caused it to persist right up to the revolutionary changes of modern times.

If we ask why this has been possible, two tentative answers come immediately to mind; and these may help to explain the apparent anachronism of a scale of values, that seem to have had their origin in pre-Christian times, existing alongside a familiarity with some of the latest developments in modern engineering. The first is the split between town and country. There has always been a certain tension between the dwellers in the town and the country dwellers; and it may be argued that in recent years the split has been deepened rather than repaired by the physical spreading of the town into the countryside. The newer culture has always been identified with the town; and in the

past some of the ineptitude of town-born and town-operating admini-
strators in their attempts to educate the countryman has only confirmed his instinct to cherish his own culture as closely as circumstances
would allow. Again, it cannot be doubted that the more sharply defined class-stratification of most rural English communities has helped
to differentiate the two cultures and to keep them more or less rigidly
apart. For the rural 'upper class' is by definition committed to the
newer culture and to its successive development: if it were not its influence would soon begin to wane. To the ordinary countryman, however, the man who is governed, this is an added reason why he should
be resistant to the new culture; and if he could be brought to speak—
or perhaps whisper—his own views on this situation, he would be likely
to say: 'This what you see is theirs: this what is not seen is ours.'

Folklorists have for many years been aware of the existence of this
older rural culture and can point to a large body of primitive customs
and usages surviving to the present-day even in some of the 'advanced' areas of the British Isles. But the folklore aspect is not the
only one: much of the oral tradition is, as one would expect, concerned with agriculture; and the handing down by word of mouth of
the findings of a long experience of wrestling with nature and the soil
is as old as speech itself. Moreover, many of the craft practices and
their secrets were passed from father to son in this way; for apart from
the question of literacy both policy and custom demanded that as
little as possible should be written down.—This will partly explain
why, up to the present century, literacy was never held in high regard
in rural areas: it was not economically necessary.—The craft of bard
in ancient Britain (the Hebridean story-teller is one of his descen-
dants) is the most notable example: the bardic craft meant, above all,
learning by heart an immense unwritten literature of traditional
verse, and the bard's reputation rested primarily upon his accuracy
in reciting it. Among other ancient craft brotherhoods dating, it is
believed, from Romano-British times,[1] trade practices and secrets
had no other means of preservation except an accurate learning of the
craft-lore by the initiates.

[1] Lewis Spence, *Myth and Ritual in Dance, Game and Rhyme*,
Watts & Co., 1947, p. 158.

This is the reason why so much primitive literature is in verse: the rhythm of verse makes it so much easier to remember; and didactic verse at first did the service of prose which was in most literatures a much later development. And though in England not much traditional material—apart from the ballads and the nursery rhymes—has come down in verse, enough remains of the old gnomic verses and aphorisms dealing with agriculture and the weather to suggest that they are fragments of a much larger corpus, and that at one time this was one of the main methods of handing down farming experience. When Tusser wrapped his precepts in durable home-spun verse he was, therefore, guided as much by the need to fit them to the actual limitations of the country folk, most of whom must have aspired to hear rather to read his numerous *Points*, as to conform to a long-standing literary convention, dating back to Virgil and Hesiod.

Much of the oral tradition has been centred in the plough and the horse and we have evidence that there was in Britain a very ancient craft brotherhood connected with them both.[1] Lady Wentworth in her study of the Arab horse has shown[2] how the horse played a great part in the traditions of Islam; and some of her remarks are apposite to our subject if only to illustrate how two separate cultures similar to those postulated above existed in Arabia:

'It must be insisted on that, as Lady Anne Blunt explained, all later traditions founded on Islam must be treated in a totally different class to the primaeval unwritten tribal traditions unknown to townsmen and scribes. As a Muteyr bedouin said to her, "these things are written in books but we took them with our hands," meaning that books were unreliable, but the firm traditions which were passed word for word from generation to generation and sung to the "rebab" over the camp fires are those which remain unaltered. This may seem strange to our ideas in which stories passed from one to another are proverbially incorrect as "Russian scandal", but in Arabia the poet-singer to the "rebab" (lute with one string and a bow) is a recognised authority who dare not for his life deviate by a word from the known

[1] Thomas Davidson, 'The Horseman's Word,' *Gwerin*, Vol. 1, No. 2, Basil Blackwell, 1956, and sources cited.
[2] *B.O.H.*, p. 141.

facts. Should he err, he is forever disgraced. No one reads or writes, therefore their memories are acute to a degree practically unknown in Europe.'

The present writer has met in Suffolk at least two countrymen whose memories, while not perhaps as well trained as the Arabian bards', were in their way equally remarkable. One of them was Joe Row, of the village of Blaxhall. His memory was so acute that Tom Jay, another Blaxhall man, said of him: 'We allus used to say owd Joe fare to remember things that happened afore the day he were born,' implying that like Tristram Shandy he had knowledge of events that happened at least as far back as the time of his conception. The other was Robert Savage of the same village: the information he gave about old farming practices, as known to himself and as told to him by his father and his grandfather, is continually being re-affirmed in every detail by researches into agricultural records dating back to the eighteenth century.

Herman Biddell found the same amazingly accurate memories among the grooms and horse-leaders he interviewed while getting material for the first volume of the stud-book; and he admitted that a large proportion of the earlier material came by word of mouth. He said: 'To this class (the grooms and the leaders) more than any other the Association is indebted for the material which has made the Suffolk Stud-Book something more than a mere registry of pedi-grees.'[1] He first got together a number of these old grooms and leaders in 1862, as already stated; and he realised that the information they had was invaluable. He started discussions and took notes, but it was not until after the Association had been founded and the pro-ject of the stud-book given its blessing that he began systematic and detailed inquiry throughout the county. One of his first jobs was to visit the old grooms on their own ground, painstakingly to go over the descriptions of horses they gave him and check them with newspaper advertisements and horse-cards wherever possible.

The most outstanding of these men was one who gave Herman Biddell much of the information for Volume One. He was John Moyse of Framlingham. 'Barber' Moyse was born in 1789 at Stradbrooke, the centre of 'High Suffolk' and a big breeding district for horses; and he was later apprenticed to a barber at the nearby town of Halesworth. Not long afterwards he started a business of his own at Earl Soham; but here, in addition to barbering, he took up colt-breaking, later giving up the barber's business altogether and becoming a horse-dealer. He settled in the town of Framlingham, but his horse-business failed and he was forced to put up his barber's pole again. He lived until he was nearly ninety, and the Suffolk horse was his study and his passion throughout his life. His memory was so marvellous that Herman Biddell characterised him as, 'literally speaking, a walking stud-book'. And he goes on to say: 'It was not, however, till a search through the files of the county papers of the last seventy years had tested his accuracy that the full force of his memory became apparent.' Descriptions of many of the early horses in the stud-book are supplemented by Moyse's memory of them. He liked a horse with sound feet, and however attractive a horse otherwise looked, he counted him of little worth if he failed to come up to his standard of 'good fa-et'. He gave great help to Herman Biddell but unfortunately when his task was in its later stages, 'Moyse was mortal and Moyse died', and Biddell was forced to leave many blanks which would have been filled in had the old man lived to see the stud-book's completion.

Another of the old grooms contacted by Herman Biddell in 1862 was Charles Row, the groom at Butley Abbey. Charles Row was *the* man at the Abbey; and it was said at the time that the fame of the Butley stud was due as much to the skill of the head groom as to the judgment and resources of his master. Charles Row was in charge of two horses already mentioned: Duke 296 and Ripshawe 294, two of the stable kings of his day:[1] 'but the crowning point of his glory was when, in 1851, Duke was first, Ripshawe second, and all the world behind the pair; and this under the very eyes of her Majesty from the castle walks of Royal Windsor. There it was the judges caught a lecture. "Trot on, my man." Row was no athlete: nothing of old Mr Catlin's was ever put out of its pace, man or beast, and so Row kept his charge well in hand. "Run on, you with No. 407." "What

[1] *S.H.S.B.*, Vol. 1, p. 13.

d'ye want to trot him for? Why, you mayn't run such horses as these." And the merest apology for a trot was all they got out of the pair. But judges in those days were not quite so bent on action; Duke passed muster—won—and Row was in ecstasies. The castle grounds were thrown open for the men. Those marble types of perfect form—the human figure in classic beauty—pleased him not. "Proper nice place," but he "wondered the Queen let *such things as them be in her garden*".'

Daniel Pattle of Catawade was another outstanding leader Herman Biddell visited. He was a cheerful, broad-shouldered but rather stooping man of eighty-five when he first met him; and in spite of his age and the fact that he had three years previously 'burned a thousand' of the horse-cards that would have assisted his memory he gave a great deal of valuable information. He was able to tell Biddell about Smith's Horse 1110 of Parham. Like Crisp's Horse of Ufford he was another powerful 'father of his nation'. Daniel Pattle had been at Thomas Coke's famous sheep-shearings at Holkham in Norfolk, the precursors of the agricultural shows; and he had travelled a horse for three seasons in that area. The horse was a good one, and he did well with it in spite of the fact that it was quite blind: 'Yes, sir, he was blind as a bat of both eyes, and no one ever found it out but a boy. When we came along the road the little rascal sung out, "Master, your horse is blind!" "Go away," said I, "he's all right." He saw me chuck the bridle when we came to the stones.' Daniel Pattle also travelled a Suffolk horse in Yorkshire for three seasons, and 'brought his master home a fortune'. But he, too, died before Biddell had finished his task. The day he went to call on him for the second time he found the hearse at the door; 'and they buried the old man while I waited at Manningtree Station for the train back to Ipswich.'

John Lancaster was another of the grooms Herman Biddell interviewed; and this name is a further example of the continuity of the families connected with the horse in Suffolk: a descendant of John Lancaster, and his namesake is groom at Morston Hall today.

Herman Biddell repeatedly affirmed his debt to these old grooms who gave him the information on which he was able to build the intricate structure of the stud-book, and his great regret that he had not been able to take down *all* the relevant memories of some of these old men is a measure of the value he placed upon them. Horses were their life and the horse-pedigrees had become absorbed into the already rich folk-tradition that had accrued around the horse. To remember a pedigree came as naturally to them as remembering a process and was not so much a conscious task as an effortless conforming to an age-old practice. William Groom has given one of the ways the old horsemen used to identify a horse and confirm his pedigree: 'My father could tell a horse's stock by looking at him and sizing him up for a couple of minutes. He knew the Suffolks so well and all the horses that were travelling in these parts that he could pick out a horse's breed by studying him. Then he'd tell the leader: "This horse has got So-and-so's and So-and-so's breed in him"; and when they looked at the horse's card they always found he was right. The eyes used to tell him, chiefly—the way they were set in the horse's head. If he sold a horse he could tell the new owner the pedigree off by heart—back for generations; and he'd always be absolutely right.'

The pedigrees were added to the other secrets of the old horse-man's craft, not to be discussed with anyone not of 'the brotherhood', but freely given to a man like Herman Biddell who was a 'horse' man himself and was sacrificing three years of his life to collect the pedigrees and verify those that had never been written down. He took down memories that went back to the late eighteenth century, to the time when the 'old breed' was just beginning to emerge from the initial stages of a grooming that was to take it to the show-rings and parade grounds of the world. It may, in fact, be said that to a large extent the Suffolk breed of horse today is a vindication of the accuracy of the old oral method of handing down factual knowledge, and to Herman Biddell's skill in recognising and verifying it.

After his tremendous labours[1] the stud-book appeared in 1880; and although he served as secretary for a further nine years, this was the high point of his achievement—one might say the high point of his life. When he retired from the secretaryship the Society made him a presentation[2] and in his speech of thanks he gave a glimpse of his feelings while he was preparing what was to become his most lasting monument:

'If there is one thing which goes to a man's heart straighter than another, or affects him more deeply than the love and gratitude of his own family, it is the appreciation of the men he has known all his life, socially and in business. You don't know what my feelings are on this occasion. It was often said to me in the days when I was hard at work upon our first publication: "How can you give up three or four years of the best part of your life to a job like that for other people?" But I remembered then, as now, the grand words of Scripture—"No man liveth unto himself".'

He lived until 1917. Raymond Keer remembers him in his later years. He kept his interest in Suffolk horses right up to the end, and often visited the Red House stud at Rendlesham: 'a gruff, kind-hearted man—tall, and always wearing a long black coat that was

[1] His writing work and his serving on deputations and committees must have cost him dear. One of his old workmen told the writer: 'Herman Biddell wasn't much of a man about the farm: they used to call him a *spear-grass* farmer.'

[2] *S.H.S.B.*, Vol. 5. (1890).

almost touching the ground in front owing to his stoop and his bent shoulders'. Yet in spite of all his good qualities, his stubbornness and strongmindedness had a negative side, and in themselves would prevent any attempt to paint an ideal portrait of the man. Ultra-conservative in his outlook and intolerant of views he did not share, his part[1] in the 1874 dispute with the newly formed agricultural unions must be set against the breadth of his understanding and his farsightedness when he was dealing with the purely technical aspects of agriculture.

Before leaving Herman Biddell mention must be made of a remarkable piece of oral tradition he himself was responsible for preserving and later writing down. As a young man he was driving his father around one of the Playford farms where there had once been a flourishing brick-kiln. Arthur Biddell observed: 'The Senate House at Washington was built with bricks made at this kiln: they were shipped there from Ipswich.' Herman forgot about the incident until, after his father's death, he had a visit from an 'American Ranchman': the year was about 1865:

'One evening without previous notice a visitor was announced as having come from America. At that time I had begun to get used to these sudden appearances. Some led to business, and if they did not there were few to whom I was not under obligation for an hour or two's most interesting after-dinner conversation. Whether this especial visitor came after pedigrees or whether like others of his countrymen he came to learn something of Playford Hall and the man who had made its name famous, I do not remember. During the evening he asked if he might have his bag. This article when forth-coming proved to be a not over-large hand-bag which to the astonishment of the domestics was found to be the entire extent of his personal luggage.

'This was nearly fifty years ago, and judging by the deck loads of the cabs which one now sees at the steps of the Langham the travelling American does things differently at the present day. From this hand-bag my visitor brought to the surface a well-made white brick.

[1] For the full story of this see the *Ipswich Journal* for March and April, 1874.

He handed it to me and said: "This came from the Senate House at Washington (then under repair, I expect); I am led to believe it was made in the county of Suffolk. Can you tell me where it was made?" "Well," I said, "it is very curious but there are only two men on the face of the earth who can answer your question. I am one of them, and the other is a brother to whom I will introduce you tomorrow."

'Now the American landed at Liverpool, I think, on the Saturday and on the Monday he came to me. The first man he inquired of was the one who could answer his question. It struck me as a very curious co-incidence.'[1]

The brick was probably a white, very hard brick once made in certain districts of Suffolk. It was known as a Woolpit brick and is to be seen in many Suffolk buildings, notably Great Glemham Hall, the home of Lord Cranbrook.

There are numerous entries relating to the carting of bricks in Arthur Biddell's early Day Book; and Robert Sherwood, the Blaxhall farmer who was brought up in Playford, remembers the exact site of the brick-kiln. It was on Kiln Farm which was one of Arthur Biddell's farms, rented in his son's, Manfred's, name in the early years of last century. Robert Sherwood has said: 'I have not seen the brickyard for about forty years, and then only one wall was standing. I doubt if anyone could find it now, unless he knew exactly where to look. The farm is always known as *The Kell* which, as you know, is true Suffolk.'

[1] *Thomas Clarkson and Playford Hall*, 1912, p. 57.

14

The Suffolk Horse Society

The Suffolk Stud-Book Association, later known as the Suffolk Horse Society, was the first of the heavy horse societies in Britain: it was founded in 1877 and sponsored by the Suffolk Agricultural Association—chiefly by Lord Waveney, Richard Garrett and a handful of prominent breeders. Herman Biddell was its secretary until 1889; then came Fred Smith, son of Alfred Smith, a well known breeder of Suffolks with a stud at the Red House, Rendlesham—in 'The Sands'. From him his son-in law, Raymond Keer the present secretary, took over in 1924. Herman Biddell's first job, as we have seen, was to compile Volume One of the stud-book; and nearly every year since an additional volume has been added—none, however, equalling the first either in scope or in dimension.

But in addition to publishing the stud-book the Society has always been concerned in popularising the Suffolk and in encouraging breeders and helping them wherever possible. For instance during the nineteenth century the feet of the Suffolk came in for much criticism. Herman Biddell reported: 'they were said to be brittle and otherwise defective' and 'side-bone' was a prevalent nuisance. Side-bone is the ossification of the side cartilages in a horse's foot; and this hardening eventually causes the horse to become lame, especially if he travels on hard road surfaces. A stallion with side-bone is almost certain to transmit the defect to his progeny. Therefore the natural remedy was to prevent the suspect stallion from breeding. The Suffolk Agricultural Association, and later the Suffolk Horse Society, adopted the method of stringent examination of all show horses by a veterinary surgeon: and however good a horse, he would not be awarded a prize if the 'vet' found any suggestion of side-bone in him.

Even today it is rarely that a heavy horse passes out of the show ring without at least one of the judges bending down and feeling round the coronets of his feet for this defect. The 'vet' later makes a more stringent examination still. This 'Show' examination is in addition to the routine one conducted by the Ministry of Agriculture under the Horse Breeding Act of 1918: this demands that before a stallion is licensed he must satisfy the Minister's examiners he is free from hereditary defect.

This side-bone fault has now been almost completely stamped out; but the Society still continues its encouragement to breeders to keep up a good standard by awarding a special prize for the horse with the best feet at their Spring Stallion Show at Ipswich. 'No feet: no horse', as the traditional saying is; and later the testimony of a blacksmith will be given to bear out the truth of this. The award is given by the Suffolk Agricultural Association, and is called 'The Arthur Pratt Memorial Prize' after the Trimley breeder who did so much to improve the Suffolk's feet at the end of the last century and the beginning of this: he did his best to get a better quality horn by 'breeding out' *brackly* or brittle feet. One of his stallions, Morston Golden Guard 4234, had particularly good feet: all his progeny inherited this trait and helped to disseminate it over the whole breed.

Arthur Pratt was a friend of Martin Long, the agent of Kenneth M. Clarke of Sudbourne Hall, and assisted him in choosing the first team of six Suffolk geldings which competed at Olympia in 1909. About this time big commercial firms were entering these competitions for publicity reasons more than anything else: in this particular year Armour's of Chicago sent over a fine team of Percherons to compete. But the Suffolks took the prize. Afterwards they were sold to Bostock and Wombwell, the menagerie proprietors, and toured the country advertising the menagerie in whatever town it appeared. The combined weight of the team was over six tons, and was made up as follows:

	Tons	Cwts	Qrs	Hands
Smiler	1	2	0	17. 0
Proctor	1	1	0	17. 1
Prince	1	0	0	17. 1

	Cwts	Qrs	Hands
Dragon	19	2	17. 1
Wallace	19	2	16. 3
Boxer	18	3	16. 3½

A leading newspaper of the time described them as 'the best team of draught horses ever seen'; and a short time after they had been sold to Bostock and Wombwell one of the directors of the firm complained humorously to Martin Long: 'That team of horses you sold us is causing a bit of trouble: they're holding more of the public's interest than the lions and the tigers.'

At this period also—especially in the two years, 1912 and 1913, a great number of Suffolk stallions were exported, chiefly to the United States, Canada, Austria and Russia. In 1912 Arthur Pratt sold a stallion to the Czar of Russia for the purpose of breeding army horses: he was so pleased with the horse's strain that he sent the breeder a gold tiepin, inlaid with six stones, as a mark of his appreciation. The pin—now held by Newton Pratt, Arthur's son—is kept in a case bearing the name of the jeweller who supplied it: *Fic Boucheron Pont Des Marechaux, Moscou—Maison à Paris, 26 Place Vendôme.*

Another method the Society adopted to keep up the quality of the Suffolk horse and to help small breeders was the *Breeding Scheme*, established in 1897. Under this scheme the Society supplied a limited number of small farmers with a mare costing not more than sixty guineas. The farmer agreed to pay not less than a quarter of the price of the mare at the time of the sale; and, in return for her use, four per cent interest on the balance of the purchase money which was paid by the Society. The mare was served at each season, free of charge, by one of the Society's nominated stallions. The farmer reared the foal and delivered it on a day appointed by the Society; and at the sale he received the sum of £16 10s. for it. If at this sale the foal realised more than twenty guineas the farmer was to share the surplus with the Society; and all monies were placed to his credit in the Society's books. The *Mares Scheme* continued successfully until 1951 when the last Society mare was sold. This year was in many respects 'the farewell year' of the draught horse on many

Suffolk farms; for by this time the post-war surge in tractor production had swept most of the horse plough-teams from the land.

The latest method the Society has evolved for encouraging breeding has grown out of the new situation caused by the great drop in the number of working horses on the farms. When the horses went from the land the older horsemen soon followed: many of these horsemen had remained on the farm long after retiring age owing to the scarcity of labour during the war. These older men usually had sole charge of the horses that were left, and few of the younger hands were trained in horse-management. Therefore those farmers who continued to breed horses soon found that few skilled men were left to break their colts in, and they ceased to breed for this reason.

To get over this difficulty the Society decided to establish a breaking-in centre for colts. They found an experienced farmer who undertook to keep Suffolk fillies and geldings on his farm and break them *to all gears* before returning them to their owners. The colts are sent to the farmer—Sidney Buck of Combs, near Stowmarket—at varying ages, though as he said: 'Thirty months old is the best age for breaking a colt.' When they reach Potkiln Farm the colts have already been *gentled to lead*—trained to wear a halter or a headstall and to allow themselves to be led. A horse-gentler is the old Suffolk term for a man who breaks in colts, and this term is more in keeping with Sidney Buck's methods and his philosophy: 'You don't *break* a horse. No horse is born bad: he is made bad. If you treat a horse right he will have a lovely mouth and will give no trouble.' William Spalding, a horse-leader who sometimes helps him, says the same: 'The lighter the hands the better. You should be able to hold 'em with a thread—hold 'em with your little finger. You don't pull at a horse, you guide it. It's the same with any kind of horse, light or heavy. What a young horse needs is a man with light hands—very light hands and plenty of confidence.'

William Spalding, while illustrating the process of *gentling*, showed a special way of tying the halter—with a knot under the horse's chin, instead of the usual place at the side, making it impossible for the horse to work the knot loose. The device was one he copied from the gypsies: and a halter tied in this way is known as a *chapped halter*.

The introduction of the colt to the bridle and bit is critical: this step is the crucial one in the horse's whole career. If a hard-handed 'breaker' gets hold of a colt during this stage the horse's mouth quickly becomes desensitised and undesirable response-patterns are formed, and he will be difficult to handle all his life. The bridle (*dutfin* in the dialect) has a special wooden bit fitted with *keys*. These

keys—loose pieces of iron attached to the centre of the bit—give the colt something to champ upon, thus producing the necessary *lathered mouth*. The flow of saliva, or *lather*, following the champing, mini-mises the friction of the bit against the sides of the mouth. The bridle is kept on for three days. Then the collar and the plough-traces are placed on the horse. The traces are tied up to the harness and the colt is thus made conscious of them against his sides, exactly as he would be when drawing a plough or a harrow. Wearing this trace-harness he is left to stand in the stall all day. Then he is fitted with the full cart harness or *fill-gear* and is left to walk about the yard for two or three days to get used to it.

The next step is to harness the colt to a log of wood and to let him drag it in order to get the feel or 'pull' of a load. On the first day out— the first working day on the farm—the colt is harnessed in every gear he is likely to use: 'This is important because a colt will always re- member what has happened on his first day; and if possible you must give him on this day everything he has to do during his life.' He is also harnessed alongside an older, more stolid horse who will steady him and hold him back if he plunges too precipitately forward. After they are harnessed for the first time, the colts are washed down with salt water to prevent *galling*—the breaking of the tender skin by the unaccustomed friction of the harness.

Sidney Buck's overall procedure is this: after the colts have been broken to all gears—usually by the end of their first week on the farm—he works them for a week. In the third week he eases off; and then works them again steadily during the fourth week, by which time they are, as a rule, ready to be handed over to their owners. The scheme is well patronised and markedly successful, the Society con- tributing a quarter of the cost of training each colt approved and sent to the farm.

In the days when the horse was the chief power unit on the land colts were broken in on each farm in a way very similar to the above, which is in the main the traditional Suffolk method. But an account of colt-rearing and training on the farm is included here because of the additional detail gathered from horsemen who worked during the time of the full 'horse regime'. The account is chiefly Arthur Chaplin's:

'On the farm where I worked most of my life there were five or six colts foaled every year. The head horseman got £1 extra allow- ance for every foal. This was for the extra work: taking care of the mare, sitting up with her the night she foaled and assisting with the delivery if necessary—*for getting the foal into this country*, as they used to say. (The first time I heard that expression was when an old 'un boasted to me: "I brought many a foal into this country.") You got the £1 at Michaelmas when the foal was weaned, and you'd be seeing to it up to that time, of course. A foal is born at the fore-part of the year, though it mayn't come till April. But whenever it is born it's counted as one year old on the following January; and a horse's birthday, for keeping account on his age, is always in January.'

Some foals are, in fact, born in January, but there is always a certain amount of risk if a foal is timed to arrive very early in the year. For if he is born before midnight on December 31st the foal is automatically a yearling as soon as the year ends—and that may be a matter only of days or even of minutes. At least one instance is known of a Suffolk mare foaling a few minutes before midnight on the last day of the year. When the foal was registered a few days later, it was accounted a year old; and the owner had to pay the fee for the registration of a yearling.

William Groom's experience with young, day-old foals will supplement the above: 'I've had many a hard struggle with a foal on its first day. The trouble was in getting it to suck. It wouldn't take the milk. It were too bitter. But it had to have it. It were the principle: the *beestings* or the colostrum, I believe they call it. It cleaned out the foal's stomach ready for the milk. But the little owd foal had no time for it at all.' It is interesting to note that modern bio-chemical re-search has shown that the *beest* or beestings has a very high content of vitamin A.

'We used to start breaking the colt when it was very young. We put the halter on it, the younger the better. We gentled it to lead—trained it to walk along gently and turn and turn about. At the next stage, between two and three years old, we put the harness on the colt and let it stand in the stall and walk about the yard to get used to it. When the colt was ready we took it out and placed it on the plough, alongside an experienced horse. The colt worked half-days only at the start. After it got used to the ploughing we put it in the shafts of a tumbril or a wagon; and when it was broken to all gears we reckoned it was *anybody's horse*; that meant anybody on the farm could take him out ploughing or doing any job that was wanted. If we had a really good horse we kept him out of the shafts as long as we could, so *anybody* couldn't take him out and mess him about just as he wanted. We got an extra allowance of ten shillings for breaking in a colt.'

To end with the subject of this section: The Suffolk Horse Society is still vigorous (although its membership has necessarily fallen in recent years) and the Suffolk horse classes at various shows are keenly contested. The breed is still prominent at 'The Royal' as it was during the early years of the Royal Agricultural Society's meetings, starting a hundred and twenty years ago. But it was in 1934 that the Suffolk probably reached the high point of its prominence in the shows.

In this year the Royal Show was held at Ipswich. The number of entries in the Suffolk horse section was 265. This was the largest section of any breed of horse, cattle, sheep or pigs in the Show; and the entry was double that of any other breed of heavy horse. As a climax, the whole entry of Suffolks paraded together: they had the Grand Ring to themselves—the only breed of heavy horse ever to be accorded this honour. The whole week of the Show (July 3rd–7th, 1934) was one of brilliant sunshine; and the crowds saw the Punch at his best. For in the sunlight the seven shades of chestnut found in the Suffolks come alive; and those who were present at this big parade have not forgotten the sight: the long neat lines of horses with their grooms—the strength of geldings, the solid grace of mares and the compact majesty of stallions—all spread over the ring in a warmth of colour that brought autumn to the green sward of high summer.

15

The Blacksmith

The smith was a key man under the old farm-horse economy; and the smithy in addition to being an essential and regular place of call was also a kind of exchange for horse and farming news in the district. But in order to bring back the atmosphere of a smithy of this period as well as to record something of its organisation, the experiences of two Suffolk blacksmiths have been written down—one who spent most of his working life as a smith at a time when there were 'horses only' on the land; the other, a younger man, who is still a blacksmith today.

Clifford Race (1898–1958) was born at Stonham Aspal and apprenticed to a blacksmith at Creeting. 'He was the strongest man I ever knew but he went blind through the strain of smithing. He couldn't see you if you were standing right in front of him, but he carried on at the anvil and used to feel the iron he was working.' Clifford Race volunteered for the army during the First World War and served as a farrier. When he came out he worked for some years at a stud-farm at Henley (Suffolk); then he went back to smithing and worked for many years at Needham Market, a large village near Ipswich.

'Nine of us worked at Day's the blacksmith's: two of us did nothing all day but shoeing. Most of the farms round here sent their horses to us, and there was plenty of work in the village: Quinton's, the millers, had ten heavy horses and two light ones for half-ton carts; and Sage, a jobbing-master at The Rampant Horse, kept about six horses for use in broughams and so on.

'The day started at six in the morning and went on till six in the evening—even until seven at one time. The guv'nor, the master-smith, were an old man over eighty. He were a remarkable man in his way: he went down a well to clean it out on the day he died. I believe he were eighty-six. But in his later years he didn't come into the smithy until after breakfast. So the first man in the smithy in the morning had to pick up a hammer and strike the anvil three times—just to let the old man know we were on the job. He couldn't go off to sleep again unless he heard the anvil ring.

'The nine of us were put out to jobs like this: two were on the shoeing—two more were brought in if there was a rush; the guv'nor would be making mill-bills—a tool for trimming a millstone; two were on farm-work, sharpening the tines of harrows, mending ploughs and so on; the last four were normally on outside jobs, on pumps for wells—outside work of all kinds.

'I was always on the shoeing job; but until seven o'clock each morning, until the horses started to come in, three of us would be shoe-making: two strikers and a smith. We took two old shoes; heated them and hammered them together, the strikers striking alternately; the smith holding the shoe on the anvil and using the small hammer himself. New iron wouldn't do for shoes at that time o'day. It would be too soft. The more you hammer iron the tougher it gets; so the old shoes welded and hammered together lasted much longer. They don't do that today: it would take too long. The shoes are all machine-made today. If it were a wet day the horses started to come in sharp after 7 o'clock. For on wet days the farmer said: "There's nothing for 'em to do here. Take 'em off to the blacksmith's straight away." Then we'd be working on the horses all day until about 4 o'clock when they usually stopped coming. Then it was back to *double-hammer shoe-making* until knocking-off time.

'During the twelve-hour day the two of us aimed to do thirty-six shoes, that is nine horses. Two of us averaged four shoes an hour. The town horses came in every three weeks or a month for re-shoeing. Country horses—horses that worked chiefly on the land—came in once in three months, on the average. The town horses were nearly always leg-weary, and harder to shoe. They'd lie on you as you lifted the leg: a town horse seemed double the weight of a country horse just because it were leg-weary. Another thing we noticed was this: as they were leg-weary they wore their shoes out more quickly; these town horses often did up to forty mile on the road during the day, and they got into the habit of sliding and dragging their feet. This just burned their shoes up.

'But we had one old country horse that was a bit of a nuisance—a big mare. She were a fine-looking animal, and she'd always give us trouble—but she couldn't help it, poor owd gel. She were *jink-backed*. You couldn't back her. She had something the matter with her spine. She used to stagger, and if you didn't watch out she'd come down on you and crush you while you were a-shoeing her. When I tell you she weighed over a ton, you can see why we were a bit narvous. We used to mark her up special on the calendar; and we took care to make a right good job of her: we took an extra lot of trouble with her shoes so we could keep her away as long as we could. We'd often make the owd gel go for twenty-four weeks without coming to us. She were a beautiful bay mare with feet like butcher's blocks. You couldn't go wrong when you were actually a-shoeing her. She had so much hoof you could bang the nails in anywhere you liked, and they'd all be right. The only thing you had to watch out was that she didn't start to stagger and put one of them feet down on you a bit sharp, or fell on you as she were a-swaying about with her jink-back.

'Jink-back[1] is something like slipped-disc, I should say. You can tell a horse in this condition without actually trying to back him. You just want to put your hand on him and he'll start to quiver—afraid you're going to back him. It's often caused by some accident.'

'There was plenty doing in the smithy when it was only horses on the farms. Sometimes there'd be eight or nine people standing about there swopping news—market news and just ordinary gossip. You hardly had room enough to do your job, but you daren't tell 'em to get out o' the way; or else they'd say they'd as much right to be

---

[1] Or *sway-backed*: 'A horse is said to be sway'd in the back when, by too great a burthen, or by some slip, strain, or over hasty and straight turning, he hath taken an extreme wrinch in the lower part of his back below the short ribs, and directly below his fillets. . . . He will falter, and sway sometimes backwards and sometimes sidelong.' (Gervase Markham, the seventeenth century writer on horses.)

there as you had! You had to go a-shoeing the horse as best you could. At election time it were well nigh impossible.

'The longest day I can remember at Needham smithy was the day of the Stowmarket Christmas sale—I forget the exact year. But up to then it had been a right mild winter. None o' the farmers had thought about having their horses *roughed*,[1] and they set off extra early that

morning to go to the Christmas market. I cycled over from Creeting at the usual time and when I started it were all right. The roads were wet. But when I got half-way, I had to get off my bike: the roads had frozen and were like glass. By the time I got to the smithy there were a queue of horses half-way down the street, all waiting to be roughed. The farmers going to market had come down from Barking and Ringshall and those places, and on the rough owd country roads they

[1] *roughing*: altering a horse's shoes to enable him to walk on icy roads.

managed; but as soon as they got to the tarred road in Needham street they had to stop. So they unharnessed the wagons, left them down the Barking road and brought the horses to the smithy.

'As you know there are two kinds of *roughing*: you can either put frost-nails in the shoe or you can take it off and turn the heels and the toes of the shoes up—*turning 'em up*, we used to call it. We did a hundred and seven horses that day. We finished at ten minutes to six, about our usual time. I was just takin' off my apron in the smithy when I says to the guv'nor:

'"Was that a chain a-clinkin' in the *travus*?"[1]

'"No, there's no horses in there now!"

'"That there is! I can hear them."

'We went in and saw two of Quinton's that been sent up to be shod. We had no shoes for 'em so my mate and I had to set to and make the shoes and shoe them. It was eight o'clock when we finished. I was so tired I had to get off my bike twice on the way up to Creeting and sit on the side of the road in the snow for a spell before I could go on. That was the sort of day you don't forget. I could hardly look at my dinner when I got home. We'd worked from 6.30 a.m. until 8.00 p.m. with the shortest of breaks during the day. My mate was over seventy, so I couldn't let him lift a horse's foot after "knocking-off" time: I actually shoed the two horses. But he was laid up after that and we didn't see him for days.

'Few people can judge what shape a particular horse is in better than the smith who shoes him. The farmers knew this; and they'd often come for advice: "Owd Todd is going to sell one of his horses—Champion, d'you know him? What sort of a horse is he?" "Oh, he's all right," the verdict may be; "you can't go wrong with him." Another may come along for advice and you'd tell him to leave the horse alone: "But he looks all right! What's the matter with him?" "Maybe he looks all right; but if you buy that horse you'll be buying yourself a packet o' trouble." We lost a farm's work through something like this; only it was my boss who was involved—and it turned out all right in the end.

---

[1] *traverse* or partition: screened off portion of smithy where horses were actually shod.

'The farmer's son brought a beautiful mare to be shod; and after she'd been done he asked the guv'nor what he thought on her. He studied her and in spite of her looks he told the son: "Tell your father she's a wrong 'un." When the farmer heard this judgment he was very angry, storming and swearing and saying there was nothing wrong with the mare. He refused to send his horses to be shod at our smithy after that; for once the smith's verdict got around it would be difficult for him to sell the mare. But six month's later that same mare developed some complaint in her front legs. She became a cripple, and I don't know what became of her. The farmer came back to our smithy after that, bringing a couple of his horses. "You were right," he admitted, "but I was whoolly riled when I heard what you thought on her."

'The foot on a horse is the most important part of him, you can say; and the blacksmith can help a lot in putting any defects in the feet right. Some colts used to have what is called *steeple-hoof*. It's a condition where the toe of the hoof wears out quicker than the rest of it, causing the hoof to be tilted forward. If it's not corrected right quick it leads to deformity in the front legs. If a stallion is a bit inclined that way he can pass on the defect to his stock. I used to go over to Battisford once, specially to *tip*—put special shoes on—six colts, all with steeple-hoofs. I tipped 'em for a twelve-month and they came all right afterwards. You had to be very particular about the *frog*:[1] it had to be looked at very carefully, because canker-foot would easily set in if the frog became infected. Some blacksmiths used to trim the frog each time the horse came in to the smithy; but when we were in the army we daren't touch the frog. We had to shoe a horse with *frog-pressure*, as they called it. That meant the shoe had to be on a level with the frog, so when the foot was set down the frog would be making contact with the ground. They said it was a kind of cushion to absorb the shock and it should be allowed to do its job properly. You daren't touch the frog in the army—if you were caught trimming up a frog it meant "fourteen days".[2]

'I used to prepare a lot of horses for shows when I was at the stud-

---

[1] *frog:* the horny, elastic pad in the centre of the hoof.
[2] Fourteen days, 'confined to barracks,' as a punishment.

farm at Henley—Shires they had there—and you probably won't believe me when I say that the blacksmith has won half the prizes for
these show horses. A good blacksmith will correct a defect in a horse's
foot so it would take a master of a judge to find it out. If, for instance,
a horse was "wide behind"—that means his hocks were too far apart
—a good blacksmith could help to do something about that by making
his shoes thick on the outside of the heel and thin inside. He'd look
a bit better then, when the judge walked round the back to have a
look at him. Special bevelled shoes was the rule for farm-horses that
were being shown—they made the feet look bigger. Then there was
another trick. While the horse was in the box or the meadow preparing for the show, we shod him with thin *grass-plates*; but the day
before the show we changed these for the heavy, bevelled shoes.
When the horse got into the ring he was unused to the heavy shoes
and he picked up his feet with an exaggerated lift that improved his
"action". Looking after the feet is one of the arts of showing a heavy
horse. It's easy to get a good body with plenty of fat on a horse; but
it's hard to keep the legs and the feet just right at the same time. The
art is in keeping the right balance. I've seen a horse perfect on top and
yet they'd been a-putting soft-soap into the cracks of the hoofs to try
and fool the judges. Besides, the feet are critical in another way: if
you feed a horse up too much he is likely to get fever of the feet. The
hoof goes soft, and it's as good as all over with that horse's showing
days.'

In addition to shoeing horses and doing various repair jobs, one
regular task at the smithy was the re-tyring of cart wheels. In the
summer the woodwork in the farm cart or wagon wheels tended to
shrink; and the iron tyres often worked loose. The wheels then
needed the smith's attention.

'When this happened some farmers used to say: "I can't afford to
hev the wheels done," and they'd stand the cart or the wagon in a
pond until the felloes of the wheel swelled up. The wheels would
be all right for a couple of days; then they'd become ten times worse
and they'd have to come to the smithy. We took off the iron tyres, and
cut out a small piece off each one and then welded the ends back
together. Then we fitted each tyre back onto the wheel which was

clamped down on the tyring platform. This was a circular steel plate, level with the ground, fixed permanently in the lane outside the *travus*. But first we had to heat up the tyre in the oven we'd built on purpose to do this. The oven was made of sheets of iron, in sections; and you could fit it or pin it together and dismantle it after use. It was circular in shape and we could fit it up to take any number of wheels—three or four pairs if need be. To heat the oven we placed shavings and wood in between and around the tyres which usually took about an hour to heat sufficiently. To get the tyres out of the oven two of us would have a long rod each. We'd marked every tyre, but sometimes we'd fish the wrong one out; then there'd be some swearing.

'The reason the tyres were heated was this: when we cut out the piece of the loose tyre and welded it together it was then smaller than the actual woodwork on the wheel. How much smaller we had to estimate before cutting the tyre in the first place. If it was a newish wheel and the joints between the felloes had a fair gap we'd give her perhaps $\frac{7}{8}$ of an inch; if the joints were not very loose we'd give her perhaps $\frac{1}{2}$ an inch. That meant the tyre would be that amount smaller than the actual wheel, so we had to heat up the tyre to expand it in order to get it on to the rim. Then, when the heated tyre gradually cooled, it contracted and drew the joints together and bedded itself firmly round the woodwork. There was a central spindle on the tyring platform, and the wheel was put over this and clamped down so that it wouldn't *spring*. Three men were needed to do the actual fitting of the tyre: two holding the tyre after they had taken it out of the oven, and one with a bucket of water to pour onto the felloes to stop them from taking fire as the tyre was clamped on. If it had been properly heated it would slip on without any trouble. But if the tyre had not been expanded enough, we'd have to have levers and gently lever and hammer it on, something in the same way as you'd do with a bicycle tyre. But if you hammered you had to be careful to miss the joints: the felloes were dowelled together and if you hit one of the joints the wrong way, the dowel was certain to break. The owd guv'nor was a knowing one with these tyring jobs. He weren't very brisk in the morning, and often we were a bit late getting off the mark ourselves; but he didn't mind us working beyond six in the evening—we didn't get paid for that! He'd say about four: "We'll fire the oven." It would take about an hour and a half to fix and heat up the oven; and, of course, once it was started we had to carry on with the job of re-tyring. I've known him more than once take out his watch half-way through a tyring job and say as though he was some bit surprised:

'"It's six o'clock! Wheriver has the day gone!"

'This particular blacksmith had a secret process for hardening mill-bills, the tool used for trimming or *dressing* a mill-stone, cutting out the "furrows" on the stone and making them well-defined in order to grind the corn more efficiently. It was difficult to hammer out the steel of these mill-bills, but the hardening process was more difficult still. Cold steel could not be heated more than *blood-hot*, that is beyond the point when it was a red of the same colour as blood. If it were heated more than this it would become all brittle; and great care had to be taken not to heat up the end of the bill—the cutting part—too much. If you were making a new bill you'd hammer it out and then you'd let it get cool. To harden it you then put about an inch of the first end into the fire, taking care it wouldn't get too hot. Then you'd take it out of the forge and dip it into a tub containing a special mixture; then you watched it change colour as you held it, watched it very carefully. It changed from white to strawberry then to violet. When it was violet it was the right temperature to dip into the tub a second time. When you had done this the first end was complete. To harden the other end you followed the same process; only when the second end of the bill went into the forge you had to have a ladle and pour water over the first end to stop it heating up again.

'There were sometimes as many as fifty dozen mill-bills in the smithy at the same time—many of them being re-sharpened, for the ends got *blobbed* after they'd been in use for some time. They were sent here from all over the country. A lot came from Leeds to be re-pointed. Day was one of the few men who knew the secret properly: I believe there was a man in Ipswich as well. The main part of the secret was the mixture in the tub: it was like vitriol to look at but no one knew what was in it exactly. Another secret he had was the joining of two old bills together to make a new one. He had a secret way of doing this and the customer couldn't tell that the new bill was two old ones dowelled together. Making or re-pointing mill-bills was gruelling work. You couldn't heat the steel until it was soft, so you had to hammer it while it was almost hard. They'd have mechanised hammers to the job today. After a day at this work your shoulders and arms would be all bruises. It shook you up so much; jarred your arms and your shoulders, so next day you could hardly raise your arm high enough to put your cap on.'

But it wasn't all work at the smithy. They used to have an occasional break; and even the most unlikely incident was seized upon to make some diversion in the monotony of the work.

'After bending over a horse or a job on the anvil till all your body ached you were glad of any bit of fun for a couple o' minutes to take your mind off the job. I allus remember the owd boy from Creeting College (farm) and the fly. There was a big owd fly settled on the smithy door; and this owd boy took off his hat and was just a-goin' to swipe this fly off the door. But the guv'nor dropped his hammer and said some serious: "Don't do that! Don't kill that fly. That's our pal. That's our pal!" And the poor owd boy put his hat back on sheepish like and watched the fly zooming about the smithy, giving us a look as the same time. We often used to laugh about the owd boy and the fly.'

Some of the boys who had just left school used to be *mischieful* when they brought the farm-horses in, but the smith had a few tricks to put them in their place. 'One of the things he did was this: On the quiet he'd heat up the ends of two thin iron rods. Then he'd ask one of the boys: "Can you play the kittle-drum on the anvil like this? Sounds good don't it?" After showing the boy how it was done, he'd offer him the two iron rods—the *hot ends* towards him. The boy would drop them immediately. Then the smith said innocently:

'"Well, that's a rum 'un. I can hold 'em quite well. Or maybe, the other ends got hot while I was a-tapping them on the anvil."

'"You hold the other end and see," the boy usually said, a bit angry. But the laugh was on him, and he'd be on his way to finding his proper place in the smithy—which was to stand by and watch, and not ask too many questions.'

If this treatment was not effective the blacksmith sometimes tried another trick. With a piece of chalk he mark a short vertical line on the anvil. Then with his small hammer in his right hand he placed his left fore-finger on the chalk-mark with a great show of concentration. Then he began tapping rhythmically each side of the mark with his hammer, at the same time moving his fore-finger deftly out of the way. After he had done this long enough to make it look deceptively simple, he asked the boy: 'Would you like to have a go?' The boy took up the hammer and at first very slowly tapped the anvil, taking great care to keep his fingers out of the way. Then after a bit of encouragement from the smith: 'That's right. You got the idea some quick!' he forgot his initial caution and began to quicken up his tapping. In a moment or two he dropped his hammer with a clatter and was walking about the smithy holding his fore-finger under his armpit.

A colt that was shod for the first time always provided a diversion; sometimes a not very welcome one. For most colts resented being shod and as a result the smith would be thrown about the travus before he had finished. But it was a long-standing custom in Suffolk that at a horse's first shoeing the farmer should pay for beer to be given to the smith and his helpers. The custom was probably a recognition of the special difficulty of introducing a young colt to the idea of having iron shoes hammered on to his hoofs.

'We used to call it *First Nail*—a shilling extra on the price for shoeing a colt for the first time, a shilling for the men as beer-money. As soon as the smith started on the colt his mates used to say: "This is the *beer-nail*. This is the beer. If you bend it, mind, you git no beer!" When the colt was shod we sent out for the beer and put our coats on and sat round with the farmer's man and drank it. Some farmers used to try and get out of paying *First Nail*. But if they didn't pay up, we got it out of 'em in another way—by putting an extra shilling on one of their bills. Some weeks we'd have as many as ten or twelve colts coming in. One farmer used to bring three colts at a time. That was too many. For with a young colt you'd git flung about middling sharp—and with some on 'em you arned your beer-money. Though a smith allus has a spark in his throat and cin drink a pint o' beer at any time.'

This ceremony of *First Nail* was usual in the blacksmith's shops in this district; and on it the very old custom of *Shoeing the Colt* at harvest time would appear to have been founded. This was a kind of primitive initiation ceremony of a newcomer into the harvest-field. Charles Bugg of Barking has described it:

'Your first harvest and the first field you went into when you were a boy the men took you and turned you up and drove a nail into the bottom of your shoe. They would go on driving in the nail until you shouted: "Beer!" When you shouted *beer* they stopped hammering the nail because it meant that you'd agreed to buy each man a pint o' beer out of your first harvest money. If a boy wouldn't shout, they drove the nail right in until it reached his foot, and then he'd pretty soon sing out.[1] There used to be a lot of clubbing up and beer-drinking when I were a lad. Then there was some bother on this particular farm—some fooling about and one on 'em put a fork through a cow's bag. That was the end of that: no clubbing after that.'

Allen Cobbold (born 1904), the other blacksmith mentioned, lives at Battisford, near Stowmarket. His grandfather and his father were blacksmiths at the same forge near Battisford Straight; and the tools he uses for the shoeing of a horse are the same as those his grandfather used. 'A hammer, a pair o' nippers, a rasp and an *unclencher*—for taking off the old shoe—is all you want for shoeing.' He still used the old fashioned pear-shaped bellows in his smithy. But in most other respects the picture has completely changed. In the first place the blacksmith no longer makes his own shoes, welding them from the old ones, as already described. He now buys machine-made shoes from an iron-merchant in the nearby town. A traveller comes round to the smithy 'about once in three months' and he gives an order for the shoes he requires.

'I used to buy my shoes by the ton, but now I buy them by the hundredweight. That will give you some idea of the position today. Six or seven years ago I had about hundred and fifty farm-horses to shoe: now I've got not many more than a score—and this score is taken from a much wider area than before: a blacksmith packs up and I take his district over. As I see it, what is happening now is that

---

[1] cf. the phrase, 'paying his footing;' see *A.O.S.*, p. 293.

as soon as a horse on the farm dies he is not being replaced. There are only a handful of horses left in the farms round here; and with these they don't go on like they used to. The horses are baited at seven o'clock when the men go to work: they don't have a horsemen specially to bait 'em. Another thing has changed: the price of having a horse shod. When I started work, shoeing a horse cost two shillings. Today you couldn't do it for less than thirty.'

In some counties the travelling blacksmith—complete with mobile smithy in a van—has been introduced to meet the need in areas where the village smith has disappeared altogether.

The Harness-Maker

Like the blacksmith the harness-maker has seen a great deal of his trade fall away from him during the last twenty or thirty years. In the days of the horse every town and most big villages had at least one harness-maker: the tradesmen now left in the county of Suffolk can be counted on one hand. There is, however, one harness-maker still working in this, the Stowmarket, district; and he has specialised all his life in making harness for farm-horses. Sidney Austin (born 1888) of Finningham took over his father's business when he was a very young man and has kept it going ever since, completing a period of about a hundred years since the business was first opened. When horses were the sole power on the farms Sidney Austin had five men working in his shop: today he has one.

During his half century or so in the harness trade he has chiefly been concerned with making the three main gears required by farm-horses. First the *thiller* or *fill-horse gear*,[1] consisting of *dutfin* (or bridle), collar, seals (mostly of wood, also called the hames), saddle and breechings and leading rein. This gear had no traces, only a small chain[2] fixed to the seals and hooked to an attachment on each cart-shaft. Next was the *cart-trace harness* (called, also, the *hames-* or *hem-gear*). This was practically the same as the fill-gear except that it had a cart-trace leather instead of saddle and breechings. The cart-trace *back* or *leather* was fitted to the top of the collar and, ran down the centre of the trace-horse's back: it was a broad band of leather about four inches wide. On the cart-trace *back* decorative sewing, done to a traditional pattern, was the rule. A *pricking iron*—a chisel-shaped implement with points or teeth at regular intervals on

[1] *A.F.C.H.*, p. 224. [2] The *fill-bells* or *tug: A.O.S.*, p. 292.

the blade—was first used to mark out the pattern and to ensure that the stitches were uniformly placed. The back also had an octagonal brass-plate as a decoration. The traces for the *leader* or trace-horse were chains weighing between sixteen and twenty pounds a pair. A *set-stick*, three feet ten inches wide, was used with the trace-gear to keep the chains apart and prevent them from nipping the horse's flanks. When he was in the plough the whipple-tree prevented this from happening.

Lastly, he made the plough-harness. This was made up of collar, with seals, dutfin and a simple *plough-back*, a light leather band fixed

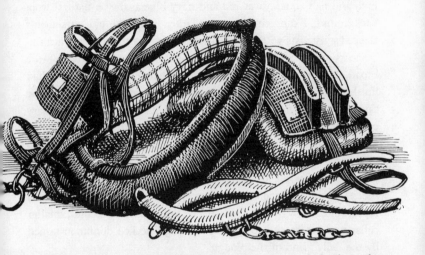

to the top of the collar and running down the horse's back to the crupper, and having a transverse piece of leather across the haunches. Fixed to this, on one side only, was a metal loop through which passed the *cord* or rein: the other cord passed through a similar loop in the harness of the horse working alongside. The traces in the plough-gear were also chains, and weighed between seven and ten pounds.

Cart *head-stalls*—called *head-collars* when made for light horses— were made of leather $1\frac{1}{2}$ to $1\frac{3}{4}$ inches wide. The horse wore the head-stall in the stable, also in the meadow if he was difficult to catch. The hames or seals were fastened at the top by *top-bands* or top-latches, and at the bottom by *throat-bands* or throat-latches. These are bands of leather, once cut in the shop from the *half-backs*—a hide cut in half; but now they are machine-cut in the factory. They used to cost twopence each: today they are sold at four shillings. This difference in price is also shown in the cost of relining a cart-horse's collar: fifty years ago it cost half-a-crown; today, thirty shillings. The same kind of woollen cloth, called *collar-check*, is still used. Arthur Pluck, the Stowmarket clothier, recalled the old type of collar-check: 'It was a rough flannel—a *union* type, about 75% wool and 25% cotton; a mixture for hard wear. The traditional check, which was about an inch and half square, was red and navy blue against a natural wool background. I can remember my father lining the old horsemen's sleeved waistcoats with this collar-check. It gave them extra warmth.'

Occasionally Sidney Austin made show bridles and *rollers*—the broad, leather bands around the stallions' girth. After a stallion had finished *travelling*, he was sometimes castrated and put to work on the farm. A special collar had then to be made for him as the ordinary collars were too small. The biggest collar the saddler was ever called upon to make was a 32-inch one (this is the inside measurement, a line from withers to throat). But the average stallion's size was a 28-inch collar, while for the average gelding or mare the collar was in the 23–26-inch range. Often, however, a stallion lost weight so rapidly after a few month's working on the land that a second, smaller collar was necessary—so quickly was high-necked dominion tamed by the daily grind of the plough.

Sidney Austin confessed it was a very difficult job to measure a horse for a collar: he preferred keeping a good stock of collars of varying sizes, and trying half a dozen or so of these on a horse until he was suited. In this way he got as good a fit as if the collar were specially made. He also made an amount of donkey-harness when the donkey was popular in the Suffolk villages. A donkey's harness was not unlike a small pony's. But it had one big difference: a donkey's head is so large that, if an ordinary collar were made to slip over it, the collar would be much too big for the neck and the shoulders; therefore a *breast-collar*—a thick band of leather across the breast—was used to take the draught.

The farm- or cart-horse collar was stuffed with straw, as it still is today, and padded with *collar-flock*, coarse, purple-dyed wool made from old rags which have been torn and shredded up. As one watched a collar being repaired with flock in Sidney Austin's workshop, the *flok* of an earlier chapter came to mind; and it was not difficult to picture the fifteenth century Norwich carter doing a similar job after his long and wearing trip to Ipswich.

When the harness-making business was in its hey-day, the shop— like the smithy—was the meeting-place for farmers in the district. They were continually calling to have jobs done or merely to have a chat. The harness-maker remembered one particular farmer who always insisted on having the collars for his horses made in a special way—with extra padding at a certain point. This meant extra work, and the collar-makers did not accept this attempt to alter the traditional pattern of their job with very much grace. The farmer knew this and spent long hours leaning over the half-hatch door—which still remains—on the surface, just chatting idly, but in reality keeping an admonitory eye on the way his collars were being re-lined. The collar-makers always rejoiced when that particular farmer's harness had been completed.

Some farmers, however, arranged to have their harness repaired at the farm. This was usually done just before harvest, a suitable time for two reasons: there was a lull in the farming rhythm at this period and therefore little of the harness was in use; again, it was being checked at a critical time, just before it would be submitted to the greatest strain of the year. The harness repairers packed all their gear into a trap drawn by a pony and made their way to the farm. 'It was a job remembering to put every tool we needed in the trap; but we used to manage somehow. We generally spent two days at a farm, and perhaps another day at an 'off-hand' farm belonging to it. We repaired the harness in a barn; and as soon as we'd finished with a set the farm-workers oiled it with black harness-oil. We looked forward to going out to the farms: it was a break from work in the shop. They looked after us well, giving us tea, and beer for those who wanted it, home-brewed beer. I didn't use to take it myself but I recollect some of it when I first went out to the farms as a lad of sixteen or seventeen.

One of the men showed it to me: it was thick as treacle, almost too thick to pour. They used to put lumps of beef into it after they had made it and were ready to cork it down for harvest: the beer would eat the meat right up, *feed on it*, as they used to say.'

But one of the pieces of horse-equipment that has not been seen in Suffolk for years was sold from Sidney Austin's shop: this was the straw-hat once worn by the farm-horse. They were not, however, made in this district. The hats were often worn at harvest time, as much—one suspects—to add colour to the scene as to prevent the horse from getting sun-stroke. Yet some farmers held that the straw hats attracted the flies away from the horses' eyes and face, thus preventing them from getting restless while, for instance, the corn was being loaded on the wagon. The netted ear-caps, decorated with picturesque coloured tassels, which sometimes enclosed the horse's ears, also served the same purpose.

As often happens, however, one of the most interesting links with the past is in a word connected with the craft: 'They used to call us *knackers* years ago, because we used to *dress* our own leather: the horse-slaughterer—knacker, as he's called today—and the harness-maker were in one business. The harness-maker took the whole hide and dressed or tanned it himself. Most of the leather used in the harness-business today is ox-hide, though, not horse-hide. But we do use some horse-leather. I've got a piece of white horse-leather here: we use it for stitching up collars and making a good firm job.'

Arthur Chaplin had also heard both usages of the word *knacker*:[1] 'Thet owd harness will hev to goo to the knacker's;' and, in discussing an old horse: 'I'll give you a knacker's price for him—£1 a leg.' It appears that £4 was the average price given for an old horse by the knackers. Sir John Cullum in his eighteenth century parish history notes that that the word was used for 'the person who makes harness, collars and leather furniture in general for the farmer.'

One product of the horse-slaughterer's has not been forgotten. After the horse-flesh had been boiled the grease was preserved and

[1] 'Sending one for "a pennorth of knacker's brandy", alias *strap-oil* is a favourite joke on 1st of April' (*A.O.S.*, p. 295); *knakkr* (Icelandic) meaning a saddle.

found its way back to the farm for use on the wagons. The horse-grease was considered much better than the manufactured grease of later years. 'With the knacker's grease you'd only need to grease the wheel after two or three journeys: with the processed stuff they'd be a-shrieking after one. It used to froth up in the hub of the wheel and would last a long time.'

The same horseman contributed a note about the buckles on the harness: 'There were two kinds of buckles: the old kind, made of iron, and the brass ones which were much better. The iron ones became rusty and got hard to undo; and this was a big fault if you were in a muddle and got a horse down and wanted to get the harness off him quickly. This happened sometimes when you were on a muck-hill. If the muck had rotted up, occasionally the horse went down up to his knees, then he'd lunge forward with the load right on top of him. You got the harness off right quick and got a trace-horse to hitch to the back of the cart to pull it off him, or else your horse would soon get smothered. I've had to cut the top-latch to release the seals because I couldn't free him in any other way; or with a hammer and a cold chisel cut the staple holding the saddle-chain to the shaft because the horse's full weight was on the side where the chain was usually slipped off. "Horse down on the muck-hill!" was a cry you'd have to attend to pretty quick; and it made the job easier if the harness had all brass buckles.'

Most harness-dealers kept whips which the horsemen bought as part of their own equipment. As a rule each horseman had two or three: 'a good top-whip—the long whip—cost seven-and-six, which was a lot o' money; but it was a useful whip to have to reach the leading horse in a team. A brass top-whip, without a lash, was no good for anything, except show and to keep the flies off—a good decoration. The short-handled whip—with a heavy, corded leather lash and a small length of *huntsman's cord*, knotted, at the end of it—was the *larner*, the *night-school* whip. You could keep a horse awake with this.' This is the whip the horsemen used to make the spectacular crack: 'If you knew how, you could crack it on a frosty morning so you could make echoes ring in the trees along the roadside.' Using this same whip the horsemen also held competitions in the stable: 'We used to set up a pin on a door, and if I couldn't put thet pin down after two lashes of my whip, I'd drop the whip on the floor. Standing at the right distance from the target was the trick.'

In discussing the different gears used by farm-horses one horse-man pointed out that in his early days there were very few double-shafted wagons about: 'But some horsemen preferred to have the single shaft even when there was a double-shafted one to be had: they'd take the second shaft off. My father used to do this and harness his four horses *at length*. When he had them all this way there was no hope of reaching the leaders with a whip. All had to be done by command—obedience to the word of mouth. To get your horses trained for this you had to have plenty of patience—you had to talk to 'em, talk to 'em all the time. They understood. *Four at length* was a test of management and training. For instance, if you wanted them to turn off the road into the homestead gate, the leading two or three horses had to be trained to pass the gate some bit before they stopped. They then came back round and through the gate gently. There ha' been a pretty muddle if they'd turned straight in as soon as they come to the gate-post.'

The skill needed to manage a team of four horses *at length* was often displayed in the show rings. Teams *at length* entered the ring with two grooms walking on the off-side of each team. There were no driving reins and the horses were controlled by two whips—one placed over the crest of the second horse, the other over the crest of the leader. The team did evolutions—figures-of-eight and so on—in the ring; and it was a point of honour that no part of the horse or the harness was touched by hand, all control being by slight movements of the whip, and whispered words of command inaudible to the crowd. These displays by teams of four *at length* were kept up until the 'Thirties.

It is worth recording that a team harnessed in this way was named in Suffolk: the *lead* or *forhoss* or *forhust* (fore-horse); the lash-hoss; the pin-hoss (the *body* in some counties); and the *thiller*, or *shaft-hoss*.

17

Additional Horse Gear

Included in this section are those pieces of farm-horse equipment not already touched upon. In his sixteenth century list of *Husbandly Furniture* in the *Five Hundred Points*, Thomas Tusser wrote down items of farm equipment that were in use in his day. Much of this equipment was used in Suffolk until recent times: in the first of the following two verses the items mentioned are concerned with farriery and harness-repairing:

> *A buttrice and pincers, a hammer and nail*
> *and aspern, and scissors for head and for tail*
> *Whole bridle and saddle, whitleath and nall*
> *with collars and harness for thiller and all.*

A buttrice is a knife, an aspern a file. Nall (cf. nadder for adder) is an awl. Whitleath is white leather—leather dressed with alum. Sidney Austin, the harness-maker, still uses strips of whitleather to repair—with the help of an awl—the collars of farm-horses as already stated.

> *A pannell and wanty, pack-saddle and ped*
> *a line to fetch litter and halters for lead.*
> *With crotchets and pins to hang trinkets thereon,*
> *and stable fast chained, that nothing be gone.*

A panel was a 'kind of rustic saddle'; a ped was a pannier or basket, usually slung in pairs over a horse's back; a wanty was a broad girth of leather by which the load was bound to the back of a horse.

An item the working horseman often carried with him in the field was a false- or split-link. If a *chain* or trace broke, a false-link was at hand to repair it. 'They were something like a key-ring in design only they were the same shape as the trace-link. We used an S-hook in a similar way. The ends could be nipped together to form a false-link; but we didn't usually do this on the trace. I had one on the horse's bit so when he had a nose-bag, as the *Shires* used to have, I could prise open the S-hook and let the bit hang free so he could feed properly. We used to make 'em in the smithy before the '14–18 war, and sell 'em at a penny each.'

Sometimes in the field a ploughman had difficulty with one horse working too close to the other, thus affecting his ploughing. To keep the horses apart he used a questionable device, called a *tuttle-box* in some counties. This was fixed on to one of the inside traces: by means of a pointed wooden pin, or even the sharp end of a nail, the horses were pricked in the flanks if they came too close together. 'It were a cruel thing to do. They'd fix a nail or a piece of wire through the plough-trace—anything sharp to keep the two horses apart. I knew a horseman who once had a mare in his team. They'd stopped breeding on her; but when she was *in season* she used to lay over to the horse alongside her. The horseman fixed a nail in her trace—but it wouldn't hev done for my boss to hev seen him—he'd hev had marching orders right quick.'

Not all of the old horsemen were models of patience and kindness: some of them—probably a small minority—used practices that were undoubtedly cruel, and would certainly be illegal today. One of the most drastic of these was their treatment of hard-mouth. If a horse had been unskilfully broken in and mishandled afterwards its mouth became hard and insensitive. Usually this was done by excessive pulling on the reins, on the assumption that a horse must be stopped by force instead of by *association*—a reflex action following gentle pressure of the bit in the mouth. This reflex action could be properly instilled in a colt only by adequate training or *conditioning*, and later intelligent handling. That is the reason the horse-gentler was so insistent on the use of light hands for a colt who was being trained to the bit. Once the hardening process had set in the damage was difficult to undo; and some horsemen resorted to the make-shift method of making the side of the mouth responsive by physical means. One practice was to rub it with the edge of a milled coin which would temporarily make the mouth tender and more susceptible to the pressure of the bit. Another method was more questionable still: before the adequate registration of poisons some horsemen used corrosive sublimate of mercury, a deadly poison, to make the side of the horse's mouth tender. Two chemists who came into the Stow-market district of Suffolk between thirty and forty years ago were amazed by the practice and refused to sell the chemical for this pur-pose.

One of the recognised forms of restraint for a horse that did not behave itself among the other horses in the yard was the *clog*. 'You'd always find a *master* horse in a yard; and if there was a new comer, the owd master often got the new horse into a corner and let out at him. When this happened the head horseman said: "Put tha' owd clog on har, bor," or something like that. We made the clog in this way: we got a piece of ash; bored a hole in each end of it; and then bent it to form a loop. After we'd tied it in position with cord, we boiled it; so it would always keep that shape. This loop was placed round one of the kicker's back legs, and a piece of iron threaded through the holes to keep it in position. A short length of chain, with a piece of wood like a policeman's truncheon attached to the end of it, was fixed to the iron on the leg. The kicker dragged this piece of wood round the yard with him; and when he started his bad habits and let out, the clog *naturally* came back and gave him a sharp rap across the hocks. He soon got tired o' thet.'

Hobbles or hopples were made on the farm in an improvised way by looping a long piece of sacking, or tough cloth, around the forelegs in the manner of a figure-of-eight and tying it securely. In the old days it was not unusual to see a team of horses hobbled on the road to prevent them from moving on. Herman Biddell gave an instance. John Julian of Boat's Hall, Laxfield, one of the early breeders, owned several well known horses. 'He was chiefly celebrated for driving his four stallions in a team together, and tradition draws a picture of the four standing by the alehouse door each with a fore-leg strapped up while the teamster himself stepped in to see who was in the room with the sanded floor. In 1813 he advertises the four Boxer 755, Briton

758, Bumper 759 and Bly 753, and there is, I have heard a painting (I expect by Hobart) of the quartett in a waggon, somewhere still in existence.'[1] Pictures of a team of four horses in a wagon must have been very popular during this period. William Groom of Claydon has a painting of a similar subject done by a village artist: it dates from early last century and is valued as a family heirloom. The horse, Boxer, in Julian's team was a son of Smith's Horse of Parham and a direct descendant of Crisp's Horse of Ufford. He must still hold the long-service record above all Suffolk stallions: he *travelled* for twenty-five seasons before retiring.

Another recognised implement for restraining a restless horse while he was being treated was the *twitch*. This was a simple device— a holed stick and a looped cord. The loop was placed round the horse's lip, or even the ear, and twisted until it was tight, holding the horse in the same way as a ring through the nose holds a bull.

The show-horse often had special items of equipment associated with the special nature of his task—which was to look convincing and to show brisk action immediately when called upon to do so. Herman Biddell has revealed how a special bridle was made for a famous horse to correct a fault that would have lost him marks in the show ring. The horse was Manchester Boxer 298, father of Catlin's Duke 296: 'He was a good reddish chesnut, but his ears were so bad, so drooped, that old Row had a special bridle made to keep them up, which so altered his appearance that as soon as the new invention was put in practice he became quite a different horse to look at.'[2] Another showhorse device, used in at least one stud, was a *mask* or hood made of leather. This was fitted on to a horse's head while he was in the horselines prior to going into the show-ring. The mask completely blinded him. But when it was taken off just before he was led into the ring, his eyes were full and staring, giving him that animated look the judges like to see in competing horses. In the same stud a *neck-band* of padded leather, weighted underneath with lead shot, was kept tied under the jaw and over the crest of a horse that 'was a bit thick in the *glands*' in an attempt to correct this fault.

At horse-sales and horse-dealers' stables one implement was con-

[1] *S.H.S.B.*, Vol 1, p. 616.   [2] *S.H.S.B.*, *Vol.* 1, p. 647.

stantly seen years ago; though it is rarely used today. This is a *measuring stick* for measuring a horse's height. In appearance it is like a thick walking stick; and in fact it was used for this purpose, but in the shaft of the stick is concealed a steel rod with a short steel arm hinged to its top. The rod is taken out, thus extending the stick; and, the small arm resting horizontally on the horse's withers, the height in hands is read off on the gradations marked on the steel rod.

There are a number of items linked with the doctoring of a horse. Most physic is administered to a horse in the form of a ball. The ball is introduced direct into the back of his throat, and he has little choice but to swallow it. Some 'vets' used a *gagging-* or *balling-iron*—an iron frame to keep the horse's mouth open—while the ball was shot into the throat with the *physic gun*. The old type of horseman, however, rarely used this apparatus. He gave a horse the physic ball by the following method: he first held the horse's tongue out at the side of the mouth and then, taking the ball between his first two fingers of his other hand, he deftly slipped it into the gullet. One horseman was very scathing about the use of physic guns: 'I once see a vet use a gun and show up the real fault of it. It stands to reason if you shoot something hard against the back of a horse's throat, it will bounce back. It's bound to. That's what was happening with this chap; and there were about half-a-dozen balls on the floor of the stall before he left off. Then I did it in the old way. I got a pliable hazel-twig; stuck a ball at the end of it, and with my fingers on top, bent it so it went right round the corner and into the horse's gullet.'

A method of drenching a horse commonly used in Suffolk farms was as follows: The horseman threw a looped rope across an overhead beam in the stable. He then placed the loop in the horse's mouth, getting someone to pull the free end of the rope. As the horse's head was pulled up he dropped his lower jaw, and made it comparatively easy for the horseman to pour the drench down his throat. The bottle containing the drench was made of tin.

The 'vet' occasionally had to use a file on a young horse with a *wolf's tooth*. This is a second tooth which instead of growing under the primary, middle tooth pushes its way out at the side. It cuts the horse's cheek; makes eating difficult and therefore causes him to go thin. A horseman described how a 'vet' filed down a *wolf's tooth*, dipping the file now and then into a bucket of water, which he had beside him, to keep the file cool.

Under his *December Husbandry* Tusser wrote:

> *Ere Christmas be passed let horse be let blood*
> *for many a purpose, it doth them much good.*
> *The day of St Stephen, old fathers did use,*
> *if that do mislike thee some other day use.*

Blood-letting has fallen out of use long ago, but some of the implements connected with this practice are occasionally discovered in out-of-the-way villages in the county. One of these is a *fleam*, a kind of knife for opening a horse's vein. Allan Jobson had a specimen, along with the small hammer with which it was used, in his collection of tools at the village of Westleton.

The two verses which follow the above passage from Tusser show how baiting the horses of the farm and the proper measuring of their corn from the granary was equally important in his day:

> *Look well to thy horses in stable thou must*
> *that hay be not foisty, nor chaff full of dust;*
> *Nor stone in their provender, feather, nor clots*
> *nor fed with green peason for breeding of bots.*
>
> *Some horsekeeper lasheth out provender so,*
> *Some Gillian spend-all, so often doth go*
> *For hogs-meat and hens-meat, for that and for this,*
> *that corn-loft is emptied, ere chapman hath his.*

An inventory[1] of the 'Implements of howsehould and husbondry late of Arthure Coke of Bramfeild in the County of Suff. Esquyor deceased' (made in 1629) shows how important and ubiquitous horse-gear was in those times: items of horse equipment seem to have been scattered all over the house. Among other items there were:

In the Parlor: one payer of newe Spurrs   ijs   od
              a snaffle (bridle)   ?

[1] *Proceedings of the Suffolk Institute of Archaeology*, Vol. xxv (1952) p. 268. Transcript by Francis W. Steer.

ADDITIONAL HORSE GEAR

In the Hall: j leather Sadle for a great horse
& parte of the furniture xxvs o
j pillion (saddle) iijs o

In the Kytching: j pillion cloath iijs iiij
v horse locks (?) v keyes viijs o
ij bytts with bosses vj
j payer of stirrupps viij

In Mister Cokes Chamber:
iij brydles with silver
buckles ?
ij payer of spurrs... ?
& ij nitingales (martingales?) ?

In the Hall Vaunce Ruff (*vaunce* roof or attic)
a woman's sadle vjs o
ould harneis for ij Coach ?
horses

In the Stable Chamber:
j Anvile vjs o
j greate symthes (sic) vice
& j beake iron xxvjs viijd

The scale of Arthur Coke's husbandry may be gathered from the
number of horses and the amount of farm gear:

In the Stable: j stoned Flaunders horse v *li* os. od
j hand barrowe, j Carte roope,
ij Tubbs, j pytchforke & j
brydle vjs vjd

In the Cartehouse:
j Carte, j Cartebooke, j Crud[1]
barrowe (wheelbarrow) and j
Tumbrell iij *li* xvs od
ij payer of Harrowes & j
plough xijs

[1] Also *crudburra*: *A.O.S.*, p. 290.

In an other Stable:

      j Stoned Colt   v *li*   os   od

Before passing to the next section an unorthodox use of a piece of horse-gear, a use once common in Suffolk villages, should be recorded. In the village of Blaxhall at Whitsun, a fair was regularly held in the village inn. Blaxhall Ship Inn Fair took place on Whitsun Wednesday. A club existed with its centre at the inn and the landlord was the treasurer. Members of the club saved up during the year to celebrate the Fair. (An annual outing to the seaside has long ago displaced this occasion). Some of the money saved went in prizes for the various competitions held during the day. One of the most popular of these competitions was *Sneering through a Horse-collar*. *Sneering* is the dialect for making an ugly face; and the best—or the worst?— *sneerer* took the prize. There was at one time a kind of folk tale relating to this game in Suffolk: A curious old lady, seeing the horse-collar hanging up in an unusual position, exclaimed peevishly: 'What's this for? What are they a-dewin' with this here?' She poked her head through the collar and was immediately awarded the prize.

Sneering through a horse-collar was a sport that was not confined to Suffolk. A bill, preserved in the Cambridge Folk Museum, records the Cambridge *Coronation Festival Rustic Sports:* these were held to celebrate the coronation of Queen Victoria and the date was Thursday, 28th June 1838; the place—Midsummer Green, Cambridge. One of the items in the sports was:

'A GRINNING MATCH: or Which is the Ugliest Phiz?

This Match will be contested by men of all ages and all complexions—all description of physiognomy—and every degree of ugliness and beauty—whether short or tall, little or big, lean or fat, young or old, green or grey—and must be performed according to the normal customs on these occasions, exhibiting in Grimaldian excellence and bold relief, the various contortions of the 'Human Face Divine' by peeping through a *Pegasian Cravat*—or as the vulgar would profanely designate it—a Horse's Collar! The party who shall be declared the winner will be rewarded with a bran new pair of

Velveteen Trousers and a New Wipe. The other competitors will be rewarded with a gallon of Sam Moore's regular right-sort, Head-strong, Out and Out, Strong bodied, Ram-Jam, Come-it-strong, Lift-me-up, Knock-me-down, How-d'ye-like-it, Genuine Mid-summer Green Stingo! and a new Hat each.'

Although none of the other Blaxhall competitions is connected with horse-gear, they are included as examples of the way farm workers and their wives enjoyed a *frolic*. *Races* were a prominent part of the fair. These were held on the road outside the inn and the distances were: one mile, a half and a quarter of a mile. Trees along the road—some of the old people still remembered which particular trees—marked the starting points; and all the races finished at the inn. The prizes were packets of tea, sweets and beer—as men women and children competed. At one point of the fair it was the tradition for the landlord to go upstairs with a frying pan full of *Hot Ha'pennies*. He scattered these from a window onto a sandy area just in front of the inn door. The antics of the children as they scrambled and tried to pick up the coins were one of the highlights of the day. *Drinking the Hottest Cup of Tea* was a competition reserved for the women. All the leather-tongued gossips competed; but one woman was invariably the winner. She had a *fake*—a trick: just before the contest started she smeared her mouth well with butter. While the women were com-peting the men were *Bowling for Nine-pins* at the back of the inn. Then in the evening the fun continued inside the inn: drinking and *Singing the Old Songs* to the tune of the 'cordion'. Folk songs—many of them connected with the sea—were the chief items. There was also *Stepping* or *Dancing*. *Stepping* has always been a feature of this par-ticular village and it is still practised to a certain extent today. In the old days the boys learned to *step* on two bricks. A great deal of the stepping seems to have been improvised but it also contained the remnants of old dances. One of these was the *Candlestick Dance*: 'You first tucked up your skirts between your legs and you danced backwards and forwards, round and about and over a lighted candle-stick. The tune was *Jack be Nimble, Jack be Quick* played over and over again on the 'cordion'. If you put out the candle you were finished. I learned this dance from my mother. It's a very old dance. The men wore high-heeled boots at that time o' day. They were lovely boots; and they danced to the 'cordion' usually; but if there was anything special on they had a fiddler.'

Priscilla Savage of Blaxhall gave most of the above information and she commented: 'You had to make your own fun at that time. Nobody hardly went out of the village; and it was up to people to make their own enjoyment. Whitsun week was a jolly time. Blaxhall folk used to say: "I like Whitsun Monday (Framlingham Fete), I like Whitsun Tuesday (another local frolic); and o' course I like Whitsun Wednesday; but *damn* Whitsun Thursday!"' It was back to earth, on that day, in the fullest sense of the phrase.

18

Horse Brasses and Other Ornaments

The common explanation for the use of the brass decorations on a horse is that they are survivals from the time when the horse was considered susceptible to the evil influences of witches. The decorations, it is claimed, were amulets or charms to render ineffective the power of the evil eye. As such they undoubtedly have a very ancient origin. These ornaments are mentioned in the Old Testament and received short shrift as superstitions.[1] They were known in pre-Roman times, and in Nubia horse-trappings have been discovered with pieces that were undoubtedly amulets. The crescent, a symbol of the moon, was the most common type of charm associated with horses, and the design survives in the modern commercially manufactured horse-brasses. The horse-shoe, still in common use as a charm—nailed, points uppermost, to buildings—is said to have acquired this use through its approximation to the shape of a crescent. The crescent is an ancient symbol: it was associated with Isis, the Egyptian goddess; and also with Diana, the Roman goddess who was linked with both the moon and with horses. She was also the goddess who presided over child-birth, and Roman matrons wore a crescent ornament as a charm against evil influences. The circular form of design, a symbol of the sun, also figured in old horse-trappings and is still a common *motif* in modern brasses—the rayed-sun design and derived figures such as the wheel. The heart is also a frequent symbol, said to have been used by the ancient Egyptians to protect a horse's owner.[2]

[1] *Judges*, viii. 21: 'ornaments that were on the camels' necks' (Revised Version: 'crescents or ornaments like the moon').
[2] H. S. Richards, 'Horse Harness Ornaments,' *B.O.H.*, p. 768.

Yet this common desire to attribute an obscure origin and mysterious purpose to the decorations given to a horse seems to override their main purpose which was certainly decoration itself, and a natural love of colour and display. Pomp and wealth have always been associated with the *fine* horse—the war-horse, the coach-horse, the circus-horse and the race-horse—and with these the love of display in decoration has taken various forms. That the heavy horse's decorations became specialised in horse-brasses was probably due to the weight of these extra trappings: an authentic brass-set is very heavy and was worn only on ceremonial occasions,[1] and only a heavy horse, not called upon to show much *action*, was suitable for wearing it. Again, the brasses' durability would commend them to grooms and carters; for, once purchased, they did not need replacing and were, in fact, handed down from father to son as family heirlooms. Conversation with many horsemen in Suffolk has not brought out one statement about the symbolic meaning of horse-brasses; and experience here suggests that decoration was the chief, if not the only, motive for their use. The observations of two horsemen appear to sum up the general attitude:

'Scottish farmers went in for decoration of their horses more than Suffolk farmers did—although we had brasses to a certain extent.'

'We've never heard of any of those beliefs (in brasses as amulets). We know nothing about such superstitions here.'

From early history, ownership of the horse was the mark of an aristocratic class; and a horse's decorations were a visible sign of the owner's wealth and status. Any ritual significance of the decorations would be secondary to this. This appears to be confirmed by the earliest and most extensive hoard of horse-trappings discovered in Britain. Although there are ninety pieces in the hoard—some functional, such as buckles, terrets and slides; and others decorative—none of these decorative pieces has any resemblance to the ritual amulets described above. One decoration, however, a series of convex, circular discs, marked with concentric rings, is identical with the brass ear-pieces worn by present-day cart-horses; and this design might well have had a symbolic meaning, possibly connected with the sun.

[1] Christina Hole, *English Folklore*, p. 82.

The hoard was discovered in north Wales at Parc-y-meirch (The Park of the Horses), Denbighshire sometime before 1868. It has been dated to the Late Bronze Age—the second phase: 750–400 B.C. The trappings were made of a leaded bronze and were all cast. The finest objects in the collection, now divided between the National Museum of Wales and the Hull Museum, are two sets of circular bronze discs attached to rings. There are six discs in each set. They hung suspended by small loops through which the rings were threaded; and while their main purpose was undoubtedly ornamental, their jingling also served to draw attention to the horse's approach, exactly as do the bells still seen occasionally on the saddles and bridles of cart-horses. Their circular form and the loops or hangers in these discs suggest that they are the prototype of the present-day 'face-brasses' which have long ago lost their function of jingling and making a pleasant noise.[1]

The designs of horse-brasses may be divided into two classes: *pattern brasses* of abstract or geometrical design, and *figure subjects*— the horse itself, for instance, either *rampant*, as often as an heraldic subject, or *passant*, perhaps linked with the cult of the horse that has left its traces in the horses cut into the chalk hillsides of Southern England. The manufacture of horse-brasses is highly commercialised today, and approaching two thousand different designs are known. On this scale the horse-brass is a product of the Industrial Revolution: it is stated[2] that few brasses were made commercially before 1800 and they did not become popular until the accession of Queen Victoria when several new patterns were made to celebrate her Coronation. The old hand-made horse-brass is extremely rare today.

Many of the present-day brasses are made in Birmingham, but one aspect of the industry shows that it has not altogether outgrown the 'hand-made' stage from which it evolved. A recent newspaper article[3] gave an account of an interview with a Birmingham housewife who 'finishes off' horse-brasses that come to her as rough castings from a local foundry. She has been doing this work for forty-two years. Each

[1] T. Sheppard, 'The Parc-y-meirch Hoard,' *Archaeologia Cambrensis*, XCVI, Part 1, June 1941.
[2] H. S. Richards, 'Horse Harness Ornaments,' *B.O.H.*, p. 768.
[3] *The Western Mail*, 22nd November, 1957.

brass is taken through seven different stages of polishing and filing before it is ready for packing—the whole process taking between ten and twenty minutes.

Horses on Suffolk farms wore brasses, both pattern and figured on the head—a *forehead* or *face-brass* hanging between the eyes on a pad of leather—and on the *martingale*. The martingale worn by a heavy

horse is a broad band of leather hanging from the bottom of the collar over the chest and fixed to the belly-band. The strap is ornamented with a number of brasses—three, four or five were the numbers met with in Suffolk: 'You didn't choose the brasses separately. The martingales were usually made up in the harness shop, the brasses already on 'em. You picked the set that took your fancy.'

'On the *necklace*, a strap of about eighteen inches in length lying

on the clean side of the neck—the mane is allus on the right side—
there were a lot of heart-shaped brasses, enough to cover it.

'The *leading-rein* had brass on it, too: it was all covered with brass
studs. The leading-rein was looped round the seals when you were not
using it and left to hang; sometimes there'd be *hounces*[1]—a red tassel
—fixed to the end of the rein. Now and then we'd have a small apron
o' leather, a half-circle in shape with a fringe or a tassel on it. This
was fixed by straps to the back of the collar and stood upright. On
special occasions we had the *swing-gates* or *swingers*—the brasses fixed
between the ears at the top of the dutfin, or on top of the saddle. They
were mostly small face-pieces swinging in a circular frame, or a small
bell with a plume.'

These are often referred to as *flyers* or even *terrets*—but a terret is
properly a rein-ring. *Latten bells* a kind of bell-flyer made from *latten*,
an old type of brass, were once made in sets of four; and each set was
called after the team horse to which it was fitted: the *lead* might have
five bells, *lash* and *body* four, and the *thiller* three. *Ear-pieces* were
decorated, enamel bosses or occasionally a round, cone-shaped brass
like the pieces in the Parc-y-meirch hoard. If a horseman put the
tassels on the leading-rein or the saddle, also the tasselled pad of
leather on the collar, it drew the comment: 'I see he's got his *hounces*
out today.' But the large pad of leather, fastened on to the hames or
collar, is more properly called the *housing*. In dry weather this apron
of leather stood stiffly up; but in wet it lay back on the horse's withers,
thus keeping them dry. Its purpose, therefore, was not entirely decorative. The wool in the housing proper was variously coloured,
chiefly red, yellow, and blue.

'On special occasions we used to decorate the tail with a whitleather thong—pipe-clayed to keep it spruce. You bound up the tail
with the thong, "binding one and leaving one"; so you got an alternate brown and white pattern by binding one width and leaving the
tail show through for the next. Or we sometimes bound up a tail with
three yards of *tail-binding*, red braid about two inches wide, done
tightly and tied at the bottom of the tail so no hair was showing. Then
we bound white and blue braid in alternate strips on this red

[1] *A.F.C.H.*, p. 205.

background. The mane was usually tied up with bast and decorated with ribbon.'

Bung or docked tails were very popular in the early days of the Suffolk horse. John Julian, the early nineteenth century breeder, had a team of four horses, all with *bung'd*[1] tails; but there may have been another reason for this tail-docking in addition to a desire to be in the fashion. E. P. Simkin, a Stowmarket chemist, has a small clothes brush made by a local man who went round the farms collecting horse-hair to make brushes. The brush has been in constant use for thirty years and shows no sign of deterioration, chiefly because the tufts of hair were *wired in* at the back of the brush, in the old hand-made style and not glued as most brushes are today. Horse-hair was once in great demand for brushes, the padding of furniture and so on; and it was also extensively used for binding plaster on walls and ceilings. For instance, Playford churchwardens' account book for May 31st 1821 has: 'Lime and hair. . . . 5s. od.' as one item in a list of expenses incurred for repair-work in the church. There appears to have been more than one way of collecting this hair from the farms. In the Museum of English Rural Life at Reading an old bill, dated 9th May, 1838, is preserved. It advertised a reward for anyone giving information which would lead to the arrest and conviction of 'some evil disposed Person or Persons (who) did, in the Night of Tuesday, the 8th Instant, break open the Stable of Furzefield Farm, in the Parish of Shermanbury (Sussex) in the occupation of Mr *Thomas Page* and maliciously *Cut Off* and carry away THE HAIR from the TAILS OF 3 CART HORSES.' Therefore, tail-docking may have been a matter of policy—of getting the cut in first—rather than a particular desire to conform to a fashion which people like Sir John Cullum had already roundly condemned.

[1] Probably called after the *bung* or stopper in a wooden barrel. The stump of the tail, denuded of hair, resembles this in shape.

Part Four

FOLKLORE CONNECTED WITH THE HORSE

19

Care of the Horse

The traditional lore connected with the horse can be treated under two headings: first, the *care* of the horse and then his *management*. Although the distinction is to a great degree artificial, it is convenient here to deal separately with these two aspects of the traditional material.

Some of the herbs used by horsemen on the farms have already been mentioned. Their use as remedies is undoubtedly very old, and it is likely that the gypsies had a great deal to do with disseminating the traditional knowledge of the use of herbs as horse-medicines. Brian Vesey-Fitzgerald has stated[1] that the best horse-doctor he ever knew was a gypsy; and, in fact, in many parts of Britain—particularly Wales—the gypsy horse-doctor is consulted in preference to the 'vet', even today. Vesey-Fitzgerald has listed a number of the old gypsy herbal remedies for disease in horses, and some of the remedies used by the old horsemen on Suffolk farms were similar. In order to show how extensive the use of herbs was here, a list of those used on one Suffolk farm is given.

The common agrimony was much in use as it kept the horses in condition. It grows on banks and hedges and has little yellow flowers on a long stem or spike. Vesey-Fitzgerald records that agrimony was one of the tried remedies of the gypsy horse-doctor, Stanley, who gave a strong infusion of this herb to cure the fever that sometimes accompanies cracked heels. Burdock was also a favourite herb for conditioning the farm-horses. This is the plant from which country boys take the burs to stick to one another's garments: 'I laughed when

[1] Brian Vesey-Fitzgerald, *Gypsies of Britain*, Chapman & Hall, p. 150.

I saw a man had a bunch of burdock leaves hanging up on his shed to dry. The leaves are not the best part of the plant: it's the roots you got to use. But it wouldn't do to tell him: he'd say: "Dew yew think I don't know my own business!" and he'd stick a swear into you as soon as look at you. Keep it to yourself. Keep it quiet; that's how we used to go on.'

The horsemen used ragwort for the same purpose. But one of the best remedies used on this farm was the leaves of the 'saffron tree':[1] 'There are two kinds of tree—male and female. In the male there is a kind of catkin that sticks up: in the female the catkin hangs down. The female is the one to use. Every time the guv'nor came to the farm—it was an 'off-hand' place—I used to watch the groom who brought him. As soon as the guv'nor had started on his round of the farm, the groom went to one of the saffron trees near the gate and took enough leaves for the week. I tried it on our horses and it were wunnerful stuff. But the trees got blown down in a gale; and I told myself I'd get a couple of those trees and grow them in my own garden. But I looked all over the county and down in Hertfordshire as well but I never did come by a tree like it.'

Elecampane was another of the herbs in frequent use: 'We used it to keep 'em on their feed. After the horses had worked very hard, they'd often have no desire to eat: they were too tired. This herb helped to give them an appetite. It has a long, broad velvety leaf; and it was the leaf we used.' Elecampane is a very old remedy, and not only for horse-sickness. The doctor in the old mummers' play, *Saint George and the Dragon*, used this herb as his cure-all. He comes forward, it will be remembered, when Saint George goes down before the Dragon's uninhibited assault, and he offers to cure the champion of his wound. Father Christmas asks warily: 'What is your fee?' and in one version of the play the doctor replies:

> *Fifteen pounds, it is my fee,*
> *The money to lay down;*
> *But since 'tis such a rogue as he,*
> *I'll cure him for ten pound.*

[1] Probably *sassafras officinale* (*laurus sassafras*) which has medicinal properties.

I have a little bottle of Elicumpane;
Here, Jack, take a little of my flip-flop;
Pour it down thy tip-top;
Rise up and fight again.

George Fox, the Quaker, also favoured the herb when he was imprisoned in the draughty castle of Scarborough in 1665; he said: 'One time when the weather was very cold, and I had taken great cold, I got a little elecampane beer.'[1] His jailers, however, filched it, and he was deprived of its comfort. The herb must be a very strong one as, it will be noticed, *little* is the emphatic word in both cases.

Feather-few or fever-few was another herb used on the same farm: 'It's a plant with leaves that turn yellow and it has a small white flower. We used it for curing colds and giving the horses an appetite.' Culpeper lists the plant and recommends it because it 'purgeth both cold and phlegm'. The horseman used rosemary for taking away all smells: the full significance of this property of the herb will be seen later. 'If you've been *hulking* (disembowelling) a rabbit, just rub your hands in rosemary: it will take away all smells. Besides, it's a real owd cat-charmer. Rub some rosemary on your trousers and all the cats will come brushing against you.' Valerian is reported[2] to be a herb with similar properties.

Celandine was used to clear a horse of worms. 'The plant was dried and fed in the horse's bait. A horseman on one of the farms not very far from ours had some difficulty in getting celandine. So his son brought a plant from another village, and he planted some in his father's garden. When the old man left the farm he gave the plant to me; but he said: "Don't yew tell anybody about it. It wouldn't dew for ma' son to know I'd given it away." '

Horehound was a herb that was much used for 'keeping horses on their feed'. The horseman added: 'One of my mates used to drink horehound every day. He said it kept him in trim.' Horehound was also given for colds in both horses and men. Rue—meadow-rue—was also a herb in constant use: 'It stinks but it's useful herb to have.'

[1] *The Journal of George Fox*, Dent Edition, p. 238.
[2] Reginald Hancock, *Memoirs of A Veterinary Surgeon*, MacGibbon & Kee. See whole of Chapter xiii.

Belladonna, or deadly nightshade, was used for curing a horse with a cough. 'We mixed it up into a thick syrup—an electuary—then we brought the horse's tongue forward, and placed the belladonna right at the back of it with a wooden spoon. When we released the tongue the horse swallowed the medicine.'

Arthur Chaplin recalled how jealously the secrets of cures and conditioning herbs were guarded. His father, Frederick Chaplin (born 1862), was renowned for the beautiful coats his horses always had. They were referred to by his mates as 'owd Fred's mouse-coated ones' because they were as sleek and as silky as a well-fed mouse. 'They allus look tidy,' they said. But one day when Arthur was a young boy, one of the mates was bold enough to ask: 'But how do you get 'em like thet, Fred?' The answer was prompt if rather cryptic: 'Cribbage and time; jes' cribbage and time.' After the man had gone Frederick Chaplin said to his young son: 'Thet will fox him. He'll most likely think I mean the herb.' Thyme was, in fact, used in the old horseman's medicines as one of the constituents of the 'drawing oils' (see later, p. 264); but as Arthur Chaplin explained: 'The answer wasn't altogether bluff. The truth was hidden in it, like it often was with horse matters. It said in other words: "*Crib (steal or acquire) all the food you can for your horses and give them plenty of time to eat it.*" My father was jes' having a knock at those chaps who stayed in bed till the last moment and didn't give their horses enough time for a proper bait before turning out.'

Even when they used roughly the same herbs or remedies the old horsemen's methods of administering them differed. Many ground up the leaves of the plant after it had been dried, and mixed the powder with the horse's chaff: roots also were grated into the bait. Others, however—the more knowing ones—prepared an infusion of the various herbs at home: 'They boiled them up in the copper, just like brewing beer; and they took a bottle at a time to work and sprinkled it on the horses' bait. If something went wrong, and the vet had to examine the stomach afterwards, he'd find nothing there. When the herbs were given this way, no one could put any blame on the horseman.'

Most of the herbs favoured by the old horsemen had the sanction

of generations of successful use, and even in these days of anti-
biotics and other wonder-drugs they are not altogether to be despised.
In fact, medical science may yet get help from an open-minded
appraisal of some of these traditional remedies. To give an example:
long before the discovery of penicillin it was the custom in parts of
southern England to slice up a number of apples each autumn and
then hang them in the attic: 'A rich growth of penicillin-type mould
developed all over the cut surfaces. During the winter months if anyone started a sore throat or signs of fever he would be given one of
these apple-slices to chew.'[1] The writer has come across two instances
in Suffolk where a trivial and seemingly irrelevant condition laid down
for the preparation of old remedies had a sound scientific basis.

A man had a very troublesome ulcer on his leg and it did not respond to treatment. A gypsy, calling at the house by chance, prescribed the herb called house-leak or sengreen, but stated that it
would be no use unless the dried herb was made up into an ointment
using fresh dairy-cream as the base. On another occasion a gypsy
cured a bad case of eczema in a child by prescribing a more-or-less
orthodox ointment; but she enjoined that the ointment must be made
up using *home-made* lard. In both instances no reason was given for
the choice of these fats; but they were specified because with these
there would be no danger of the cures being rendered ineffectual as
often happened, through the use of commercial fats that had been
adulterated, even in the smallest degree, by common salt or other
preservatives.

One cure that was strongly linked with the old horsemen in Suffolk
was the *hoss-iles* or embrocation. A bottle of horse-oils was accounted
a good cure for rheumatism or for a tight chest. 'If you had a cold in
the chest, you rubbed it with *hoss-iles*—they'd soon loosen it up for
you.' The usual ingredients of the oil were: yolk of egg, spirits of
hartshorn and white vinegar. Bryony root as a tonic and a herb to
make the coat shine has already been mentioned. 'It has a big root—
as big as a coconut. It was ground up and mixed with the bait. But
you had to be some careful with it, not to give too much.' Another
similar plant found in the hedges and used for the same purpose was

[1] *Ibid.*, p. 191.

mandrake. According to one recipe the roots were dried, and in the meantime a number of earthworms were procured, placed in a bottle and buried in a muck-heap. After a while the worms turned to 'oil'. This was then mixed with the grated roots of the mandrake: a little of this mixture rubbed on a horse's coat was guaranteed to make it shine as splendidly as the coat of the finest groomed show-horse.

Cummins, or cummin seed, was used as one of the ingredients of a physic ball, with ginger, caraway seeds and 'anise seed' mixed with treacle to give the ball the required consistency. An old farming book[1] states that the horsemen were once very fond of giving the horses sanfoin seed in order to make them fat and make their coats sleek and fine. The seed was much too dear to make a practice of feeding it to the horses; and where it was used, it was probably without the farmer's knowledge. The same source gives a number of herbs and seeds, some with exotic names, as constituents of physic balls: coriander seeds, sweet fennel seeds, grains of Paradice, mithridate, oil of juniper, London philonium and liquorice powder.

Clifford Race, who worked for some years on a stud-farm where Shire horses were bred, contributed two or three old remedies: 'If a horse tended to have a coarse *feather* (the hair on the legs) we wiped the legs down with a paraffin rag. It would make the feather silky for a day or two so someone examining him wouldn't notice the coarseness. The paraffin took the grease away—but only for a spell. It's not got rid of as easy as that. It's probably due to the horse's particular breed. If a stallion has a coarse *feather* it's not a recommendation, as his family is likely to have the same fault. Suffolks don't give trouble with grease, but with Shires we had to be careful. We washed their legs every fortnight; and two days after washing them we dressed the the legs with a special mixture of linseed oil, sulphur and paraffin. We grew our own linseed on this farm, and used it a lot as a cure for colds. The head-groom was very particular about the legs—with Shires you've got to be. The only way to keep them free from grease is to see they're absolutely clean. We had to rub down their legs, getting between the hairs with the tips of the fingers. Every now and then we had

[1] Thomas Potts, *The British Farmer's Cyclopaedia*, 1809. See under 'Artificial Grasses'.

to show our hands to the head-groom: if the finger-nails weren't worn right down to the skin, he knew we weren't a-doing our job properly.'

'We went to this farm at Henley one Michaelmas; and by January all the horses had got *strangles* (a glandular complaint). We didn't try to give them medicines. We turned them all out on the meadows. As they nibbled the bit of grass that was there, their heads right down, all the filth came away from their nostrils. They were in the meadows for a week without nothing to eat except the bit o' grass they could crop for themselves. We saved every one on 'em.'

20

Management: The Whisperers

The management of his horses was a skill in which most of the old horsemen took a great pride. In this as in the grooming of their horses and turning them out for a special occasion there was a great deal of rivalry among farm horsemen: the man who could control his horses in such a way as to compel them to do exactly what he wanted without the least show of effort on his part was held high in honour among his kind. Occasionally the horsemen had a chance to try their skill one against the other in informal contest such as the following:

'Arthur Chaplin's father was with a number of other horsemen in The Crown at Stowupland—this was well before the First War, more like the end of the last century—and they were arguing about who had the best control of their horses. To settle it they took the horses out of the shafts of the wagons and tumbrils and so on, and decided to have a kind of trial outside on the road. Frederick Chaplin happened to have a horse in a tumbril: he took him out of the shafts, and sent him away up the road as though he were a-sending him hoom without his cart. Then he stopped him with a whistle, and with another whistle got him to come right back. Then he did lots of other manoeuvres with him outside the pub, just whistling him to come this way and to go that. After the others had had their turn they got the horses into the pub yard, and put them through their paces there. But that's where the trial finished: one of the horsemen was a-showing how he could back his horse to the inch. Well, he backed him to the inch all right—but it was an inch too far. The horse put his rump through the pub window. It cost them more than the price of a few pints to pay for that!'

The ability to control a horse undoubtedly ran in families, and in-volved—as well as the handing down of secrets—the careful school-ing of the son by the father, both by means of precept and direct example. For example, Arthur Chaplin's grandfather, born during the early part of the nineteenth century, also had a great reputation for his power of control over his horses. When he was a young man he saw an advertisement requesting a leader for a Shire stallion in Essex. Now it had got around the farms that this particular horse was a vicious one, and had in fact killed his previous leader. No one was anxious to apply for the job; but when Chaplin heard about it he looked upon this horse as a challenge. He, therefore, went into Essex and offered his services to the breeder. The breeder agreed to let him try the horse but warned him that as soon as he opened the door of his box the horse would come out at him. Chaplin thought about this, and before he approached the stable he put on a long, white shep-herd's smock. He waited till dusk then went to the stable and opened the door suddenly. As soon as the horse saw the unexpected white figure before the doorway he backed away, momentarily puzzled and suspicious. Chaplin immediately followed up his advan-tage by dropping on to all fours and boldly crawling towards the stallion that was now retreating towards the other corner of the box. And his initial shock tactics were successful: he gained control of the horse, and retained it by ringing the changes on all the tricks he had learned at home. He travelled successfully with the horse for a season and then returned into Suffolk.

Some time afterwards a farmer in his home district near Stowup-land 'sent his son to Barnum and Bailey's circus or menagerie to learn all about horses'. He paid £50 for the privilege. But after he had been back at the farm for some time he admitted quite freely that 'owd Fred Chaplin was still some bit in front on him'.

In the Barking district of Suffolk, one horseman whose name was Moore is remembered for his outstanding ability to control his horses by means of the whistle; and they used to respond to his whistling like sheep-dogs. He had only to whistle in a certain manner as he went down the lane to the field where the horses were grazing for them to be at the gate waiting for him. Two instances have also been recorded in this area of a horse that had been trained to enter a public house at a whistle from his master, to drink a proffered glass of beer, and then to back out at the word of command to the position outside the door where he had first been halted. But this latter trick was a pub-parlour exhibition once practised in various country districts. The nearest approach to the trick the writer has seen was a donkey drinking stout. But the donkey was too fastidious, or merely unwilling, to enter the bar; and the drink had to be brought to him outside on the pavement.

The control of a farm-horse by the horseman's cracking of a whip above his own head in the manner of the circus ring was also exhibited by an occasional horseman to satisfy his vanity and to enhance his reputation for control; and the various tricks in the field—leaving his two horses plough without touching the *cords*, or even releasing the handles of the plough—were all part of that emulation between the leading horsemen in a district. All these skills were the result of 'use' and long training and, like the schooling of horses which perform in the ring, are remarkable only for the endless patience, the compact understanding between the horse and his master, that lies behind the performance.

Yet in the folklore of the countryside it is not the straight-forward methods of training that are most noteworthy but the semi-magical control over horses said to have been possessed by a class of men known in many areas—but not, as far as is known, in Suffolk—as the 'whisperers'. They are so called from their alleged practice of whispering a few ritual and magic words to the horse they wish to control. The exploits of some of the more famous whisperers have been written down. As long ago as 1648 it was recorded that a Sussex horseman, John Young, had the art of controlling horses by means of the whisper; but the most famous whisperer is probably James Sullivan, an Irishman who was born towards the end of the eighteenth century;[1] 'James Sullivan of Cork, a horse-breaker was an ignorant, awkward rustic of the lowest class. He gained the singular epithet of Whisperer by an extraordinary art of controlling in a secret manner and taming into the most submissive and tractable dis-

[1] *Miles's Modern Practical Farriery*, quoting 'The Horse', Youatt, 1843.

position, any horse or mare that was notoriously vicious and obstinate. He practised his skill in private and without any apparent forcible means. In the short space of half an hour, his magical influence would bring into perfect submission and good temper even a colt that had never been handled; and the effect, though instantaneously produced, was generally durable. When employed to tame an outrageous animal, he directed the stable, in which the object of his experiment was placed, to be shut, with the orders not to open the door until a signal was given. After a *tête-à-tête* between him and the horse during which little or no bustle was heard, the signal was made; and on opening the door the horse was found lying down, and the man by his side playing familiarly with him, like a child with a puppy dog. From that time he was found perfectly willing to submit to any discipline, however repugnant to his nature before. . . . I observed that the animal seemed afraid whenever Sullivan either spoke or looked at him. . . . He seemed to possess an instinctive power of inspiring awe, the result perhaps of a natural intrepidity, in which I believe the greater part of the art consisted.

'A faculty like this would have, in other hands, made a fortune; but Sullivan preferred to remain in Ireland.'

Sullivan's best known exploit was his taming of *King Pippin*, a notoriously vicious horse, at the Curragh in 1804. A man who had offered to put on his bridle had been seized by the horse and shaken like a terrier shaking a rat. He was saved only by the amount of clothes he had on his back. It appears that it was the custom of the Irish peasant to show off his wardrobe on occasions such as this, and if he had three coats he put them all on. After this incident they sent for Sullivan to subdue the horse. He shut himself up with him all night, and in the morning the horse was following him about the course like a well-trained dog. He won a race at the same meeting, and remained docile for three years. At the end of this period his bad habits returned; he killed a man and was destroyed. Sullivan claimed that his secret came from a soldier he had once befriended. He was bound by oath never to reveal the secret told to him by the soldier. Whatever the secret was it was thought to have died with him, for although his son pretended to some knowledge of it, he did not in fact possess the *charm*. Sullivan, it is reported,[1] died about 1810, having considerably shortened his life by whisky drinking.

Jumper, a Yorkshireman, also became well known for his ability to control a horse by merely whispering into his ear; and Herman Biddell mentions a man of similar reputation who had taken to giving exhibitions in London:[2] 'Barthropp's Hero 88 never was a pretty horse. . . . In temper he was a brute, killed one man, kicked the end out a horse box or two, and was sent up to London on foot to make an exhibition before one of Mr Rarey's[3] audiences, when that clever horse-breaker was performing his wonderful feats in the metropolis.'

The power of the 'whisper', whatever it was, appears to have been

real and numerous attempts have been made to explain it rationally. Among the latest to demonstrate a remarkable control over animals, a power analogous to that said to have been possessed by the old whisperers, is Mrs Barbara Woodhouse: it is worth noting that she obtained her secret—probably as Sullivan's soldier had done—from a primitive source. This is her account of it:[4]

'I used to live in the Argentine, on a lonely cattle *estancia* 100 miles from my nearest English neighbour. I spent my time breaking the wild horses from the herd of 6,000 on that *estancia*. Whilst doing this

[1] *Notes and Queries*, Vol. 185, p. 54.
[2] *S.H.S.B.*, Vol. 1, p. 653.
[3] J. S. Rarey, an American who visited this country in 1859. *See Haydn's Dictionary of Dates*, Ward Lock, 1904, p. 614.
[4] 'Talking to Animals,' *Observer*, 3rd January, 1954; see also a book by the same author: *Talking to Animals*, Faber and Faber, 1954.

one day I met a very old "Guaranee" Indian, of which tribe there are very few left now. I stopped to talk to him about the beautiful little mare he was riding, and he told me that his tribe do not have to break in their horses the way we do; they just catch them with a lasso, and then stand near them, with their hands behind their backs, and blow gently down their nostrils. The horse understands this as "How do you do?" in its own language, and returns the greeting by approaching the human being and sniffing up his nose. From that moment the horse has no further fear, and the breaking in is simply a matter of showing the horse what you want.

'I tried this simple trick on a horse that was a killer; three men had lost their lives trying to master her, and I bought her for 15s. It worked. She stopped trembling and came slowly up to me as I blew down my nostrils, whilst standing quite still in the corral where she had been penned for me. She raised her head until her nose touched mine. I blew gently up her nose and then put my hand out to caress her. She never moved. I fondled her ears and her neck and then stroked her all over. I went to the house for my saddle and bridle and saddled her up. She stood quite still; I mounted her and away we went. I never want a more glorious creature. Years later I brought her home to England and she was put down in the war, after having been the most faithful mount of myself and my children.

'This trick I employed on all the future horses I broke out there, and I used to reckon to get a horse going nicely, having never previously been handled, in two hours.'[1]

Mrs Woodhouse's experiences may well have a bearing on the 'power of the whisper', and the method may have been used in this country in earlier times. Charles Dickens appears to be describing it in one of his novels: 'We got out; and leaving him to hold the pony, went into a long low parlour looking towards the street, from the window of which I caught a glimpse, as I went in, of Uriah Heep breathing into the pony's nostrils, and immediately covering them with his hand, as if he were putting some spell upon him.'[2]

Part of the background of this novel, *David Copperfield*, is said to

[1] See also William Youatt, *The Horse*, 1853 edition, note on pp. 443-4.
[2] *David Copperfield*, Chap. XV.

be East Anglia; and at first glance Mrs Woodhouse's method would seem to have some importance for any inquiry into the methods of the 'whisperers' who have operated in Suffolk within fairly recent times. (It must be emphasised again that the writer has not heard the term 'whisperers' in relation to these experts, but the term is kept merely for convenience of reference). But it is likely that neither the real methods or true antecedents of the Suffolk 'whisperers' lie in the direction indicated above. To discover these it will be necessary to go very much further back into history.

21

The Society of Horsemen or Ploughmen

Undoubtedly the whisperers were connected with, or had access to the secrets of, a very ancient order or society of horsemen that was in existence up to the late nineteenth century here in East Anglia. Oral evidence in the Stowmarket area of Suffolk is sufficient to suggest that such a society existed here and that they held regular meetings in Ipswich. But owing to the secrecy surrounding the whole organisation, details are very hard to come by; yet correlation of oral evidence and an examination of some of the practices of the old horsemen in this district show that it must have once existed in a fairly complete form. All this will be discussed later; but to clear the ground it would be as well to outline the form of the old horsemen's society as far as it is known; to define its purpose and to determine, as far as possible, its origins.

The horseman's society appears to have had its most characteristic form and to have lasted until most recent times in the agricultural districts of Scotland. Here it was called *The Horsemen Society* or *Society of the Horseman's Word*. Thomas Davidson, in an informative article[1] in a recent issue of a folklore journal, has given a summary of the Scottish evidence. The Society's main functions were to admit into its fraternity the farm-workers who had acquired the skills of their trade; and, after the initiation ceremony, to share with him the trade's secrets and to pass to him certain closely guarded oaths and passwords. Such craft societies or trade organisations were once common in England, and there is a strong likelihood, as Lewis Spence suggests,[2] that they had their origin in Romano-British times

[1] *Gwerin*, Vol. 2, 1956, Blackwell, Oxford.
[2] *Myth and Ritual in Dance, Game and Rhyme*, p. 158.

and stem from the Roman institution of the trade society 'founded on
the worship or patronage of some god appropriate to the predilections
of the craft which they followed.' Spence says of the Society of Horsemen in north east Scotland:[1] 'Down to the close of the last century
the brotherhood held secret initiations in barns at midnight with a
good deal of "horse-play", the "altar" being a sack of corn. The
initiate who was blind-folded had a "grip o' the auld chiel's hand", a
stick covered with hairy skin. "The auld chiel" is most obviously an
euphemism for some debased deity, probably confounded in later
times with that ubiquitous form "the devil" who succeeded and
absorbed a whole pantheon of ancient divinities. The neophyte was
then invested with "the horseman's word" which there is no harm
in revealing as "Both in one",[2] alluding to the harmony which was
supposed to exist between man and horse. This word, it was held,
could arrest a horse in the road so that no man could make him
budge.'

The similarity of this *reist* (or arrest) word to the alleged magic word
of the 'whisperer' will already have become apparent. But if it would
seem strange that such an ancient craft brotherhood with all its
suggestion of magic and mysticism, symbolism and secrecy, should
have survived in Britain right into modern times, one can point out
its correspondence in at least some of its aspects with the Freemasons
and, on a different level, with some of the Friendly Societies. All
these appear from the outside to have this leaning towards the esoteric,
and even the occult; and in this connection a High Churchman friend
of the writer's has stated that he did not know what the word ritual
meant until he attended a meeting of one of these semi-secret
societies.

In the same article Thomas Davidson has stated that there was a
class of horse charmers known in the Ely and Peterborough districts
until quite recently. These were known as *Toadmen*. A *toadman* was
accounted a kind of witch—male witches were common at one time
—and got his name from the ritual in which a toad or a frog was in-

[1] *Ibid.*
[2] *sic iubeo*—Thus I command thee—in the Fen districts of Cambridgeshire. *Folklore*, Vol. 69, June 1958. 'Some Folk Beliefs of the
Fens,' Enid M. Porter.

volved. Evidence of some of these practices have been found in the Stowmarket area of Suffolk. But before discussing these it would be well to ask: what was the ritual of the toad or frog's bone, and what was its purpose? The ritual is a primitive survival that is, or was, practised in countries as far apart as Scotland and India. As described to the writer by an old horseman living in the Stowmarket area, to obtain the power of the frog's bone one had to perform the following ritual: 'You get a frog and take it to a running stream at midnight, but before this you have killed it and pounded it up. You throw it into the water and some of it will flow downstream, but a part of it—a bone—will float upstream. This is the part you have to keep.'

More evidence from a village in the same district has shown that the village wart-charmer is believed to have gained his powers in this way. He followed the ritual of the frog's bone: 'He took a frog to running water at midnight and he sold his soul to the devil, and now he has the power to cure warts'. Many Suffolk villages still have wart-charmers, operating more or less openly, or more frequently only within a small circle of the 'accepted folk' in the village. But only in this one instance has the writer come across the ritual of the frog's bone associated with wart-charming.

Thomas Davidson has recorded instances of identical practices in the Cottenham district of Cambridgeshire and in parts of Cornwall. Possession of the frog's bone was believed to give a horseman absolute power over the most intractable horse that came into his care. 'With the frog's boon,' said one horseman in this district of Suffolk, 'you could do anything you like with a horse; take him upstairs if you wanted to.'

But which bone of the frog was the one preferred? The bone can be identified without much doubt both from descriptions given here: 'It was like a chicken's wish-bone in shape: my father used to keep it in his trousers pocket' (an old Suffolk horseman is the narrator), and from a passage in a book describing a piece of Indian folklore.[1] In India the frog was wrapped in a piece of white linen and given astrological benedictions. It was then put on an ant hill at sunset. The ants ate the flesh and left the bones, and two bones were then

[1] Sudhin N. Ghose, *The Flame of the Forest*, Michael Joseph, p. 151.

kept. One of these was to hook the object desired—the lover in this case; the other to reject him. This latter bone was called the shovel, and is probably the supra-scapula of the frog. The *hook* or wishbone—the bone kept by the horsemen here—is without much doubt the ilium, the chief bone in the frog's pelvic girdle. Another horseman from this area of Suffolk has given the pith of the matter in an observation: 'The frog's boon was the same shape as the frog in a horse's hoof'; and if there were any doubt about the identity of the particular bone used by the old horsemen, this similarity would appear to dispel it. For the ilium of a frog is, in fact, identical in shape to the V-shaped horny, elastic substance in the middle of the sole of a horse's hoof; and moreover the identity of name points strongly to the principle of

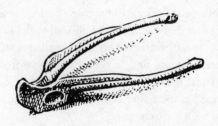

magic under which the frog's bone was supposed to operate. Frazer's first principle of homeopathic or imitative magic is operating here in at least two of its aspects: like has control over like; an object of particular shape once possessed by a man gives him the power of control over a similarly shaped object he desires very much to influence. The horseman has the frog's bone, therefore he can control the frog on the hoof: in other words, he can stop or release the horse at will. The second aspect of magic involved is this: by the possession of the bones of a dead animal, one can render another animal as immobile as death, until you wish to release him.

The ilium, it may be stated, is also roughly the shape of a boomerang; and one wonders whether this peculiar shape caused it to behave differently from the other bones when they were thrown into the stream. Is it too fantastic to suppose that its shape would carry it into an eddy, out of the mainstream, where it would revolve while the other bones were carried downstream? Only actual experiment would throw light on this; and this the present writer has not attempted.

By this time, the reader is no doubt saying: 'Where is all this farrago of superstitious nonsense taking us?' or he may be ready to make the ultimate gesture of criticism—to close the book at this particular point with an unanswerable and inexorable snap. If he has this impulse he is asked, most politely, to hold his fire and impatience; for there is in this belief of the frog's bone, as there is in most primitive beliefs, very much more underneath than appears manifest on the surface: an iceberg-like proportion of the belief, in fact its real substance, is well out of sight. This, the kernel of the belief, was the justification for all the secrecy of the old horsemen's societies—the *arcana* that it was vital for them to preserve intact and to pass on only to the initiated and the well-affected.

But before going on to discuss these secrets and how they were applied by horsemen here in Suffolk, and before proceeding to uncover the results of the present efforts to make sense of these primitive and seemingly fantastic practices, one observation should be made concerning the frog's bone. Even if it were used merely as a *charm*, its cherishing by the old horsemen would seem to be justified on this ground alone. Many times during the last war, to give an example, pilots of operational aircraft went on flights with the most curious charms one could imagine. Occasionally a member of the ground-crew had to return a child's teddy-bear or a toy dog to a pilot who had inadvertently left it in the cockpit after coming back from an operation. No comment was made at the strangeness of the mascot: the practice was accepted. For it was held, even though it was seldom openly stated, that where a man's fate hung on chance he would be flying in the face of chance if he made no effort to propitiate it. In the same way, a horseman who had to deal with a killer stallion was better able to gain control if he had the fertile suggestion in his pocket, in the shape of the frog's bone, that he could not but succeed in his task. For it has been said that no animal can sense better than a horse any nervous tension in a person who is approaching him. Nervous tension is rightly interpreted as fear by the horse; and fear begets fear and trouble is bound to follow. (Is the breathing-down-the-nose device a recognition of this? It is impossible to have full muscular tension while breathing thus.) The use of the charm is in one sense a recognition of what psychologists agree is a fact: that there is a large area of the mind that is not directly and easily accessible to reason: this is particularly true when, as in the primitive mind, reasoning is often faulty. Therefore a charm such as the horseman carried had to a certain extent a pragmatic sanction: it was used because it appeared to work—not perhaps as it was supposed to: directly on the object; but through giving confidence to the wearer and suggesting to him that he was full master of the situation in which he was about to engage. But there was very much more to the frog's bone than this—at least as it was used by horsemen, certain horsemen, here in Suffolk. In the following chapter the active principle that underlay its use will be shown, and in addition the true substance of the supposedly magical power of 'the word' or 'the whisper'.

22

The Search for the Horseman's Word

In his search for the principle behind the nexus of beliefs known
variously as the *whisper* or the *power of the horseman's word* the
writer stumbled by accident across a seemingly irrelevant fact
which proved to be the first step in a direction that ultimately led to
what is claimed to be the real centre, the holy-of-holies, of the old
horsemen's practices. The incident was this: in a small Suffolk village
a woman mentioned to another in the sort of conversation women have
in an environment where new topics of interest are rare: 'That's the
duttiest (dirtiest) house in the village! The horseman at X Farm can't
get his hosses past it. Every time he goes that way he very nigh has to
drag them past the door.' This incident lay dormant at the back of
the mind for some time and then a somewhat similar observation
brought it forward again: 'The owd hoss were all right when they
mucked out the cows with him; but you should ha' seen him when
they tried to get him to muck out the pigs! He wouldn't play at all.
He kicked and he snorted, very near tipped the cart up, and he *runned*
(ran after) the hossman, cart an' all, right across the yard. As soon as
we took him away from the pigs he were as quiet as his usual self.'
The next link came when a farm-worker mentioned that he dare not
hang a dead rabbit on the tumbril when it was drawn by one or two of
his horses. With some it was all right; but an occasional horse would
shy and refuse to draw the cart until the dead rabbit had been taken
away.

The obvious, and in itself quite undramatic, inference from these
incidents is that a horse has a very keen sense of smell.[1] But the pos-
sibilities of this hyper-developed sense in a horse and its importance

[1] cf. *Job*, xxxix, 25; 'he (the horse) smelleth the battle afar off'.

for our inquiry were not fully realised until a meeting with an old horseman in the Halesworth area of Suffolk—Walter Lovett (born 1878) of Bramfield. It was plain that he had never been in the inner circle of horsemen in the district: he did not have the *know*, or the *Word* as it was called in Scotland; but, when asked about some of the seemingly magical powers claimed by the older teamsters when he was a young man at the end of the last century, he related what proved to be a germinal incident in the search:

'I heard tell that two carters once called at The Wherry Inn in Halesworth for the usual snack and drink and bait for the horses. They put up the horses in the stable and then went into the pub. After they'd had a couple of drinks, one said to the other:

' "Shall we have another?"

' "No, I reckon we'd better see to the horses."

'But when they went to the stables they couldn't budge the horses from their stalls. They pulled and they cussed and they swore, but the horses wouldn't move an inch. After they tried for a quarter of an hour or so, an old man who happened to be in the yard said to 'em: "What's the matter on 'em? Won't they come out?—I can fix thet." He may have been the one who done it—mind you, I don't know. But he went inside the pub, and in a minute or two he came out with a jug of milk. He got this jug and put it above the lintel of the stable door and after a minute or two he say: "It's all right: you cin take 'em out now." And sure enough they led the horses out of the door without any trouble at all.' No explanation was given: no explanation was asked for at this stage; for it had become obvious that the horses' acute sense of smell was involved here without question: because milk has the property of absorbing any obnoxious or strong smell arising anywhere near it.

From this point onwards the search, instead of being a rather futile and frustrated groping about in the half-light of primitive fantasy and magic, became a consciously determined drive to get at the centre of the whole tangled system of horse-beliefs. The man who had wilfully caused the horses to refuse to come out of their stalls had used a substance that was so aggressive to their sense of smell that it was impossible to get them to cross the threshold of the stable. Such was the hypothesis at this stage. But what was the substance and where had the trickster placed it? These questions were not answered until later; but now, having an hypothesis, it was possible to work systematically towards its confirmation—or its rebuttal; to the stage where all the questions would answer or cancel themselves.

But at this point came support for the theory that the horse's sense of smell is more highly developed than is ordinarily realised. A brief inquiry into the steps in the evolution of the horse shows that at one stage of its evolution the development of a keen sense of smell was very important to its survival. When the horse was in the wild state, chiefly a plains dweller relying for his food on grass and plants near the ground, he had no protection against his enemies except his speed and his ability to apprehend danger as soon as it was in the vicinity. The horses with the best eye-sight and the keenest sense of smell, those best equipped for seeing and scenting the approach of an enemy, were most likely to survive. Therefore through the first stages of its development the head of the horse tended to lengthen: the eyes were then further off the ground, making better instruments of detection while the horse was grazing, and the nostrils had also lengthened giving him the optimum sense of smell. For this depends on the thousands of small nerves that line the nasal passages: and to increase the surface of the nostrils meant to improve the power to smell. It is part of our thesis that this hyper-acute sense of smell has survived the horse's domestication.

The next step was a discussion of the old horseman's practices with a farmer of the old school. He had never been a horseman himself, yet he had been a keen observer of their activities all his life; and he had his own theory about the way they got their seemingly magical results. The *reist* word, 'the whisper between the collar and the hames' to stop a horse and keep him on a spot until the horseman—and no other— wished to move him, was given a new meaning by conversation with this old farmer. But it is likely that this information would not have been given had he not realised that the questioner was already at the threshold of the truth before he talked with him. His first illustration showed that the hypothesis formed above was not far wrong:

'These owd horsemen, you couldn't tell 'em anything; and they'd never tell you! I seen one of 'em put a stick up in a field in front of his pair of horses, and they wouldn't budge from where they were for anybody. The horseman could go off to Ipswich and they'd still be there when he come back.'

After this the writer related to him the story told him by a horseman from a different part of the county. This was the story: 'They had about a hundred horses at .... Hall the time I'm telling you about. A man who was working up there got wrong with 'em over something or other—I don't know what happened. Anyhow he got the sack. But thet night he went up and did something to the horses. Next day not one on 'em would go near the harness. No one could do anything with 'em. In the end they had to fetch that man back for him to put it right. No one ever knew how he did it. He went in and locked the stable doors. But not long afterwards they harnessed the horses and they came out as if nothing had happened.'

The old farmer's comment was direct and to the point:

'I reckon the fellow who got the sack didn't do anything to the horses. He put something on the harness, you ma' depend. They wouldn't go near the harness because of it. When they had him back he wiped it off or put something else on it to take the smell away. But he'd make sure they wouldn't see him a-doing of it. I reckon it's the same sort of thing as when a horse won't come out of a stable. The horsemen put something on the doorpost—something that a horse couldn't bear the smell of, and wouldn't shift to go near it.'

To illustrate his theory he told another story which fitted in with the writer's, formed not long after he had heard the original story of the old man and the jug of milk:

'A horseman brought three fine horses into a Suffolk town on market day and stabled them and baited them at an inn. The stableman happened to say to him: "You got three fine horses there, bor."

' "Yes," he say, "and I know right well how to handle 'em." Now the stableman wanted to finish early that afternoon, and to do this he needed to move these three horses to a stable in another part of the yard. So after a while they decided to change the horses' stalls. But when they tried, the horses wouldn't move an inch. Then one man who was more in the know than the rest said:

' "I know the way to shift 'em!"

'And he did. He got a bottle of vinegar; poured some in his hand and smeared the muzzle of each horse with this as he moved him from his stall. The horse couldn't smell nothing else when he did this; and they got 'em all out without any trouble.'

The same man gave another facet of the old horsemen's activities, still observed—it may be noted—from the outside:

'The horsemen would never tell you their secrets. But if you listened and watched, kept your ears and your eyes open, you could put two and two together. I was in a pub in Stowmarket once; and I got to know a bit of their business. There were a couple of men talking about some stuff to give the horses, and a third man who was listening said: "If the stuff cin do thet, I'll go out and git some from the chemist's." But when he came back he said he'd been to every chemist in the town and none of 'em had got it. "Give me a pint," said one of the men, "and I'll go out and git if for you." He returned with the stuff within five minutes. You see, the chemist wouldn't give it to anyone, only a man they knew—one of the regular horsemen.'

The old horsemen would not allow anybody to take liberties or impinge on what they considered to be their craft preserves; and they were fond of putting the uninitiated in their place. The following incident is typical of a number related to the writer: 'The stockman on a farm said to one of the horsemen: "I'm going to take one of your horses into Stowmarket early tomorrow: I'll take him afore you git back from breakfast, so you don't want to bother." The next morning the horseman fed the horses at his usual time and went home for breakfast. When he returned the horse was still there.

' "What's the matter with him?" the stockman asked in despair; "he won't come out!"

' "Won't come out," said the horseman, "'course he will!" And with a word he led the horse out of the stable.'

One thing was very soon established: only a very small proportion of horsemen during the last half-century were in possession of *the know*, as one old farm-worker referred to the secrets of his craft. The horsemen who had it, guarded *the know* jealously and would pass it on to no one: least of all to those who were working on the same farm. One horseman revealed this at a very early stage in the search, and at the same time confirmed that some 'stuff' or substance was in fact used when, at this point, only a very tentative theory had been formed about the real nature of the 'magical practices'. On being asked about the horseman's strange power to control horses at a distance, when the horseman was not actually present himself he said:

'Some used it, but I never used a piece of the stuff in my life. I always managed my business without any of it. Someone tried it on me once, but I knew enough to get out of that!' And to the further question: 'What did you use?' he replied with a twinkle in his eye: 'Only a drop of water—just cold water.' The incident could be reconstructed when later more was known about such happenings. Probably a fellow-horseman had placed some of the 'stuff' on the doorpost of the stable thus preventing him bringing out his horses. But although he was not in possession of the full secrets, he knew enough to wash down the woodwork before attempting to force his horses out of the stable.

One horseman in the Stonham Aspal district told of a similar incident: A horse-dealer or jobber had sold two of his geldings. The head groom told one of the men in the stables: 'These two horses are going away tomorrow, and I'm not a-taking them. But the man who is, will have to wait till I get here afore he takes 'em out.' But the man who took the horses the next morning did not wait. He harnessed them up and brought them out of the stable; and he passed the horseman as he was coming out of his cottage. 'Mornin', Bill,' he shouted. But the horseman kept a sullen silence, put down by the other man's knowing quite as much as he did.

One further example will add emphasis to what has already been written about the jealous guarding of precedence among farm horsemen. The incident happened on a farm in the Ipswich area about fifty years ago: 'There were a big chap working on this farm. I believe he were the second horseman, or maybe he were the second's mate: a big, cross-grained fellow. He were one of the Brethren—with God on Sunday and with the devil the rest of the week. He started taking his team out in the morning as soon as he were ready, right out of his turn. No one said nothing at first. Then one morning, one of the baiters said kinda quiet like: "He's not allus a-going to do thet, is he?" The next morning the big fellow had some trouble with his horses. He couldn't get them out of the stalls. He cussed and swore because he couldn't get them harnessed up; and there were the horses, getting into the other horses' stalls as he were laying into 'em. There was a regular rumpus. But all the rest of the men turned out as usual and just left him to manage it as best he could. He niver gave any more trouble after thet.'

The horseman did not go into details about the way the lesson was taught, but from what has already been stated the reader can infer the actual procedure.

These incidents illustrate some aspects of the old farm life that are worth dwelling on briefly. They confirm the impression, already discussed, that only a handful of horsemen, at least within the last fifty years or so, were within the inner brotherhood of the craft; and these possessed the secrets that were held, one supposes, by members of the craft society when it functioned regularly. Confirmation of this came from two particular horsemen who later revealed information that demonstrated that they were outstanding, and held secrets very few horsemen in the district knew of. One of these gave some details about the horsemen's society that used to meet in the town: 'My grandfather used to go to it and the horsemen from Bush Hall, Akenham Hall and Thurleston Hall used to go with him. Both my father and grandfather told me this. There was some sort of ceremony to join, I believe; but it was all before my time (He was born in 1886). They met to have a chin-wag amongst themselves.'

Bits and pieces of evidence collected about this society suggest that many of the secrets—probably the traditional medicines and cures, chiefly—were actually written down. The book was available, so it is reported, for certain horsemen at a cost of £5—a mint of money in the days when the average farm-worker's wages were twelve or fourteen shillings a week. Basil Brown, the Suffolk archaeologist, who once farmed in north Suffolk, has also heard of the existence of this booklet; but he was unable to secure access to the particular copy he knew of. Recently, too, the writer has been informed[1] that the secret of 'The Horseman's Word' has been offered for sale by a man—a ploughman—in Scotland; and this seems to suggest that the Society has broken up even there where it flourished more strongly than in other parts of Britain.

One other aspect is this: the secret of 'the horseman's word' gave certain horsemen a positive economic advantage, and they were very careful not to jeopardise this advantage by giving their secrets away. The more they knew, the more skilled they were, the better they could do their job and the more likely they were to hold it; and in the agricultural depression of the end of the last century and the pre-war years of this, possession of *the know* was a very real advantage indeed. The set-up on some of the farms during these years, as related by the old horsemen, was anything but idyllic; and the description they gave of the rivalry, back-biting and sometimes open malice that existed, even among the men themselves, should be taken into account when there is any impulse to depict the countryside under the old order as a haven of peace and rural contentment. The scene was not as it looked to visitors from the town—the Corydon and Amaryllis seekers—who even now are convinced that the Golden Age is immediately behind us.

But what was the relation of the farmers themselves to the practices of the horsemen? In most cases they appear to have known nothing of them. Like the shepherd the head horseman had a very responsible job. He was usually given a free-hand by the farmer who did not interfere with the actual technique of looking after the horses. As long as he was assured they were treated well and were kept in good condition, he knew that it was best to interfere as little as possible. Certainly, few farmers would belong to the horsemen's society even if they knew of its existence. Some, however, were aware of unorthodox practices and gave out that anyone caught using 'stuff' would immediately be given the sack. But on the whole the farmers were forced to err on the side of trust rather than suspicion; for once a farmer's suspicion became overt the smooth running of his farm would

[1] Personal communication from Mrs Leslie More of Newbridge, Midlothian.

greatly be hindered. The horseman had the 'whip-hand', in more senses than one. The following incident will illustrate this:

'A farmer had a horseman who couldn't pass a pub. So he told the policeman at B.... to look out for him: if he ever saw the horses standing outside a pub, to get the horseman out of it and send him home. One day the policeman saw this farmer's horses standing outside The Fox. He went inside and said to the horseman:

' "You better get back to the farm."

' "Yes, I will: when I'm ready."

' "If you don't get going now I'll take the wagon and the horses back myself."

' "Right. In that case I'll be here till stop-tap!"

'The policeman went out and tried to lead the horses back to the farm. But he couldn't get them to move an inch. He returned to the pub and told the horseman: "I can't shift 'em."

' "No more you will. They'll go when I'm ready," ' and he quietly finished his drink and took the horses home without further trouble.

23

The Frog's Bone

During the search the writer talked with dozens of horsemen up and down the county of Suffolk; and he soon learned to distinguish the ones who were likely to have secrets of the inner-circle of the craft. That this circle was still in existence—if not in formal operation—was apparent to him on one of the first occasions when he talked to a horseman who, he was sure, was more likely to have *the know* than anyone he had so far met. Wishing to indicate that the horsemen's secrets were not entirely unknown to him, and that the revealing of information would not, therefore, be entirely a breach of the craft's secrecy he gave a rather gratuitous explanation of an incident—similar to those already given—where a horse was *reisted*[1] or stopped by apparently magical means. He was immediately met with the sharp challenge: 'Who told you that?'

But in the weeks that followed when the old horseman came to recognise that the questioner's motive was no more sinister than to record the past farm-economy in all its aspects, he became less cautious; and he grew sensible to the argument that while at one time giving his secrets away would have been equivalent to letting someone 'take the bread from his mouth', as one horseman put it, at present, when a full 'horse economy' had gone from the farms, the secrets could be of little material advantage to anybody. Moreover, as there was now no working horseman to pass his secrets to, unless he told them now they would soon go into oblivion.

For at this stage the inquirer was still puzzled by one apparently unassimilable fact. The *reist* phenomenon, the control at a distance, had been explained at least to his own satisfaction; and, judging from

[1] A Scottish dialect word.

the old horseman's reaction when he heard it, his theory was the right one. But how did the frog's bone fit into the picture? When the old horseman was first asked if he had ever come across the frog's bone, he shook his head and said bluntly: 'Never heard of it.' Here was a lesson the questioner should have learned long before this: it is almost useless for a folklorist to ask the direct question—at least in a cold and purely 'informative' atmosphere. The real information comes of its own accord, is nourished by a kind of involuntary flow between the questioner and the questioned; and when the time is ripe it comes unannounced, with all the freshness of a discovery and with the same conviction of rightness that accompanies the poet's inspiration.

So it was with the old horseman. After a number of talks extending over a few months, one winter's evening the true secret of the frog's bone was revealed. But first of all, the searcher had to sit humbly under a mildly astringent and admonitory lecture. The horseman rolled himself a cigarette; trimmed the shreds of tobacco from its ends and threw them into the fire: 'Now look, you've been hearing things! Someone round here has been telling you things about the horseman's business—about stuff and chemicals, the frog's boon and all thet. Well, you don't want to believe half on it. It's someone who's heard a bit of it and is making the rest of it up. Now I'll tell you about the frog's boon. . . .'

At this point the horseman paused to take another shred of tobacco from the end of his cigarette, and the effect was both dramatic and painful. Painful, because the inquirer sensed that here he was about to learn a vital fact that would quicken most of the others; and yet at the same time he knew that in the long seconds that were passing before the old horseman would start to speak again, there was plenty of time for him to change his mind, to gloss over or to retain the information he first intended to impart. But with all the solidity of his kind he kept to his first intention:

'I'll tell you about the frog's boon. First of all not one in ten thousand knows what kind of frog it comes from, or would be able to recognise the boon if they saw it—not one in ten thousand. I knew only one man in this district who had one. The frog you were after wasn't easy to come by: it were a rare kind. It were a black frog with a star on its back; and you'd be most likely to find one in a wood where they'd been a-felling trees. You'd get one, maybe, under an owd felled log or something like thet. After you'd caught it you had to kill it and hang it up on a blackthorn tree to dry. Then you took it down and treated it till it were all broke up and dismembered. Or you could clean it by putting it in an ant hill: the ants would pick all its flesh off the boons. You then took it to a running stream and placed it in the water. Part of it would float upstream; and that's the part you had to keep.'

So far the account was no different from the conventional account of the frog's bone ritual, already given by two other horsemen in the area. But what followed was the crux:

'*When you got the boon you next cured it*. You got umpteen different things and you cured the boon in this mixture. After you had cured it and dried it again, it was ready. You kept it in your pocket until you wanted to use it. *There were no charm about it*. This is how it were used. A farmer would tell a horseman just before "knocking-off" time:

' "There's a load of oil-cake to get from the railway station: will you take the tumbril down and get it?"

' "But my horse is tired: he's been working hard all day."

' "It's not the horse is tired!—But all right: I'll get someone else to do it."

'But when the farmer told another horseman to harness the horse and put him in the tumbril, the horseman found that he wouldn't come out of the stable. What you did was to rub the frog's boon on the horse's shoulder. Then whoever came to fetch him would straightway be in a muddle. The horse would go through the motions of moving but wouldn't shift an inch. To make that horse go you just had to take the frog's boon and rub it lightly on his rump.'

It will be immediately recognised that the potent principle in this, as the old horseman indicated, is not the exotic type of frog, the ritual at the stream, or even the bone itself. All these were incidental. It was the herbs or chemicals in which the bone was *cured* or steeped and the resulting odour with which it became impregnated that had the seemingly magical effect. So, as in the use of 'stuff' on stable-doors, lintels and harness, the deciding factor in the use of the frog's bone was the hyper-sensitive smelling power of the horse. The frog's bone was steeped in substances not detectable by human smell; but they were so aggressive to the sense of smell of the horse that he was as though paralysed when the odour was anywhere near his nostrils. When the bone was rubbed on the horse's rump, the odour coming from somewhere behind he was impelled to move away from it. The frog's bone, it may be mentioned, was used in the incident where the policeman tried to get a horseman out of the inn.

The principle behind the use of the frog's bone is analogous to the one that operated in that other secret *charm* of the old horsemen—the *colt-milt*.[1] The *colt-milt* or *melt* is a small, oval-shaped lump of fibrous matter like the spleen (*milt* is in fact another, older word for spleen). It lies at the back of the colt's tongue when it is in the mare's womb. The old horseman described what happened at a colt's birth:

'When a mare was about to foal, one of the horseman had to set up with her. She usually foaled at night. In the morning the farmer came in to have a look:

' "Well, I see you got a colt. Where you with her when it was born?"

' "Yes, I was here."

' "Where's the milt?"

'Then you took out the milt for him to see. The milt would show you were actually on the spot and not asleep when the colt were born. Because to get the milt you had to put your two fingers into the colt's mouth and prise it out just as it were a-coming out of the bag. Do you leave it until a moment later, the colt would swallow it.'

Like the frog's bone the milt was a good *charmer*. The old horse-man said he had a dozen milts at one time. But they were no use un-less they were properly cured. Like the frog's bone, to be effective the milt had to be cured in a mixture of 'umpteen different things', before it could be used.

'I used to laugh sometimes—I'd hear a chap say: "Well, I got the milt. Now I got a good charm. I can get the horse to follow me any-

[1] cf. Christina Hole, *English Folklore*, Batsford, p. 82.

where." But o' course the milt were useless unless it were put in the right mixture first. I've heard them boast, too, about the frog's boon that had never been properly cured. They didn't know nothing about it. They didn't have the secret. But I said nothing. It wouldn't do to say anything.'

It was from such occasions as these that the Suffolk proverb, *Quietness is best*, was born.

The reader will have noticed that there is an important difference between the uses of the frog's bone and the milt as outlined above. The action of the frog's bone may be described as inhibitory: the horse is *reisted* by the aggressive, inhibiting odour in which it is steeped. But the action of the milt is to attract the horse, to get a horse to follow it owing to the special way it had been scented. The realisation that there were two types of substance—opposite in their action—involved in the secret practices of the horsemen was another key-point in the search.

The search now moved to a chemist who was able to confirm this part of the theory. For although in the old days it is likely that the horsemen prepared their own mixtures and got most of their medicines from herbs and trees, as the gypsies do to this day, within the last few generation many have come to use the chemist's shop where many of the substances they needed were to be bought. A chemist who came into an agricultural district of Suffolk during the hey-day of the farm-horse about forty years ago described how the old horsemen came into his shop for their mixtures:

'They would sometimes have their recipes written down on an old slip of paper, in a half-literate hand. But we could usually puzzle them out. The remedies and so on were traditional, handed down for generations; and some of them had cures the vets had never heard of. They also had their *drawing iles* as they called them: aromatic oils for *drawing* or attracting horses to them. These oils were like candy to a child. A drop on a horse's tongue, and it would follow you about all day; or even the scent of it on a horseman's coat. If a horseman came in to ask for one of his chemicals, he first of all took a good look around the shop to make sure that no one else would hear what he was asking for. When I started in the chemist business as a young man forty years ago they used to come in and order their favourite powders—a stone or so at a time if they were going away for a period, to a show or something like that. The last of the old horseman who used to come to me regularly died a few years back.'

Another chemist described how the more careful of the horsemen used to make up the mixtures themselves, coming to him for only one or two of the ingredients and then passing on to another chemist, and perhaps even a third, to get the remainder. One horseman has described how he had code names for chemicals, and these were understood only by the chemist and himself. Therefore, even when the shop was full, he could ask for what he wanted without anyone being any the wiser. '*Dragon's blood* was one of the owd bluff names I used.' And it would have suited his sense of secrecy and tickled his humour immensely if one of his rivals, overhearing his request, had in turn procured the real dragon's blood—the red gum from a palm fruit. This horseman also frequently used an aromatic herb called foenu-greek but when asked for in the dialect as *finnigig* it was incomprehensible to anybody but the chemist.

The action of the *drawing oils* is typified by the following illustrations:

'The owd horsemen were very skilled,'—this from Harry Mason, the shepherd—'they didn't have to exert themselves. A horseman would go into a meadow and there'd be no horses about; but as soon as he got himself into the wind, they'd come a-running up to him, a-neighing and rubbing their noses against him. They'd rub their noses along his legs and his body. He got something sweet-smelling on him, o' course, put on specially.'

'A stallion killed a horse-leader and it was decided to have him put down. But someone suggested that a certain well-known groom should look at the stallion—a valuable one—first, before they finally decided to get rid of him: "Let Jack Francis see him first," they said. Now Jack Francis was a little man, a ha'porth of a man, bow-legged and wizened. When he got to the farm where they kept the stallion they told him: "You'd better hev something to eat first, Jack, afore you see the hoss."

' "No, I'd like to see the hoss fust." So he went into the horse's stall and immediately the horse started to nuzzle his head onto Jack's shoulder and very soon he was rubbing his head against him as though they were two old friends. After lunch he went to the horse, put a rope halter on him and led him out as if he were a child's pony.'

'The old horsemen often kept a little bottle in their hare-pocket or in their sleeved weskit. If a horseman was going to approach a strange horse he had to deal with for the first time, he'd have some of the stuff from his little bottle sprinkled over his hand. Then he went up to the horse to talk to him. But as he was standing a-talking, his hand with the stuff on it would be gently rubbing the horse's muzzle.'

Thomas Davidson, in the article already cited, quotes the story of a blacksmith from Bourn in Cambridgeshire. This man, George —— had the power to *reist* a horse. One day a farmer offended the men in the smithy by hinting that one of them had stolen some money he had lost. 'A little later the farmer drove up to the forge in a pony trap. George turned towards the road, took out his handkerchief, and held it to his nose and replaced it in his pocket. He did no more; but when the farmer was ready to leave, the pony refused to move. In spite of every effort on the farmer's part, the animal remained where it was from nine o'clock in the morning until five o'clock in the afternoon. Then the horse charmer patted its neck, and it went off quite un-harmed and unflurried.

'When asked by his co-workers how he did it, George said it was by means of a charm. He then proceeded to give, in detail, a version of the ancient charm of the frog's bone that floats upstream.'[1]

[1] *Gwerin*, Vol. I, no. 2, p. 70.

A Suffolk horseman gave the following information which un-doubtedly illumines the above: 'I used to use the *drawing oils* some bit. If I had a horse in a loose-box or in a yard and it was being a little troublesome, a little oil of —— on a handkerchief and held up would do the trick.' The handkerchief that figures in both these accounts is significant and there is no need to dwell on the correspondences. But why did George the blacksmith give his fellow-workers the rig-marole about the old frog's bone? Undoubtedly it was to put them off the scent. He could safely give away the ritual in all its details and be sure that no one could make any use of it, as long as he kept the ultimate secret to himself. He was only acting in accordance with his kind in letting people know of the ritual, because this was, consciously or unconsciously, part of the smoke-screen to the real practice and also part of the atmosphere. His real secret gave him added social status, some economic advantage and in this particular environment a great deal of power, and in no circumstances would he be ready to give it away. The similarities between the use of the *drawing oils*, out-lined above, and the motions of the so-called 'whisperers' are too obvious to need stressing. One horseman actually stated that he pre-tended to be 'talking quietly' to a horse when all the time he was in-troducing it to a soothing, aromatic oil.

The farm, it has been said, is the last resort of magic. This is pro-bably true; but we can now see that we must not interpret this word *magic* too uncritically. For it is part of magic's function to conceal its real dynamic under a smoke-screen of fustian and fantasy, precisely because magic is no longer magic if it ceases to be the monopoly of the class or section who practise it. A secret that is shared by the whole community has no realisable value, and brings no kudos—of status or actual economic advantage.

A very appropriate illustration of this principle is given by a former district officer in the British Solomon Islands, D. C. Horton, in an account[1] of primitive Melanesian magic called *The Vele Man*. The Vele men were able, it appears, by the aid of a system of magic to terrorise the populations of certain islands, thus gaining effective control over these islands for themselves. For a long time it was dif-

[1] *The Listener*, 6th January, 1958.

ficult to stamp out the terror because none of the islanders would discuss the Vele for fear of being victimised himself. Finally, however, a determined administrator, Commander Wright, stamped out the terror and the methods of the Vele men were unmasked.

The victim of the Vele men was usually someone who had offended the secret society. He was attacked at dusk, though not before an atmosphere of terror had been carefully built up. The Vele men themselves spread rumours that the Vele were in the district and they drew attention to the simulated cry of an evening bird whose presence always preceded an attack. While the whole village was in a state of hysteria the victim was singled out. 'At the right moment the Vele man would step out of the bush behind his victim, clasp him round the throat and force something into his mouth, at the same time uttering an incantation in a high-pitched shriek.' The victim, if he did not actually die of fright, died from the poison that had been thrust into his throat; for the rest of the villagers were too frightened to help him and left him alone, although it would not have been difficult to save his life by getting him to spit out the poison and giving him an emetic to induce him to vomit up any he had swallowed. But the substance itself appeared not to be directly connected with the death of the victim; and the interesting fact emerged, when the terror was cleared up, that the Vele men themselves believed they had actual magic powers, and did not associate the killing with the poison thrust into the throat of the victim.

It is likely that all the hocus-pocus connected with the ritual of the frog's bone originally impressed not only those who got to know rumours or even some details of the ritual but deceived even the men who practised it into believing that it was the carefully followed formula of the ceremony that was important and not the substances that went into the curing of the frog's bone. This view is strengthened by other discoveries here in connection with it. The frog's bone was used not only in the way already described but it was also ground up and given with other substances to farm-horses either as medicine or a 'drawing powder'. Though for this use the backbone of the frog or the toad was reported to be favoured, in addition—it is assumed—to the ilium.

The widow of an old horseman, in a village near Stowmarket, turned out his papers after his funeral and gave certain scraps of paper containing some of his old remedies to a young horseman who lived next door, thinking they might interest him: 'There was witch-craft in one of them: all about grinding up a frog's boon and mixing it with some other stuff.' An old farmer also confirmed that some of the horsemen sprinkled a powder containing a ground-up frog's bone in the horses' bait: 'I've seen a horseman with some: he kept it in a tin and he'd give a pinch now and then in the bait. The horse would come after him and always do what he wanted.' Some of the horsemen undoubtedly believed that the frog's bone was the sovereign principle in their composite remedies.

The similarity between aspects of the frog's bone ritual here in Britain and certain aspects of the Indian and South Seas magic already described raises an interesting problem in the diffusion of cultural patterns. At first sight the Gypsies appear to be likely agents in spreading the lore. The Gypsies, according to the most widely accepted theory, had their first home in India, and their interest and skill in horse-lore would provide a likely vehicle for the transmission of the ceremony of the bone. But it is more than probable that it had reached Britain centuries before the Gypsies.

The reading of a remarkably illuminating book[1] by Ronald Rose, who with his wife lived for many years with the natives of Central Australia, leaves one with the conviction that much of the material which is fashionably described as 'folklore' in Britain could be more profitably studied if it were considered as vestiges of a definite stage of social development in the past, when these fragments were part of a system of vital social practices. There are so many correspondences in pattern between 'folklore' in Britain and the actual beliefs and some of the social practices of the Australian aborigines that one is tempted to relate the origin of many of the 'folklore survivals' here to a prehistoric period when the people of these islands were similarly hunters and food-gatherers, before they had learned the use of metals.

One other point regarding the *Horseman's Word* in East Anglia needs to be discussed. Thomas Davidson has stated his belief that the

[1] Ronald Rose, *Living Magic*, Chatto and Windus, 1957.

Word was introduced into East Anglia by the influx of Scottish farmers, already mentioned, in the second half of the last century. Much evidence here in East Anglia discounts this theory altogether. In not one instance has the writer discovered that the practices described here have been associated with a Scottish farmer, or a farm that has been occupied within the last century by a Scottish farmer. Again, the writer's most reliable informant on the *Word* stated with an assurance that is backed by all the other accurate information, checked and counter-checked, given by him: 'We had it here before the Scots came down. My father was born in 1862: he had it (the frog's bone) and my grandfather had it before him.' But the strongest of all arguments for considering the practices indigenous to East Anglia, co-extensive perhaps in time with the Scottish practices and not stemming from them, is the peculiar insular character of this region. Outside influences, outside practices, such as these, do not usually weave themselves into the pattern of a folk in the bare span of a century: in East Anglia they would hardly do so in the space of a millennium.

The expression the *frog's-boon* was also used by the old horseman in another way that is worth recording: it was heard as a kind of metaphor for 'being in control'. If, for example, a horseman was in the field and the ploughing was going on extremely well, his stetches coming out neatly, with dead-straight furrows and a level 'top', his mate sometimes called out in recognition of his prowess:

'I see you got the owd frog's boon with you this morning.'

There are one or two other notes to add as a supplement to what has already been said about the *Word*. For a horseman who had the *know* it was easy for him to release a horse that had been *reisted*. He did not attempt to look for the place where the inhibiting substance had been placed. He took the shorter way, as already indicated in a previous page, and went to the horse himself, temporarily paralysing his sense of smell by introducing another stronger or more pungent substance, vinegar or gin, for instance. 'If you had a drop of gin and just rubbed it in the horse's muzzle he could smell nothing else. Or you could even blow some cigarette smoke up his nostrils. Then you could lead him past anything that had been put down.'

Apart from the necessity of keeping their secrets for their own advantage, the old horsemen probably realised, however dimly, that it was to the society's advantage that their knowledge should remain esoteric. For in irresponsible hands the real secrets of the *Word* were dangerous; and if they had become common knowledge, especially at a time when the horse was literally one of the motive forces of society, the result would have been anarchic. Even at the present time it is considered best not to disclose the names of these actual substances: to do so would not add anything to the folklore aspect of the account; but it would certainly leave it open to be used for purposes other than for those it was intended.

Finally, to balance the above account the following cannot be emphasised too strongly: in ninety nine farms out of a hundred the *Horseman's Word*—to give a comprehensive name to the whole corpus of practices—was never heard of, or even if dimly known was not known well enough to be practised. The majority of farm horsemen cared for and managed their horses by the orthodox methods; and control was by use and patient training. As the old horseman who was possessed of the real *know* has stated: only one or two men in a district would have it; and often where it was openly talked about, discussed and even claimed to be practised, the self-styled practitioner boasted he had the *Word* merely to gain extra status among his kind. In most instances what he had was the husk and not the kernel. Yet, although the practice of the *Word* in the farms of Suffolk was exceptional, it is included here and discussed at length even at the risk of giving it a false emphasis. For at this point of time folklore deals with the exceptional; and what appears to be exceptional in one area or country, when taken in relation to the whole field—that is, the world and all its peoples—reveals itself as the manifestation of an universal type or pattern and, therefore, valuable data for recording.

24

Additional Folklore Linked with the Horse

Under this heading is included all the folklore material collected in the course of the search, but not to be explained under the theories advanced in the previous chapters. Most of this is written down without value-judgment or comment whatsoever; and the reader can ponder, mock or dismiss it—whichever he pleases. But it is included here, first of all because it would be questionable to record only the data that fitted in with a particular theory; and again because similar phenomena have been reported from other areas and recording them here may help towards their final explanation. It will also serve to show that even the most exhaustive investigation in this field still leaves a number of questions to be answered:

'A man told me—and he's not given to making up tales and thet sort o' thing—he saw a horseman in the field make a few turns with his hand and there was something a-shinin' on the handle of the plough "I dursn't go near it," he say.' Similar incidents to this one (from north Suffolk) have been reported from elsewhere, and are associated with the phenomena known as plough-witching.[1]

'One of these witchmen (men connected with the frog- or toad-bone ritual) was once walking in the village street when he saw a very old man trundling a full wheelbarrow. The old man was making a very hard job of it. So the witchman stopped him and asked him where he was taking it. The old man told him. Thereupon the witchman took off his cap; made two or three passes with it. The barrow immediately went of its own accord to the old man's destination.' This was from the Woodbridge area.

'A farmer not far from Ipswich came into possession of a toad's

[1] *East Anglian Notes and Queries*, Vol. XII, (1907–08), p. 215.

bone. It was the back-bone of the toad and was supposed to have magical powers. But the bone got the master of him, after a time, and he were afraid it were a-driving him crazy. It got so he had only to make up his mind to get a muck-fork, say, from another part of the yard for the fork to start coming to meet him. So he threw the toad's bone away.'

Very early in the researches into the *Horseman's Word* we came across three or four references to alleged magic practices with a fork stuck in a muck-heap: 'An owd horseman could stick a fork into a muck-heap in a certain way; then you could hitch a horse to it, and the horse couldn't budge it. But after he'd unhitched the horse, the horseman could go up to the fork and take it out with one hand.'

'They used to teach the horses to *draw*[1] by hitching them to a fork stuck deep into a muck-heap. If they got the horse to draw gently at first, and not pull at it sudden-like, the fork would stay in. The muck would fly all over the place but he wouldn't shift it. They reckon it were the special knack the horseman had of putting the fork into the muck.'

Some of the horsemen had the reputation of curing warts. As already stated, in a village near Stowmarket the wart-charmer is said 'to have sold his soul to the devil' by means of the frog's bone ritual. Another wart-charmer, a horseman in the same district, cured a woman's warts by rubbing them with a certain substance; and some have claimed to have cured warts by rubbing them with a live toad. The toad, since is itself wart-like, was thought to cure warts on the homeopathic-magic principle of like curing like. But if interfered with—anyone picking up a toad will notice this—it exudes an irritant fluid: some believe it is this fluid that effects the cure, if cure there is.

The writer has known two village wart-charmers in Suffolk. Each had real powers of curing warts. The method of cure was this. The charmer, when first approached by the patient, asked how many warts he had. The number was critical, so he said; and if the warts were wrongly counted the cure might not work. When the patient had told the number, he was assured that the warts would now go. One charmer, however, was accustomed to tell his patients: 'Don't be in too much of a hurry. If it's still there in a fortnight, don't worry: it will go.' Both charmers stated that the charm had been passed on to them many years before by an older person. While they kept this secret they held the power: as soon as they disclosed it to anyone the power would pass on to that person. Here, although no material principle is involved—no substance or actual medicine of any sort— we cannot write off the wart-charmers as practising magic, in the derisory sense. If the modern forms of treatment by hypnosis and suggestion are magic we can call wart-charming by the same name. For it appears that we are here in the psychosomatic borderland, and some skin ailments respond better to treatment by suggestion than by surgery or physic. Warts have been treated by hypnosis in experiments in a London hospital,[1] and it is reported that a country doctor has referred patients with warts to the village wart-charmer who has a more certain and less troublesome form of cure.

In the inquiry into the *Word* we discovered in two or three different villages the belief that the hoof-parings of a horse—particularly the parings from the frog—have the power of attracting dogs. The first came from a blacksmith: 'Often in the *travus* a dog would be snapping at the parings from the hoof while I was shoeing a horse. One old fellow told me: "You keep a piece of the frog in your pocket, bor, and you can get a dog to follow you, or you can manage the fiercest one you meet." ' The two other sources confirmed this and one old horseman added: 'We used to trim up the corns on a horse's leg—you know, the pieces of bone-like warts that grow out from the side. The dogs liked these parings. You could keep one or two parings in your pocket as a *charmer*. But they whooly *ponged* (smelled).' This is similar to a practice reported from the Midlands: a piano-tuner who was nervous of the dogs which he often met in going round the various houses, always kept a piece of dried liver in his pocket, be-

[1] 'Skin Conditions and Hypnosis,' by Hugh Gordon, Skin Physician to St George's and the West London Hospitals: article in *Health Horizon*, Autumn 1955.

lieving that the smell of this would make the most sullen dog well-disposed towards him.

From all that has previously been written here it is not surprising to discover that horses were once believed to be very susceptible to the powers of witches. Hag-stones—stones with holes in them and pieces of metal, sometimes a key, attached—are still to be seen hanging up outside farm buildings in Suffolk.[1] The hag-stone, a charm against witches, was hung up on the stable door: the writer, has seen a hare's foot, pinned to a door, serve a similar purpose in south Wales. The idea was to prevent the horses from being hag-ridden. But farm-horses in the old days were sometimes unaccountably tired for two entirely different reasons: from their surreptitious use by smugglers —this was frequent on the Suffolk seaboard; and from the *horse-play* that sometimes accompanied initiation to the 'Horseman's Society', when the initiates, fresh from the ceremony, rode the horses about the fields at night, mainly, it appears, out of devilment.[2]

The *fairy-loaf*[3]—the sea-urchin fossil—is reported by some to have been carried by the old horsemen in their pockets as a charm; and they have associated the term *fairy-* or *farcy-loaf* as a charm against the particular disease of farcy, or glanders, in horses. The writer has not been able to find an instance of this, and undoubtedly *farcy-loaf* is a mis-hearing for *pharisee-loaf*; for in the Stowmarket area of Suffolk fairies were once called *pharisees* or even *ferrishers*[4] and as the *loaf* was well known as a charm in another connection it is not difficult to see how the wrong association came about. But none of the horse-men in this area has heard of the sea-urchin fossil being linked in any way with horses.

A well-documented instance of primitive imitative magic has been reported in Suffolk, and we have recently heard of a similar occurrence in Cambridgeshire: A horse pierced his hoof by treading on a nail; the horseman, in addition to treating the horse's hoof, preserved the nail. He cleaned and greased the nail daily to prevent the wound from festering.

[1] Horseshoes served the same purpose.
[2] *Gwerin*, Vol. 1, No. 2, p. 73.   [3] *A.F.C.H.*, p. 212.
[4] *History of Stowmarket*, Hollingsworth, 1844, pp. 247–8. Also Lady C. Gurdon, *Folklore of Suffolk*, p. 33.

Conclusion

It would be much easier, and safer, to leave this section out altogether. Conclusions are dangerously near to commitments; and it is not the fashion for a writer to commit himself to anything, least of all to pointing out what he considers to be the likely developments of trends implicit in the period studied and the historical facts assembled. Facts, it is said, should be left to speak for themselves; and it is too often considered sufficient to get together massive, magpie collections whose very weight would seem to excuse the writer from forming any conclusions about them. But facts are merely disparate objects unless they serve a purpose that will vitalise them and give them some sort of being; and a work is only half a work if it stops at this stage of collecting and recording. Like the man in the Thurber cartoon who falls noticeably short of his full human stature in the satisfaction he shows in 'knowing nothing except the facts,' a study that proposes to offer no more is cutting itself off from the most vital source of communication with its reader. Moreover, it will only tend to strengthen the error that history is solely the *technique* of finding, establishing and recording facts. Facts are the proud blazon of this type of study; but sterility is too often its sub-title. It is hoped that what is written below will be productive of something, if only disagreement.

In cultivating the land man has always been compelled to adapt his methods to the type of soil, the prevailing climate and the tools he has at hand. A change in any one of these, forces him eventually to change his methods, and by changing his methods to change—in a greater or lesser degree—the organisation of his farming, and finally the community associated with it. For example, the climatic changes in Britain during the last few centuries B.C. gradually caused the giving up of the system of ploughing and cross-ploughing associated with the square Celtic field, and demanded in its stead the ploughing of the soil in ridges necessary to drain it in the succeeding period of wet, temperate climate that has persisted until the present age. The new, heavy plough with iron coulter and share was developed on the continent and brought here by the Belgae, a tribe who came to Britain about 50 B.C. This was the type of plough that was used all through the Middle Ages and even into the eighteenth century. The weight of this plough needed a team of four, six or eight oxen to draw it; and the ox has become the symbol of the collective, subsistence farming of the Middle Ages. There are two main reasons[1] why the horse was not used in the plough during early times: he was too small and had not the strength to draw such a heavy implement; and again, the breast-collar which he wore made it difficult for him to breathe when given a heavy task. It was not until the invention of the hard collar, sometime during the twelfth century, that the horse was able to put his full strength into the drawing action. Horses were used in the plough here and there after this date, as we have seen from the Norwich records; but it was not until the release of the 'great horse', following the change in the mode of warfare, that it was possible to develop a larger horse suitable for the plough. This change roughly coincided with the beginning of the break-up of the old feudal and manorial economy and the introduction of the commercial farming, farming for the market, that over the next few centuries was to displace the old subsistence farming almost entirely. The change-over from oxen to horses was made easier by the development of the lighter ploughs, notably the Norfolk and the Rotherham, in the seventeenth and eighteenth centuries. The enclosure movement helped to complete this change, and the horse became the typical draught beast of the 'individual' type of farming that had its heyday in the nineteenth and early twentieth centuries. Since the coming of the tractor the horse has largely been displaced from his main task of ploughing the land and, where he has been retained, he now does some of the marginal tasks that were previously allotted to him during the era of the ox. One of these jobs was harrowing: for this horses were used from very early times. It was a job the horse was equal to,

[1] *Y.A.G.*, p. 196.

and one that the ox, accustomed to the steady, resistant pull of the plough, found particularly uncongenial[1] owing to the jerky, spasmodic movement of the harrow over the furrows. The wheel, therefore, has come full circle; for on many farms today, one of the few jobs left to the horse, expecially in the heavy land districts, is to draw the harrow, thus eliminating the need for taking the heavy weight of the tractor on to the prepared seed-bed.

The square Celtic field cultivated by the light, primitive plough drawn by a pair of oxen; the long strip of the open-field worked by the heavy, Belgic type of plough and a large team of oxen; the small, multi-form, 'patchwork-quilt' field of the post-enclosure era, cultivated by the lighter, better designed all-iron ploughs drawn by horse-teams—all show that a certain method of cultivation tends to demand a certain shape of field and size of holding. What is the shape and size of holding 'natural' to the new era of the machine farming we have entered during the last thirty or forty years? The majority of farms in East Anglia, as in most areas of the country where arable farming has predominated, appear to have taken their present size and shape during the eighteenth and early nineteenth century enclosure movement—probably much earlier in Suffolk. The fields were blocked out then in sizes that were best suited to their working by horse teams; and, in the main, these same fields are still in existence today under full tractor cultivation. Put in another way: the tractor is being confined and compelled to work in restricted units, of unsuitable shape, that were designed for or evolved under an entirely different economy. Figures show that agriculture in the United Kingdom is the most highly mechanised in the world:[2] 'one tractor for every 50 acres of ploughland as compared with 120 acres in the U.S.A.';[3] and one 'cannot escape the conclusion that farming here is over-mechanised—not, be it noted, because too many processes have now been taken over by the machine—but for the reason that

[1] *The ox is never wo*
   Tyll he to the harrowe goo.
[2] Rene Dumont, *Types of Rural Economy: Studies in World Agriculture*, Methuen, 1957, p. 387.
[3] *The Times*, 1st September, 1958, puts the proportion even higher: 'There is (in Britain) one tractor to every 38 acres of arable land.'

each individual machine is doing far less than it is capable of doing. Field units and farm units are so small that in few instances is the machine being worked to anywhere near its full potential. A number of small farms are grossly over-capitalised, each holding equipment whose aggregate could be halved if it were shared on a co-operative basis.

If there is a lesson to be learned from the study of farming history it is this: the optimum size of unit of cultivation for arable land in any given area depends on the tools and methods used for its working. No one knows what is the best size of unit for the mechanised farm today: it would be rash to make an estimate when so many factors are involved and the tide of mechanisation is still flowing. But it can safely be said that it is many times larger than the average unit worked in the arable areas at present; and if it were possible to plan the farms of the future in units best suited to the machines, the agronomist would have to think in terms of thousands rather than in hundreds of acres.

It will be objected at this stage that this is mere copybook, and that the academic approach has no relation to the actual needs of the land or the people who work it. But now that farming is almost fully commercialised, it cannot hope to escape the same laws of growth that have governed other sections of industry and commerce. Farm mechanisation is one of the last products of the first industrial revolution; and that means, unless it is centrally guided and controlled, farming as an industry is certain to take the same course of development as any other industry in this country: the increasingly large-scale organisation of its productive units and the progressive elimination of the small producer. A poor prospect for the small farmer and the small-holder? Here is a quotation from a newspaper serving one of the most highly mechanised arable-farming areas in the country: 'In Britain three out of every five farmers work fewer than 50 acres. They are there because they love the land, and they love the independence that the land gives them. But they are a doomed race.'[1] Yet the position is not as desperate as this. It will be desperate if the machine is allowed to dominate farming, as it most certainly will unless there is a bold re-organisation of agriculture as a whole to meet

[1] *East Anglian Daily Times*, 3rd December, 1957.

the new conditions. Unless an attempt is made to do this the machine will take on a dynamic of its own and appear to push the small farmers out of their holdings by its own ineluctable force.

The formation of large co-operative units of small farmers is not only desirable but inevitable if the small farmer is to survive: the alternative is that he be allowed to suffer in the same way as the cottagers and peasant farmers did during the enclosure movement— the last analogous, large-scale change in the countryside. These were swept to one side by a movement that was thought as impossible of control as a thunderstorm; and on one side they remained, getting scant sympathy and little help as some of history's unavoidable casualties. Historically the return to an era of collective farming would seem inevitable; a farming organised by the local community as it was in mediaeval times, but with the addition of centralised guidance. This was the embryo system, with local agricultural committees and central control, that worked during the last two wars; and the new farming that is bound to develop with the increased momentum of the machine will demand that some such system be adapted more fully to serve its needs.

If the farmer objects that this is merely *controls* writ large, and is the ultimate challenge to his independence, the objection can be answered by one bold statement: With farming for the market as it is today, there is no independence, and the issue is simply this: Which is the better: to be a member of a planned, co-operative unit of small producers with some sort of guarantee of a return for·his labour and some safeguard against a bad year, or to be at the full mercy of a pair of tyrants, the market and the weather, both or either of which is capable of turning him out of his holding within a couple of seasons?

The re-organisation will only be possible, given a clear-sighted policy and vigorous State action. Whether it can be accomplished without the State taking over the full control of the land is doubtful. Dr. C. S. Orwin, writing nearly thirty years ago,[1] was of the opinion that, apart from any questions of politics, nationalisation of the land is inevitable if we are to control the economic forces set into motion by

[1] C. S. Orwin, *The Future of Farming*, Oxford Univ. Press, 1930, p. 128.

the industrialisation of farming by the machine. The argument seems to have more cogency today, especially in the face of the opportunist, Budget-to-Budget, almost day-to-day, agricultural policy of the major political parties whose watchword appears to be: *We don't know where we're going, but we're going there fast*. Even if farming were simply an industry, it would demand vigorous and far-sighted action now. But farming is more than an industry: it is a way of life, and the need for such action is, therefore, doubly urgent.

But what will be the place of the horse in the new farming? We have seen that in agriculture more than in any other industry the old methods and old forms of cultivation tend to survive alongside the new, and that even in comparatively small countries as in Britain different regions develop at different rates. It is likely that the horse will still be used in agriculture in these islands for many years to come; and the whimsical forecast given to the writer by an old ploughman will take a long time to be realised: 'Horses are dying off on the farms and they're not being replaced. Before long, if you want to see a farm-horse you'll have to visit the zoo; and in about twenty years' time you'll see me a-settin' in there (pointing to his cottage) and doin' my ploughing by radio-control.' It will take many years for the second industrial revolution to reach the farm: even when it does the horse will probably be there to welcome it.

A report[1] made recently by the Economic Commission for Europe confirms that the horse is not likely to disappear from agriculture in the foreseeable future and draws the conclusion from a study of the figures that the present decline in horse numbers may reach a point where increased mechanisation will not meet all agricultural needs. This is already true of many of the farms in the heavy land districts of East Anglia. Farmers have discovered that a pair of horses are invaluable for certain processes when it is impossible for a tractor to go on the land. A farmer of heavy land in Suffolk is able, if he still has a horse or two, to drill his spring seed much earlier than his neighbour who has only tractors: he can use his horse-drill when the land is too wet for the tractor to go near it. The same applies to harrowing and hoeing.

[1] *Effects of Farm Mechanisation on Horse Numbers in European Countries*, United Nations, Geneva, 1958. See pp. 19, 48–9.

In the Fen districts of East Anglia where large crops of vegetables are grown, horses are still used in fairly large numbers for hoeing, carting and harrowing; and there is an additional reason in the Fens why the horse is likely to be in demand for many years to come. The land there is usually well below the level of the road, and in wet conditions only a horse is capable of drawing a load up the short, sharp-rising ramp to the highway. A tractor is quite useless for this job during the greater part of the year. Similarly, the usefulness of the horse for carting jobs on farms in Suffolk is continually being re-discovered: for tractors bog themselves down in conditions where a horse can draw a loaded tumbril with comparative ease. The Suffolk horse is ideal for these marginal jobs: his relatively low food-intake keeps maintenance costs to a minimum, and the absence of *feather* on legs makes him easier to keep clean in the muddy conditions in which he is proving indispensable.

To sum up: in pointing out the likely place of the horse in the farming of the future one does not want to indulge in any backward-looking mysticism or to imply that the tractor is the 'villain of the piece'. The tractor is both the implement and the symbol of the machine age of farming, but not until the social and technical implications of its use on the land have been fully taken into account will the tractor be doing an unfettered job and working at its full potential. Even then it is probable there will still be a place for the horse alongside it.

One conviction kept intruding itself upon the writer while he was collecting the material for this book: 'You are only touching the fringe of the work that needs doing.' This is the sort of inquiry that should be conducted by a team, backed by a university and having considerable resources at its disposal.

Representatives of at least four universities have in fact been working in East Anglia in recent years (Cambridge: archaeology; Leeds: the dialect, and agricultural history; London: folklore; Leicester: local history). But this is no substitute for a planned and co-ordinated study of the area undertaken by one university. The dialect, the farming history—including the study and collection of old farm tools—the folklore and folk-culture of the region are too interrelated profitably to be studied apart. Dr W. G. Hoskins of Oxford, in his pioneer studies of the history to be traced in an actual landscape, also in his work on the history of domestic architecture, has started a vigorous school of open-air historians who are as much concerned with the actual, physical area studied as they are with the books and documents concerning it in the libraries. This type of approach, extended to embrace the oral tradition and conducted by a team organised by a single university or school of studies, is most likely to be fruitful in East Anglia or any other homogeneous region.

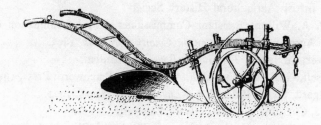

SELECTED WRITTEN SOURCES

Biddell Family, The, *The Biddell Papers*, Ipswich Borough Archives.

Biddell, Herman (Editor); *The Suffolk Horse Stud Book*, Vol. 1, 1880.

Cullum, Rev. Sir John, *History of Hawstead (Suffolk)*, 2nd edition, 1813.

Darby, H. C., *The Domesday Geography of Eastern England*, Cambridge University Press, 1952.

Ernle, Lord, *English Farming Past and Present*, Longmans, 1922.

Evans, George Ewart, *Ask the Fellows who Cut the Hay*, Faber and Faber, 1956.

Finberg, H. P. R. (Editor), *The Agricultural History Review*, The British Agricultural History Society.

Fox, A. Wilson (Assistant Commissioner, Royal Commission on Agriculture), *Report on the County of Suffolk*, 1893.

Frazer, Sir James, *The Golden Bough*, Macmillan.

Fussell, G. E., *The English Rural Labourer*. Batchworth Press, 1949.

Haggard, Sir H. Rider, *Rural England*, Longmans, 1902.

Hole, Christina, *English Folklore*, Batsford.

Payne, Ffransis, *Yr Aradr Gymreig* (The Welsh Plough), University of Wales Press, 1954.

Peate, Iorwerth (Editor), *Gwerin* (A Journal of Folk Life), Basil Blackwell, Oxford.

Ransome, J. Allen, *The Implements of Agriculture*, 1843.

Ransome, Sims and Jefferies (Ipswich), Archives and publications, notably: *Ransome's 'Royal' Records*, 1939.

Raynbird, Hugh and William, *The Agriculture of Suffolk*, 1849.

Reyce, Robert, *The Breviary of Suffolk* 1618, edited with Notes by Francis Hervey, Murray, 1902.

Seebohm, Frederic, *The English Village Community*, Longmans.

Spence, Lewis, *Myth and Ritual in Dance, Game and Rhyme*, Watts, 1947.

Trevelyan, G. M., *English Social History*, Longmans, 1942.

Trow-Smith, Robert, *English Husbandry*, Faber and Faber.

Tusser, Thomas, *Five Hundred Points of Good Husbandry*, edited by Dorothy Hartley, Country Life.

Vesey-Fitzgerald, Brian, *Gypsies of Britain*, Chapman and Hall.

Vesey-Fitzgerald, Brian (Editor), *The Book of the Horse*, Nicholson and Watson.

Watson, Sir James A. Scott and May Elliot Hobbs, *Great Farmers*. Faber and Faber, 1951.

White, *Directory of Suffolk* (for articles on nineteenth-century agriculture.

Wright, Joseph, *English Dialect Dictionary*.

Young, Arthur, *General View of the Agriculture of the County of Suffolk*. Third Edition, 1804.

FILMS

The two following films, both directed by Mary Field, were made in the Peasenhall district of Suffolk in 1935. They are strongly recommended for the accurate picture they give of certain aspects of Suffolk farming prior to full mechanization:

> *This Was England*
> *Spring, Summer, Autumn and Winter on the Farm*
> (a Series)

Both films were made, and are distributed, by G. B. Instructional Ltd.

Index

287